The African Sermons

The Albert Schweitzer Library

Albert Schweitzer at Lambaréné
© Archives centrales Albert Schweitzer Gunsbach

The
African Sermons

Albert Schweitzer

Edited and Translated from the French by Steven E. G. Melamed, Sr.

 SYRACUSE UNIVERSITY PRESS

First Edition 2003

03 04 05 06 07 08   6 5 4 3 2 1

The paper used in this publication meets the minimum requirements
of American National Standard for Information Sciences—Permanence
of Paper for Printed Library Materials, ANSI Z39.48–1984.∞™

Library of Congress Cataloging-in-Publication Data

Schweitzer, Albert, 1875–1965.
[Sermons. English. Selections]
The African sermons / Albert Schweitzer ; edited and translated from
the French by Steven E.G. Melamed, Sr.
p. cm.—(The Albert Schweitzer library)
Includes bibliographical references and index.
ISBN 0–8156–2920–6 (alk. paper)
1. Sermons, French. I. Melamed, Steven E. G. II. Title. III. Series.
BX4827.S35A5 2003
252'.04—dc21
2003000498

Manufactured in the United States of America

This book is dedicated to my beloved wife, Antonia,
in grateful appreciation for her enthusiasm, encouragement,
critical thinking, tireless assistance, wisdom,
and most of all, love.

Steven E. G. Melamed, Sr., is a teacher and clergyman. After attending Public School 89 and the High School of Music and Art in New York City, he earned a B.A. at New York University and an M.A. in English at the City College of New York. He also received an M.Div. degree in religion from Princeton Theological Seminary and a Ph.D. in humanities from Florida State University. He teaches humanities and philosophy at Tallahassee Community College in Florida.

Dr. Melamed is also an ordained Presbyterian minister who served in that capacity at the First Presbyterian Church of Watervliet, New York, for nine years and at the Church of Universal Fellowship in Orono, Maine, for seven years. He is a member of the Presbytery of Florida for the Presbyterian Church (U.S.A.).

Contents

P A R T   F O U R   The 1931 Sermons

Preface

THIS EDITION represents my translation of transcriptions that comprise the sole surviving record of seventy sermons Albert Schweitzer preached to the African people in Lambaréné, Gabon, from 1913 to 1935. Although there are other places where he writes about what he did and said in the worship services at his hospital in Lambaréné, these texts are the only record, however imperfect, of his spoken words.

The idea for this project began in the summer of 1990 when my wife, Antonia, and I were traveling through Europe. While we were in Switzerland, I told her about my lifelong interest in Albert Schweitzer.

"Did you know that he lived in Alsace, not too far away from here?" I asked.

"Then why don't we drive over there?" she replied.

I made a few phone calls and reserved a room for the night in Kaysersberg. The next morning I asked some questions at the little museum next to Schweitzer's birthplace. I was given the name of the Albert Schweitzer Fellowship, at that time located in New York City. The secretary of the fellowship, Estelle Linzer, referred me to Jackson Lee Ice of the Department of Religion at Florida State University. In 1991, Professor Ice invited me to apply to the doctoral program in the humanities and offered to be my dissertation adviser. I wanted to study with him, and I was very sad that he died before my studies began.

Later that year I went to New York City to attend a United Nations conference on the relevance of Albert Schweitzer's philosophy of Reverence for Life to the modern world. There I met Rhena Schweitzer Miller, Albert Schweitzer's daughter, who has championed her father's legacy and promoted his philosophy of Reverence for Life throughout the world.

I spoke of my long-standing interest in her father's work. "Could you give me any ideas for a suitable project?" I asked.

"Yes," she said, "I have certain sermons of my father's which may be of interest to you. Many of these have never been published. It would make a good project. They are in French. Your French is good, no?"

"Oh, I think so," I said, with some hesitation. And so I began my work.

Rhena Schweitzer Miller made a typewritten transcript of nine sermons from 1913–14 in her possession and sent them to me. She also sent me transcripts of three other sermons from the same period as well as thirteen from 1930. I subsequently located fourteen sermons from 1930 at Syracuse University that she had provided that institution some years earlier. Without Rhena Schweitzer Miller's trust and personal involvement in this project, this book never would have been written.

At Florida State University I asked David Darst, professor of romance languages and humanities, to be my major professor for the dissertation. He monitored my work and checked my translations. I collected transcriptions of the original French sermons and made English translations of thirty-eight sermons from Lambaréné, thirty-five of which had never been published. These were all the sermons available in the United States. In 1997, I was awarded a Ph.D. in Humanities from Florida State University; my dissertation was entitled "Albert Schweitzer's African Sermons 1913–1914, 1930."

Knowing that there were more sermons in Europe, however, my wife and I visited the International Albert Schweitzer Center at the Maison Albert Schweitzer in Günsbach, France, where we met Sonja Poteau-Müller, the director, curator, and chief archivist of the Schweitzer collection (Archives centrales A. Schweitzer). The Albert Schweitzer Center occupies the very house that Schweitzer built to be his home in Günsbach, the town where he spent most of his youth. The house is now a museum containing many of Dr. Schweitzer's personal effects, including his Nobel Peace Prize. It also contains the extensive Schweitzer archives.

Mme. Poteau-Müller was surprised to learn that the Central Archives did not possess the sermons that were available in the United States. She arranged for me to meet with Professor Jean-Paul Sorg, who had published six of Schweitzer's African sermons in the journal *Études Schweitzeriennes* and in a book he edited, *Albert Schweitzer: Humanisme et Mystique* (1995), which contains an extensive anthology of Schweitzer's writings and one sermon. Mme. Poteau-Müller transcribed copies of fragments of handwritten sermon notes that Rhena Schweitzer Miller had given to me. Without Mme. Poteau-Müller's continuing assistance, I never would have been able to complete this project. I thank her.

I am also grateful to Antje Bultmann Lemke, whom I visited the following year at the E. S. Bird Library at Syracuse University. She introduced me to its extensive Schweitzer collection and was helpful in many ways. In addition, I would like to thank John Fruehwirth, managing editor of Syracuse University Press, who has worked very closely with me, and Bettie McDavid Mason and Marian Buda who spent countless hours helping me with their superb technical expertise.

Finally, my dear wife, Antonia Melamed, has devoted a tremendous amount of time and energy to this book during all phases of its production. I value her critical analysis, attention to detail, and editing skills. She has been a true helpmate and deserves first place in the list of those who have aided me along the way.

Textual Notes

ALBERT SCHWEITZER's African sermons have been drawn together from three sources: the personal collection of his daughter, Rhena Schweitzer Miller; the E. S. Bird Library at Syracuse University, Syracuse, New York; and the central archives at the Maison Albert Schweitzer, Günsbach, France. Six of the sermons from Günsbach have been edited and published by Jean-Paul Sorg, most in the French journal *Études Schweitzeriennes* and one in his book *Albert Schweitzer: Humanisme et Mystique* (Sorg 1995, 352–55), but the remaining sixty-four are hitherto unpublished.

Fortunately, there are calendar dates for almost all of the sermons. I have therefore listed the sermons chronologically, assigning a number to each sermon entry for convenience.

In most cases, the sermons have no real titles. The title "Humble Yourself" on Schweitzer's manuscript sermon notes for 4 January 1914 is a notable exception. The few other "titles" are either generic indications of the Sunday in the church year on which the sermon was given or brief allusions to whatever biblical text Schweitzer was using for the theme of his sermon that day. Of those sermons without anything in the title position, some have notations in German indicating the text and/or the particular day in the church year (e.g., the First Sunday in Advent, Easter, Pentecost); such notations may possibly be Schweitzer's but more probably were added by the transcriber. In some cases, the information about the text and day is simply provided within the sermon itself. On the basis of this information, I have been able to provide "titles" for those sermons that had none.

In some sermons whose earliest extant source is a typescript, there are various gaps in the typewritten text. In some cases, disjunctive syntax indicates that the transcriber missed some of the text. In these instances I have inserted spaces in brackets [ ] to indicate that text is missing. In other cases, however, there are gaps even though, syntactically, no text seems to be missing. In these cases, therefore, I have simply ignored the extra spaces; apparently, the old typewriter used for typing the transcriber's notes occasionally skipped.

The earliest sermons, from 1913 and 1914, are sometimes in form simply sermon notes rather than prepared manuscripts. (Sermon 8 is unusual in that there exist both notes by Schweitzer and a transcription of the actual sermon he delivered.) Many of these sermons are fragmentary and thus full of bracketed spaces indicating missing text. All the 1913–14 sermons are from Schweitzer's handwritten manuscripts. Sermons 1–6 and 10–12 were transcribed from the typewritten French text by Rhena Schweitzer Miller; sermons 7–9 were transcribed by Mme. Poteau-Müller.

The Lambaréné sermons were delivered in simple, colloquial French and were never intended for publication; assistants sitting in the congregation wrote down Schweitzer's words while he was preaching the sermons and later transcribed their notes. The sermons from 1930–33 were not written out by Schweitzer. They were preached extempore. While it is possible that Schweitzer preached from notes, none have been found, and there are no photographs of him doing so. There never were any original manuscripts for these sermons.

From 1930 on, assistants transcribed Schweitzer's sermons, sentence by sentence, during the time the sermons were being translated into the two local languages while Schweitzer was preaching. The handwritten transcriptions made during Schweitzer's oral delivery were then typed by the transcribers themselves. Although some of these transcribed sermons are fragmentary, most are fairly complete and thus provide a record of Schweitzer's actual words.

The transcriptions are occasionally marred by omissions and by errors of grammar and style. The errors in French are more likely to derive from the transcribers than from Schweitzer, who simplified his French in order to be understood. He did not wish to speak over the heads of his listeners, whom he knew to be illiterate. Though he used a simplified vocabulary, few in the audience could understand him without a translation.

The transcriber's pen often faltered. There were times when Schweitzer's words were hard to hear or understand. Moreover, concentration was often difficult at his out-of-doors worship services. Even so, the transcribers did a superb job under adverse circumstances. We are indebted to them for taking the time to perform this laborious task. Today we would record such services with electronic equipment, but how many people, even today, would take the time to transcribe not only the preacher's sermon but also the prayer at the end?

The transcribers performed a labor of love, by any standard of measurement. Marie Secrétan, a laboratory technician, transcribed the sermons of the years 1930 and 1931; as Mrs. Gustav Wyott, wife of Schweitzer's nephew, she also transcribed some later sermons (Poteau-Müller, letter to the author, 5 February 1998). Miss Jeannette Siefert transcribed those from the years 1933 and 1935. Another transcriber who should be recalled is "Mrs. Canada" (Mrs. C. E. B. [Lillian] Russell), whose monkeys were permitted to roam about freely during the service and whose name is occasionally mentioned in the sermons.[1] There was always someone present in Schweitzer's audience willing to write down his words. There was enough time to do this because native translators repeated each sentence of the sermon in two tribal languages.

Schweitzer lived and wrote long before the concepts of "inclusive" language and "multiculturalism" appeared. His expressions of race and gender are simply those of his time, and in my translations I have not attempted to change them.

It should be noted, so that the reader can be selective, the contents of the sermons vary markedly: the early 1913–14 sermons tend to be fragmentary and orthodox; the middle sermons from 1930 are often dogmatic and moralistic; and the later sermons from 1931 to 1935 are usually quite pastoral and reflective.

1. Mrs. C. E. B. (Lillian) Russell—known as "Mrs. Canada" because she had orchards in that country—was not a nurse but a volunteer who donated her time and resources to Schweitzer in the work of the hospital. She stayed in Lambaréné on several occasions between 1907 and 1916. During her sojourns there she took charge of the workers who were clearing the forest and building hospital buildings. Like Schweitzer himself, she loved animals—especially monkeys, who followed her around and were allowed to roam about during religious services. Fluent in German and French, she also served as Schweitzer's translator in England.

Introduction

ALBERT SCHWEITZER (1875–1965) was a man of genius and ability whose lasting contribution to humanity included deeds of kindness and enduring works of scholarship. He is best known for his work as a doctor in Africa. He was the first physician to establish a hospital for the relief of suffering in the interior of French Equatorial Africa. It was a heroic and pioneering effort. According to Rhena Schweitzer Miller, in a letter to the author dated 13 February 1997, "When my father came to Gabon in 1913 there were medical facilities in the cities but not in the interior" (letter to author, 13 February 1997).

Schweitzer's hospital in Lambaréné became a model for others to imitate. The wealthy American William Larimer Mellon was one of those who fell under Schweitzer's spell (Byers 1996). In 1947, after reading about Schweitzer's work in Africa, Mellon was inspired to leave his comfortable life and take up the study of medicine in order to establish a hospital in Haiti, one of the poorest places in the world. Mellon founded his Albert Schweitzer Hospital at Deschapelles, Haiti, in 1954. Other hospitals continue to be built in imitation of Schweitzer's in Lambaréné.

Although Schweitzer's work as a physician remains his landmark contribution to humanity, he did not see this great effort as his principal gift to the world. "[W]hen you portray me," he would often say to those who interviewed him, "it should not be as the doctor who ministers to the sick. It is my contribution of Reverence for Life that I consider my primary contribution to the world."[1]

It was this ethical philosophy, which he termed Reverence for Life, for which he most wished to be remembered. The original German phrase

---

1. Schweitzer often repeated the sentiment expressed in this remark.

"Ehrfurcht vor dem Leben," signifies more than simple respect for life; it expresses a religious awe in the face of the mystery and miracle of life. Life is precious, said Schweitzer, and may be taken only if there is no other choice, and only after careful thought. From his childhood on, Schweitzer showed a profound respect for all life: "There slowly grew up in me an unshakable conviction that we have no right to inflict suffering and death on another living creature unless there is some unavoidable necessity for it, and that we ought all of us to feel what a horrible thing it is to cause suffering and death out of mere thoughtlessness" (Schweitzer 1963, 52).

This conviction was the motivating force behind his mission of mercy to Africa, and it formed the basis of his philosophy of life. Schweitzer believed that in order for people to have reverence for life, human reason itself must be transformed. There must first be a change in the way human beings perceive life. Then a transformed mind and heart will express itself in deeds of moral action: "According to the teaching of Jesus, men are to be gripped by God's will of love, and must help to carry out that will in this world, in small things as in great things, in saving as in pardoning. To be glad instruments of God's love in this imperfect world is the service to which men are called, and it forms a preparatory stage to the bliss that awaits them in the perfected world, the Kingdom of God" (Schweitzer, 1939, 13–14).

Disregard for life begins with the thoughtless taking of animal life and concludes with the slaughter of millions of human beings without remorse. The taking of any life was problematical for Schweitzer. As a physician he knew that to save one human life he had to kill millions of germs. There was no other way to save a human being. Even so, the necessity dismayed him. He was forced to confront this issue day after day in Lambaréné. Some of the animals that lived in the hospital compound needed to eat the flesh of other animals in order to survive. Nonetheless, he was never happy about having to kill some animals to feed other ones.[2]

During the last decade of his life, Schweitzer did not want to make political statements or to interfere in the affairs of nations. It was not in his nature to "get involved." However, he was persuaded by his colleagues and friends to protest the testing and use of nuclear weapons. He eventually

---

2. In a letter to the author dated 13 February 1997, Rhena Schweitzer Miller informed me that "My father, in his later years, was a convinced (not reluctant) vegetarian."

spoke up, but only after a lifetime of avoiding political pronouncements and entanglements (Jack 1984, 88–91).

Schweitzer was born in Kaysersberg, Alsace, on 14 January 1875, the first son of Louis Schweitzer, a Lutheran pastor, and his wife, Adèle, and reached maturity in nearby Günsbach. There, at the parish church, he first played the church organ and heard his father preach the gospel. He studied at the University of Strasbourg, where he was awarded a Ph.D. for his work in the philosophy of Immanuel Kant. Schweitzer also earned the licentiate degree in theology and in 1900 was ordained curate at St. Nicholas Church in Strasbourg.

In 1905, after a brilliant academic career, Schweitzer turned to the study of medicine. He had resolved to devote his life to the service of humanity. In 1912, after earning his medical degree, Schweitzer resigned his position as professor of philosophy and theology at Strasbourg, to the dismay of his family and friends. He traveled with his new wife, née Hélène Bresslau, to Lambaréné, Gabon, where they established a hospital for the purpose of relieving the physical suffering and distress of the African people. The Schweitzer Hospital is still there, much larger now, but still bringing help to people in need and providing medical care for the relief of suffering and pain. Over the entrance, in French, are the words of Jesus from the Sermon on the Mount: "Heureux les miséricordieux, car ils obtiendront miséricorde" [Matt. 5:7, Blessed are the merciful for they shall obtain mercy].

In recognition of his humanitarian work, Schweitzer received many honors, including the Goethe prize awarded in 1928 by the city of Frankfurt, Germany, and the Nobel Peace Prize in 1952. Distinguished also as an organist, musicologist, and theologian, he frequently received prizes and honorary degrees in those fields as well.

In addition, Schweitzer was a prolific writer in many fields throughout his life. A selected list of his books includes: in philosophy, *The Religious Philosophy of Kant* (1899), *The Philosophy of Civilization* (1923), and *Indian Thought and Its Development* (1934); in biblical scholarship, *The Kingdom of God and Primitive Christianity* (1901), *The Quest for the Historical Jesus* (1906), and *The Mysticism of Paul the Apostle* (1931); in music, *The Art of Organ-Building and Organ-Playing in Germany and France* (1906) and the two-volume work *J. S. Bach* (1908); in theology, *Reverence for Life* (1966, posthumously); and in medicine, *The Psychiatric Study of Jesus* (1913) and *On the Edge of the Primeval Forest* (1921). He also wrote an autobiography,

Out of My Life and Thought (1933); a book on Goethe, *Goethe: Five Studies* (1961), and a treatise against the dangers of nuclear weapons, *On Nuclear War and Peace* (1958). Most of these works have been translated into English, and many are still available today in republished editions.

An Alsatian by birth, Schweitzer chose to do most of his scholarly writing in German. He spoke both German and French as a child because Alsace was bilingual, but German was his primary language, the language spoken at home. French was his second language, and although he spoke it well, it was not so easy for him to write and publish in French. However, Schweitzer's mentor and friend, the great French organist and composer Charles-Marie Widor, with whom he studied in Paris, suggested that he write a scholarly essay on J. S. Bach in French, and it evolved into a book-length study. Of this experience Schweitzer wrote: "To write the book in French at a time when I was also lecturing and preaching in German was an effort. It is true that ever since my childhood I have spoken French as readily as German. I always used French in my letters to my parents because that was the custom in my family. German, however, is my mother tongue, because the Alsatian dialect, which is my native language, is Germanic" (Schweitzer 1990, 63).

Schweitzer struggled with his French style, commenting later that "Like everyone who writes about art, I had to wrestle with the difficulty of expressing artistic opinions and impressions in words" (Schweitzer 1990, 64), and this difficulty was compounded by his discomfort with written French, which he felt to be constraining. "I can best describe the difference between the two languages," he remarked, "by saying that in French I seem to be strolling along the well-kept paths of a fine park, but in German to be wandering at will in a magnificent forest" (Schweitzer 1990, 63).

Although Schweitzer had reservations about his French style, Widor was pleased with the Bach book, and after it was published in 1905, critics in Germany encouraged Schweitzer to do a German translation. Instead of translating, however, Schweitzer finally rewrote the Bach book in German, in the process doubling it in size. When it appeared in 1908, it proved a great success.

Why Schweitzer Went to Africa

Albert Schweitzer was at the pinnacle of his career as a professor, author, musician, and pastor when he suddenly announced to his family and friends, in a letter mailed 5 October 1905, that he intended to study medicine and go to Africa as a physician. This letter left him with "hard battles to fight with my relatives and friends" (Schweitzer 1990, 86). To them it seemed to come without warning, but in fact Schweitzer had been considering this move for nine years.

One summer morning in 1896, he had awakened with the thought that he must give something to others in service:

> While outside the birds sang I reflected on this thought and before I had gotten up I came to the conclusion that until I was thirty I could consider myself justified in devoting myself to scholarship and the arts, but after that I would devote myself directly to serving humanity. I had already tried many times to find the meaning that lay hidden in the saying of Jesus: "Whosoever would save his life shall lose it, and whosoever shall lose his life for My sake and the Gospels shall save it." Now I had found the answer, I could now add outward to inward happiness. (Schweitzer 1990, 82)

For eight years he inwardly debated what form this service to others would take. Finally, in the autumn of 1904,

> I found on my writing table in the seminary one of the green-covered magazines in which the Paris Mission Society (La Société Evangélique des Missions à Paris) reported on its activities every month. . . . Without paying much attention, I leafed through the magazine that had been put on my table the night before. As I was about to turn to my studies, I noticed an article with the headline "Les besoins de la Mission du Congo" ([The needs of the Congo Mission] in the *Journal des Missions Evangéliques*, June 1904). It was by Alfred Boegner, the president of the Paris Missionary Society, an Alsatian, who complained that the mission did not have enough people to carry on its work in the Gabon. . . . The article concluded: "Men and women who can reply simply to the Master's call, 'Lord I am coming,' those are the people the church needs." I finished my article and quietly began my work. My search was over. (Schweitzer 1990, 85–86)[3]

3. In this quotation from Schweitzer's autobiography, he is inconsistent in his translation of La Société Evangélique des Missions à Paris, using first "Paris Mission Society" and then "Paris Missionary Society." Henceforth, the name will be translated as "Paris Missionary Society."

Schweitzer ignored the arguments of friends and family, and at age thirty he entered medical school.

Getting to Africa as a missionary was not easy for him. Schweitzer's unorthodox views on the divinity of Christ and his liberal interpretation of the historic doctrines of the Church made him suspect in the eyes of the Paris Missionary Society (Schweitzer 1990, 94, 114–15). The society thought him unfit for work even as a medical missionary because he might undermine the Christian efforts of the missionaries and corrupt the souls of the African people. Its members finally allowed him to go to Lambaréné, but only on condition that he be "muet comme une carpe" [mute as a carp] and refrain from preaching. They withheld their blessing but did not stop Schweitzer from going. He raised his own funds for medical supplies and expenses but used the society's existing facilities for his activities.

It was only with a bit of luck that the Lutheran Church of Alsace had ever ordained him in the first place: "I was almost denied ordination by the synod because of my views, and indeed was told, 'because of the heresies you have already put into print, there is probably not another synod of the Lutheran Church in the world that would ordain you, but we knew your father and your teachers and so we are willing to take a chance on you' " (Marshall and Poling 1989, 203).

Schweitzer was operating far beyond the doctrinal confines of the Lutheran church. His religious truth was to be Reverence for Life: the universal application of the commandment of Jesus to love.

If we substitute *I* for *us* and *I* for *they*, this last paragraph from his book becomes a divine directive for Schweitzer: "He comes to [me] as One unknown . . . He speaks to [me] the same word . . . and sets [me] to the tasks which He has to fulfill for [my] time . . . and [I] obey Him . . . [I] shall pass through toils, conflicts and sufferings in His fellowship . . . and [I] shall learn in [my own] experience Who he is" (Schweitzer 1968, 403).

In Lambaréné, Schweitzer came to understand "Who he is." It was Schweitzer who heard his commanding voice, followed him to Lambaréné in obedience, and did his will. This effort brought him "toils, conflicts and sufferings." Schweitzer omitted the name of Jesus in his credo because, to his way of thinking, the Lord's identity was revealed only in the doing of his will.

Schweitzer among the Africans

When Schweitzer arrived at Lambaréné in 1913, Gabon was under the jurisdiction of the French colonial government. French language and culture had already been introduced into the local region. The local population was harvesting Gabon's old-growth forest for European export. In return for this lumber, the colonial government offered money to the African laborers, who then used this money to buy French-made manufactured goods. The social reality of French West Africa did not escape Schweitzer's notice. He was aware of the problems caused by colonization, and he voiced his disapproval of a social order that exploited the native population for the economic benefit of the mother country. Nevertheless, Schweitzer thought it possible that, under ideal conditions, colonial rule could promote education and the self-betterment of the local population (Schweitzer 1990, 190). He argued that since it was no longer possible for the less developed peoples of the world to avoid contact with the West, the advanced Western nations had a moral obligation to provide health, education, and welfare assistance for the peoples of preindustrialized societies.

As a physician and humanitarian, Schweitzer saw the magnitude of the medical needs of the African people. He urged more doctors to go to Africa: "Doctors must go out to the colonies as a humane duty mandated by the conscience of society" (Schweitzer 1990, 195). He believed that before independence could be granted to any colony, it was morally necessary to raise the local population to the social, economic, and political level of the colonial power itself.

From the very beginning of his residency in 1913, Schweitzer had seen that the natives were tearing down their forest in order to acquire French money for the purchase of French goods. He was not happy that the African people labored for foreign capital and were not being encouraged to develop their own economy or industrial base. According to Schweitzer, "Farming and crafts are the foundations of civilization" (Schweitzer 1990, 194), but under these circumstances farming and crafts could not flourish.

Noting with dismay that educated Africans were not interested in the development of local agriculture and craftsmanship (Schweitzer 1976, 83), Schweitzer observed in the spring of 1925, "How true it is, after all, that civilization does not begin with reading and writing but with manual labor . . . but manual work is despised. Had I any say in the matter, no black man would be allowed to learn to read and write without being apprenticed to some trade. No training of the intellect without simultaneous training of the hands! (Schweitzer 1976, 169–70)

Schweitzer advocated the moral virtue of work because he was a firm believer in the holy virtue of work. He held that everyone in this world has a vocation or *calling* (in the Lutheran sense of the word), and that this calling is holy. A vocation in this sense is not limited to those who have been set apart from the common folk by religious rites and ceremonies. The specific activity is not at issue. The nature of one's work is irrelevant, so long as one's work is done for the glory of God and for the benefit of humanity. Even if work is not appreciated, God sees it secretly and will reward it openly in his Kingdom. The joy and blessing of the Kingdom of God has already come upon us even as we work in obscurity, for all work is holy. Thus, it did not matter to Schweitzer whether he was a farmer or a physician or a scholar or a musician or a preacher. What did matter was that he had experienced a "call" to do God's will. He chose to go to Equatorial Africa because he would be able to put into practice there the principles of the Kingdom of God as Jesus had taught them.

When it came to the practical matters of social behavior, Schweitzer was flexible. With respect to the practice of polygamy in Gabon, for example, Schweitzer did not agree with the Christian missionaries. He did not see polygamy as a problem, although it was a dilemma for most white Europeans. Recognizing that polygamy was necessary in a culture in which women and children were left unprotected without the legal safeguard of marriage (Schweitzer 1976, 85), Schweitzer was sure that the practice would disappear as African society developed. Monogamy was the goal, but it did not have to be imposed by force.

After World War II, Schweitzer's position on colonialism and related issues provoked much criticism. During the 1950s, late in his life, the movement for independence was sweeping throughout colonial Africa. Suspicious of nationalistic fervor, Schweitzer was reluctant to espouse this movement. He did not see nationalism as a solution for any human problem, and he was particularly adamant that his hospital be free from such influences.

Schweitzer feared nationalism as an excuse for totalitarian policies and military aggression, for racist policies and mass murder. This fear was rooted in personal experience: he and his family had suffered much as a result of the nationalist policies of France and Germany. Because they were German nationals, Schweitzer and his wife had been interned by French authorities during World War I. Later, during World War II, his wife and daughter had barely escaped the Nazi regime.

However, his critics interpreted his opposition to nationalism as evidence of paternalism and racism. Jackson Lee Ice comments: "These accusations stem partially from several remarks Schweitzer made in his 1954 Nobel Address in which he spoke of the growth of a 'virulent variety' of nationalism among the smaller nations of the world, and its endangering 'a long history of peace' " (Ice 1994, 5).

Such criticism was fueled by the press. Some articles even accused Schweitzer of exploiting the African people in order to become a famous humanitarian (Ice 1994, 2). But who was exploiting whom? The truth of the matter was that these journalists were exploiting Schweitzer for their own purposes. (Schweitzer recognized that these writers had their own agendas, but he nonetheless entertained them graciously.)

Some of the journalists who visited him when he was in his seventies and eighties did not like his "old-fashioned" ways and described him as being a "white patriarch," an old man "out of touch" with the modern world. They also scrutinized his method of hospital care. Because Schweitzer encouraged the presence of village life within the hospital compound, he was accused of having slovenly and unsanitary facilities and promoting dangerous medical practices.

There were no medically trained Africans when Schweitzer began his hospital and for many years thereafter. As trained African personnel became available, their employment in the hospital became a point of contention. Schweitzer was used to his European staff and wished to retain them.[4] He commented: "You must remain the *absolute* master of your establishment, as I am here, otherwise you risk the sorts of complications that could cause untold trouble. You will already have enough to do with the indigent and the locally trained doctors and nurses" (Byers 1996, 30). In this respect he might be viewed as an obstinate old patriarch.

---

4. According to Rhena Schweitzer Miller, "The Schweitzer hospital was never nationalized. It is still a private international institution, and although there is important Gabonese participation in finances, work, and direction, it is not run entirely by Gabonese" (Miller, letter to author, 13 February 1997).

However, there is a big difference between paternalism and racism. Schweitzer exercised an old-fashioned brand of paternalism in Lambaréné, but he did not think that one race of humanity was superior to another. There is evidence for his paternalism, but none for his racism. Ice's evaluation is this: "His personal paternal attitude at his hospital, the result, it seems, of experience rather than prejudice, must not be translated into a stand for racism. If Schweitzer possesses an 'elder brother' attitude toward the natives, it is in the spirit 'I am my brother's elder *brother*,' and not 'I am my brother's *keeper*,' so often exhibited by the condescending air of the so-called Christian nations" (Ice 1994, 6).

We must keep in mind that Schweitzer, who was thirty-nine at the outbreak of World War I and sixty-four at the outbreak of World War II, lived long before the concepts of "inclusive language" and "multiculturalism" appeared. His language reflects the standard Western usage of his day. He uses the words *man* and *brother* to mean all human beings. When he uses the word *primitive*, it is in a positive way: not in the sense of "backward" or "stupid," but instead meaning "unsophisticated." In speaking of the African people as "children of nature" or simply as "children," Schweitzer is only employing the rhetoric of another era, when European people spoke with conviction about "the noble savage" and the inherent purity of primitive peoples uncorrupted by the contamination of modern society.

He recognized a cultural difference between Europeans and West Africans, but this cultural difference had nothing to do with racial differences. For Schweitzer there was no such thing as being "better" or "inferior." There was only the personal nobility of "goodness, justice, and genuineness of character, real worth and dignity." Only these qualities could earn the respect and admiration of the "blacks" who judged the "whites" for themselves (Schweitzer 1976, 89).

Schweitzer's response to all criticism—criticism that became particularly virulent after he received the Nobel Peace Prize—was not to respond, an act in which he found the peace of God. In a letter from 1963 to Dr. Robert Weiss in Strasbourg, he wrote:

My strategy consists of never responding to any attack of any kind whatsoever. That has always been my principle, and I have stuck to it loyally. In the long run no one can fight against silence. It is an invincible opponent. Nor does anyone have to defend me. It is my lot to go my way without combat. It is my lot to pave the way for the spirit of reverence for life, which is also the spirit of peace. I am quite dumbfounded by the fact that I have been granted such a splendid calling; as a result, I go my way, spiritually unhindered. A grand, calm music roars within me. I am permitted to see the ethics of reverence for life starting to make its way through the world, and this elevates me beyond anything that anyone can reproach me for or do to me. (Schweitzer 1992, 331)

The following quotation reveals the depth of his self-understanding, especially as he tried to maintain his temper and humility in the face of harsh criticism.

I must forgive lies directed against me because so many times my own conduct has been blotted by lies. I must forgive the lovelessness, the hatred, the slander, the fraud, the arrogance, which I encounter, since I myself have so often lacked love, and have hated, slandered, defrauded, and been arrogant, and I must forgive without noise or fuss. In general, I do not succeed in forgiving fully; I do not even get as far as being always just. But he who tries to live by this principle, simple and hard as it is, will know the real adventures and triumphs of the soul.[5]

By remaining silent amid the firestorm of criticism, Schweitzer demonstrated peacemaking and compassion. By remaining silent, Schweitzer practiced what he preached; he was living the gospel. Since he too was sometimes guilty of unworthy actions and in need of forgiveness, Schweitzer responded with peace. He answered the critics with the silence of forgiveness, compassion, and love.

Worship with the Africans

Before going to Africa, Schweitzer had been a clergyman at St. Nicholas Church in Strasbourg, a professor of theology and philosophy at the Uni-

---

5. Marshall and Poling 1989, 296. This quotation is cited by Marshall and Poling and comes from an article published in the *Reader's Digest* of October 1949. It has been quoted by Fulton Oursler in an article on Schweitzer. It appears elsewhere in books by and about Schweitzer.

versity of Strasbourg, and a writer of major works in the fields of New Testament studies and musicology. Could he become a jungle physician and make the huge transition to African life? What would he say to the African people? Would they understand him? Could they benefit from his words as much as they could benefit from his practice of medicine? Schweitzer hoped they could.

Schweitzer's background notwithstanding, the local clergy doubted his intellectual qualifications. European credentials were of no value in this new setting. Even his theological knowledge was called into question: "One day, when I had expressed my opinion on a certain point at the request of the missionaries, one of the African preachers suggested that the matter was outside the Doctor's province 'because he is not a theologian' " (Schweitzer 1990, 141–42). Schweitzer did not impose his academic and theological credentials upon them. He was a modest man in this respect. However, it was not long after his arrival in Lambaréné that he was asked by the local clergy to preach: "As I did not make the smallest attempt to disturb them with my theological views, they soon laid aside all mistrust and rejoiced, as I did, that we were united in the piety of obedience to Jesus and in the will to simple Christian activity. Not many months after my arrival, they asked me to preach, and thus I was released from the promise I had given in Paris *d'être muet comme une carpe* (Schweitzer 1990, 141).

There was no chapel at the hospital, and, because Schweitzer honored the work of the Protestant mission and did not wish to compete or interfere with it, he did not celebrate Holy Communion, baptize African infants or adults, or officiate at African weddings.[6] However, since patients and their families at the hospital could not physically attend the Sunday service at the mission station, Schweitzer did hold a Sunday service at the hospital just for them.

In an article dated 25 July 1930, Schweitzer described a typical service at Lambaréné (Schweitzer 1931). What follows is my translation of the complete article.[7]

6. Rhena Schweitzer Miller has informed me, however, that "he did baptize expatriate babies and officiated at marriages between expatriates" (Miller, letter to author, 28 November 1998).

7. The sermon was printed in *Cahiers Protestants* 2 (March 1931):3–7. This source was handed to me by Mme. Poteau-Múller in Gunsbach, France, at the Maison Albert Schweitzer in 1997. It is the only source that is known to me. I have translated it from the French.

A Sunday Service in the Virgin Forest

The missionary station is three kilometers away and one can return there only in a canoe, which creates all sorts of hindrances. Also, I am supposed to preach regularly each Sunday at the hospital. Most of the patients don't know anything about Christianity and probably have never had the opportunity to hear a missionary. They come from hundreds of kilometers away in the interior, hired for two or three years to work in the untouched virgin forest and in the marshy areas to clear away the trees to the edge of the Ogooué, and there they can't be visited by the missionaries.

To preach to our patients and to their companions is to throw seeds into the wind that will take root far away.

One Sunday, at nine o'clock, a male nurse goes by all the barracks and rings a bell to summon everyone to "prayer," as they say. Slowly the assembly gathers together at a place between the barracks, and each one finds a place in the shade of the large overhanging roofs.

It is well over half an hour before the audience is completely gathered. Meanwhile, I play on the small harmonium that has been carried out into the open air. Or perhaps Madame Russell's gramophone plays a suitable religious piece.[8] I begin with the Word, avoiding the folly of singing or beginning with prayer. The listeners are almost all pagans and speak at least six different languages. If they had to begin with prayer, the newcomers wouldn't know what that was. It is the preaching that prepares them for a prayer.

I am flanked by two translators, who repeat my discourse, sentence by sentence. The one on my right translates into Pahouin, the one on my left into Bendjabi, a dialect that the peoples of the interior all understand, more or less.

That my listeners are as quiet as European churchgoers I wouldn't claim to be the case. If, at the place where they are gathered, some are in the habit of making their fire, I allow them to prepare their meal during the service. Mothers wash and groom their children. Men mend their nets, which are suspended under the overhanging roofs. Some natives, without shame, place their head on the knees of a friend and then he picks the lice out of their hair. It is better to allow this than to interrupt the

8. Mrs. Lillian Russell was an Englishwoman who assisted Schweitzer in Lambaréné. Fluent in German and French, she was his interpreter in England. She also transcribed some of his sermons at the hospital. "Mrs. Canada" received her nickname because she had orchards in Canada. Mrs. Russell had a great love of animals, especially chimpanzees, who were allowed to roam about freely, even on Sunday.

meditation with words of discipline, since it would be necessary to repeat them every Sunday to this audience, without stopping. Sheep and goats cross the meeting while butting and bleating. Weaver birds, situated in neighboring trees, make a deafening din. Even Mme. Russell's two monkeys, who are left free on Sunday, make their thousand circuits of neighboring palm trees and tile roofs, and finally come to huddle on the shoulders of their mistress.

However, despite the fact that there is a little movement, this service is solemn, because these people are going to hear the Word of God for the very first time.

My presentation is necessarily the simplest. My listeners do not know anything about the familiar stories of our childhood. They are ignorant of Adam, Eve, the patriarchs, the people of Israel, Moses, the prophets, the Law, the Pharisees, the Messiah, and the apostles. To an audience of one hour, which tomorrow will be scattered, it is necessary to give up on teaching even the elements of biblical history. The Word of God has to be given to them out of time, so to speak. With all these questions that I cannot approach, it seems to me as if I am like a pianist who is forbidden to use the black keys.

Once we admit this simplification, everything goes better, and we are amply compensated for our difficulties by the privilege, inexpressibly grand and lovely, of proclaiming the gospel to minds and souls that are completely untouched and fresh.

As the theme of my speech, I take a verse that I explain by one or two parables and by an appropriate biblical account. At the end, I repeat the verse several times, in order to fix it in the heart and the memory of my listeners.

I avoid speaking solely of the Law. Those who preach to pagans are too tempted to use it in this way, by way of preparation for the declaration of the gospel. I seek to awaken in hearts the desire to be at peace with God. The most primitive of my primitives can understand the difference between a soul without peace and a soul at peace. And when I present Jesus to them as the one who brings the peace of God to men, and when I tell them that the Messiah is the king of hearts sent by God, they understand.

I hold myself to the most elementary experiences. Whatever my point of departure may be, I always return to the central point, which is to allow myself to be seized by Christ. So, even if a listener hears me only once, he has at least an inkling of what it means to be a Christian.

I stay as concrete as possible, avoiding vague generalities in order to explain, for example, the question of Peter to Jesus: "How many times do I have to forgive my brother? Will this be up to seven times?" [Matt.

18:21]. I lead my people with complete realism, and I describe to them, through actions, what it means to forgive seven times in a single day.[9] Here is how I did it recently [sermon of 13 July 1930]: "One morning you get up and you leave your hut. You see a man coming who all hold to be wicked. He hurls an insult at you. You remember that Jesus said that one must forgive; you remain silent instead of entering into a discussion.

"Then your neighbor's goat eats the bananas you were saving for your dinner. Instead of seeking a quarrel, you only tell him what his goat did and that it would be fair if he replaces your bananas. But if he contests it and claims that this was not his goat, you distance yourself quietly and reflect that the good Lord made the bananas to grow in your plantation, that it is not worth the aggravation to enter into an argument for some fruit.

"Then you see a man coming to whom you entrusted ten bunches of bananas to sell at the market. He brings you only the price of nine bunches. You tell him that it is too little. He retorts that you are mistaken, that you have given him only nine bunches. You are going to shout to his face that he is a liar. But you think of all the lies, known only to you, that God has forgiven you, and you return peacefully to your hut.

"You are going to light your fire, and you notice that someone has helped himself to the wood that you have gathered from the old forest, which would have been sufficient for you for a week. Once more you restrain yourself. You give up going to search the homes of all your neighbors or filing a complaint with the chief.

"In the afternoon, you are going to leave for work at the plantation and you notice that someone has taken your good machete for clearing, that someone has taken it away and replaced it with a chipped one. As for the tool, you easily recognize that it has been damaged. Then you realize that you have forgiven four times and that you will have to make it a fifth. Although the day has already had plenty of annoyances, you feel as happy as ever. Why? Because your heart is happy to have obeyed the will of the Lord Jesus.

"In the evening, you want to go fishing. You go to take the torch placed in a corner of your hut. But it is not there. Anger seized you, and you say that today you have forgiven enough, that now you are going to lie in wait for the thief. Once more the Lord Jesus masters your heart and you descend to the bank with a torch borrowed from a neighbor.

---

9. The following is Schweitzer's rendition of the same sermon in the transcriptions. It differs slightly because he is recalling it from memory, and as he does so he recasts the points he once made.

"There you discover that your canoe has disappeared. Someone has used it to seek his own fish. Irritated, you hide behind a tree to spy upon him and you promise to pay him back thoroughly when he returns, to seize his fish, to file a complaint against him, and to make him pay you to make proper amends. But while you spy on him, your heart begins to speak. It does not stop repeating to you the word of Jesus: God cannot forgive us our sins if we do not forgive others their offenses. The hard wait lasts so long that the Lord Jesus once again achieves victory. When the other one returns at the end of the day and shrinks back when you come out from behind your tree, instead of welcoming him with punches, you tell him that the Lord Jesus has forced you to forgive him, and you let him go. You don't even ask for the fish that he has caught, if he does not give them over to you himself. But I believe that he will give them to you because he will be surprised that you don't make a palaver with him.

"Then you return to your house, happy and proud to have succeeded in forgiving seven times. But suppose that this very day the Lord Jesus comes into your village, that you appear before him and that you imagine that for your beautiful deeds he is going to praise you before the whole world. Hardly. He will tell you, as he did Peter, that seven times is still not enough, that one must forgive again seven times, and yet again, and a fourth time and many other times, if you want God to forgive you all the time."

To see the faces of the listeners, one feels their attention, receptive and focused. Often I interrupt to ask them if they have given thought to the divine Word or if they have some objection to make. In a chorus they reply that the Word of God is the truth.

An evangelist who was nursed at the hospital assists at the divine service. He goes afterward to the station to tell them that the doctor preaches as well as if he, like the missionaries, had studied theology!

At the end I explain briefly what prayer consists of. Then I make everyone place their hands together for prayer. The newcomers look like the old-timers. When all hands are placed with palms together, I pronounce an extemporaneous prayer very slowly in five or six sentences that my two translators repeat with the same slowness pronounced in the two languages. Once the amen is pronounced, their heads remain bowed for a long time in posture of reverence. They only raise them at the moment when the gramophone plays a sweet melody. All remain still until the last reverberation has faded away. Then I thank my two translators and I take my leave of them, while the assistants slowly rise and disperse.

Worship with the Staff

Schweitzer also had services for his staff. Every evening he led a brief devotional meditation or vesper service. It is interesting to see the remarkable similarity between the Sunday service for the native Gabonese at his hospital and the one for his European staff. Schweitzer uses a simple order of worship and gives us a thoughtful and clear presentation of the biblical text he has chosen.

The dinner hour for the staff was held regularly at six o'clock in the evening in the dining hall. Schweitzer sat at the head table. He was pater familias, not only head of staff but also head of the Lambaréné family. "Here in Lambaréné we are like a kind of convent, and it's necessary to have a Father at the Head of the community" (Byers 1996, 60). After a moment of silence, and before the meal itself, Schweitzer would offer his standard blessing: "Danket dem Herrn, denn er ist freundlich und seine Güte währet ewiglich" [Thank the Lord, for he is gracious and his goodness is everlasting], words that begin Psalms 106, 107, and 118.

Following dinner, the tables would be cleared and a brief devotional service would be held, with Schweitzer at the head table. His staff became a congregation. The service began with a hymn or two. Hymnals would be distributed to all, and Schweitzer would select a hymn to be sung. He would walk to the piano in the room and improvise for a while before introducing the first chord of the hymn. The tune and words were familiar to all. After everyone sang he would read a passage from the Bible and then give a commentary about it. Such commentaries usually lasted between one and five minutes, but occasionally he would speak longer. After his presentation there would be a recitation of the Lord's Prayer, which effectively concluded the evening.

George Marshall, in his biography of Schweitzer, gives the following eyewitness account of the evening's proceedings as he observed them during his visit to Lambaréné in the 1950s:

> At the conclusion of the hymn, Dr. Schweitzer would walk slowly around the table to his place, seat himself deliberately, open a well-thumbed Bible to a page where he had placed a bookmark, clear his throat, announce the Bible passage, and begin reading it in both German and French. He finished the passage, announced a prayer, flipped the pages

back to another bookmark at Matthew: 7, and read the Lord's Prayer. Closing the worn Bible, he would glance around the table at the hushed expectant faces wreathed in lamplight and would begin a discussion of the passage just read. With the thoughts of the readings in their minds, the hospital staff would retire for the night, walking back to their cabins by lamplight. (Marshall and Poling 1989, 280)

Some of what was said during these devotional or vesper services is contained in the so-called *Bibellese*. This German word is Schweitzer's term for the brief Bible exposition he gave in each evening service. It means "Bible lessons" and is always plural in form. The Bibellese have never been published or edited. The manuscript of the lessons belongs to Rhena Schweitzer Miller and remains in her personal collection.

When Schweitzer discovered that Siegfried Neukirch was transcribing his verbal commentaries, he became quite upset and demanded that any written Bible lessons be destroyed. Rhena persuaded her father not to require their destruction. Schweitzer agreed on the condition that they were not published and that they remained in his daughter's possession. In a personal letter to the author dated 13 February 1997, Rhena Schweitzer Miller stated that "Siegfried Neukirch, who wrote in shorthand the contents of the Bibellese, was no member of the medical staff. He works now as a librarian, and in Lambaréné he was supervisor of maintenance and construction crews and driver of the hospital truck. The lessons of the Bibellese were given every evening after supper."

Although these Bible lessons continued on a daily basis throughout Schweitzer's career in Lambaréné, it was only during the period from 2 May 1963 to 12 August 1965, that Siegfried Neukirch managed to transcribe approximately 781 of these devotionals, writing them secretly and later transcribing his notes. Neukirch believed it was important to have a record of these events for the sake of posterity. Schweitzer was eighty-eight years old in 1963 when the first Bibellese was transcribed and ninety in 1965 when the final Bible lesson, from 12 August 1965, was given and copied, just twenty-three days before Schweitzer's death on 4 September. The Bibellese, then, are a significant record of Schweitzer's personal faith and pastoral skill.

He did not need to live in Alsace and serve a church as his father before him in order to be a pastor to his people. He could continue to live and work in Lambaréné and, by so doing, serve as a pastor to the world. In 1950, Schweitzer wrote to a minister friend in Alsace, Robert Hirt:

> For a long time I nursed the hope of returning home from Lambaréné in
> my later years and spending my twilight years as pastor of a small Alsatian
> parish. Now I see that I have to keep working here even in my old age. . . .
> Both of us value work as something precious and we are grateful to God
> from the depths of our hearts. . . . May we, as blessed people, become
> blessings for others and continue as blessings as long as God allows us to
> wander down here. (Schweitzer 1992, 214–15)

Schweitzer was successful as a preacher and pastor in Lambaréné because he had a pastoral heart. He showed himself to be a disciple of Jesus, the Good Shepherd, who cares for his sheep. Schweitzer never relinquished his pastorate, even after he left St. Nicholas in Strasbourg. Though his parish was Lambaréné it included the world. His religion hadn't changed; it had simply expanded.

Toward a Reading of the African Sermons

Two years after his arrival in Lambaréné, Schweitzer had a revelation:

> Late on the third day, at the very moment when, at sunset, we were mak-
> ing our way through a herd of hippopotamuses, there flashed upon my
> mind, unforeseen and unsought, the phrase "reverence for life." The iron
> door had yielded. The path in the thicket had become visible. Now I had
> found my way to the principle in which affirmation of the world and
> ethics are joined together! (Schweitzer 1990, 155)

Here was Schweitzer's "Damascus road experience": Paul the Apostle had had a revelation about the divine truth of the risen Christ; Schweitzer had a revelation about the sacredness of all life. On the Ogooué River near Lambaréné in 1915, it dawned on him that all life is mysterious and there-fore must be handled lovingly and with reverence. He established a new philosophical connection between rational though and biblical *agape* that he called "Ehrfurcht vor dem Leben" (Reverence for Life). "I believe that God has assigned me the task of establishing a philosophical *Weltanschau-*

ung that reconciles thought and religion," he commented in a letter from 1922, "something that will contribute to human progress: the *Weltanschauung* of the Kingdom of God. However, this philosophy has power only if I live it" (Schweitzer 1992, 64–65).[10] In other words, he had to practice daily what he preached.

Theological and Philosophical Themes

On 15 October 1913, not long before the outbreak of the Great War, Schweitzer wrote to Walter Lowrie from Africa: "The days are devoted to helping in the name of Jesus, to fighting for the Kingdom of God—actions that I call practical eschatology" (Schweitzer 1992, 37).[11] *Practical eschatology* for Schweitzer meant working daily to establish a beachhead in Lambaréné for the Kingdom of God. In that little corner of the African jungle, he would translate the "eternal ethic of active love" into deeds of medical kindness, live out the gospel of love, and promote the philosophy of Reverence for Life. Schweitzer appears to have seen each deed of selfless love as a preparation for the Kingdom of God. Each act of *agape* may have been as small as a grain of mustard seed, but once performed, it would take root and become a great and useful tree, hastening the coming of the Kingdom of God (Matt. 13:31–32).

Schweitzer believed that the ethics of Jesus' love composed the one true standard for all interactions among men and nations and between men and nature—a noble ideal worthy of the efforts of a great man. He was struck by the profundity and simplicity of his insight. "Sometimes," he said in a letter dated Palm Sunday, 1930, "I am deeply moved by the thought that I have found and can utter the philosophical expression for the ethics of Jesus' love in my doctrine of reverence for life, so that people can be led on the road to Jesus through true and profound thought" (Schweitzer 1992, 108). It was a task that engaged all his talents.

In Africa he found new inspiration as well as a new challenge: "Evenings I go to bed dead tired," he wrote in a letter from April 1913,

10. This letter, dated 5 January 1922, was addressed to "Baron Lagerfelt and Greta Lagerfelt, Duseborg, Sweden, Malung [Central Sweden]." Greta Lagerfelt was Schweitzer's Swedish translator.

11. Walter Lowrie was a doctor of theology at the American Church of St. Paul in Rome, Italy.

"but in my heart I am profoundly happy that I am serving at the outpost of the Kingdom of God" (Schweitzer 1992, 28).[12] Lambaréné became the physical expression for not only the ethics of Jesus' love but also Schweitzer's own doctrine of Reverence for Life. Although there were times when Schweitzer left Lambaréné, he did so only when necessary— for the sake of his family, to renew his European roots, to lecture, to play concerts, or to encourage others to help him with his hospital—and he would always return. In one of his sermons he speaks of the petition in the Lord's Prayer concerning the Kingdom of God: "We know that the Kingdom of God has already begun, because God has already sent the king and the kingdom into the world. This king is Jesus, our Lord, the king of hearts" (10 August 1930).

Preachers often have one sermon that they consistently preach. Schweitzer was no exception. He had one prominent theme: God is love, and we are to love each other. Jesus reveals God's love, brings peace to our hearts, and shows us how to love each other. So everyone is to make Jesus lord of their hearts because he is the king of hearts. They are to love all. For Schweitzer, this is the core of the Christian message, which he preached over and over.

Schweitzer had his own interpretation of why Jesus died. In an early sermon given in April 1914, while he was sponsored by the Paris Missionary Society, he stated that Jesus had to die "that all men might be saved." This is the standard Christian phraseology. But when Schweitzer repeated this theme in a sermon given in 1930, he modified his position. To the sentence "It is extraordinary that there is a Jesus, the Son of God, who died for men so that God forgives them their sins when they are dead," Schweitzer added, "No one can explain this because it is a thought of God" (20 April 1930). A later sermon (10 September 1933) contains the clearest statement of Schweitzer's belief. In that sermon, he quoted Jesus as saying, "I die for the sins of men. I die in order that the Lord God may send the Kingdom of God on earth." According to Schweitzer, Jesus hoped that God would send the kingdom, but the kingdom never came. Schweitzer held that God can forgive our sins without the death of Jesus. The reason why God wanted Jesus to die remains a mystery to be revealed only in heaven. Jesus died for us as an example of what it means to live for others.

12. This letter was dated only by month, not by day, and sent to Adele Woytt.

We look in vain in Schweitzer's sermons for any mention of the problems of the historical Jesus, the apocalyptic world view of first-century Judea, or the Christ-mysticism of Paul the Apostle. Although he continued to write about these topics the entire time he was in Lambaréné, they are not mentioned in the African sermons. These were specialized subjects and out of place in Lambaréné.

To the inhabitants of Lambaréné, Schweitzer presented a simple yet profound Christianity. He never asked his audience to acknowledge the divinity of Jesus. He never urged anyone to accept Jesus as personal Lord and Savior. He never told anyone that it was necessary to be saved in order to go to heaven. Schweitzer simply said that Jesus is the king of hearts who brings peace to our hearts, and that God will ultimately reward the good. He did not demand that others believe this.

Likewise, he never tried to persuade anyone to believe in the existence of God, the Holy Spirit, or the Trinity. He never insisted that one must be baptized or partake of Holy Communion in order to be a Christian. Schweitzer assumed that many in his audience had heard about Jesus from the Christian missions in Lambaréné, but he never tried to make new Christians out of them.

What he did want was for his listeners to reform their personal conduct in accordance with the teachings and ethical example of Jesus. He wanted his African brothers and sisters to be as forgiving and loving and gentle toward others as Jesus had been to the people around him. He assured them that when their lives and hearts were duly prepared, Jesus, the king of hearts, would become lord of their hearts.

Schweitzer on Palavers and Reverence for Life

There is a curious word that Schweitzer uses to describe the pointless and destructive arguments that were a normal part of tribal life in Lambaréné: *palavers*. Schweitzer detested these endless parleys as useless and ultimately harmful, and frequently admonished his audience not to engage in them.

The dictionary defines *palaver* as "a long parley, especially one with primitive natives," or "a conference or long discussion of profuse and idle talk." *Palaver*, from Latin *parabola* meaning "parable," came into English usage in the eighteenth century and is a standard word in French. Schweitzer frequently used the word to mean a pointless or fruitless conference or discussion. He did not like palavers because he felt they created more problems than they solved. Speaking of the palaver that God will have with certain "ne'er-do-wells" at the time of the heavenly judgment, for example, he would tell his audience that they would not benefit from the outcome of such a palaver. God's verdict at the heavenly palaver would not please those who had done bad things. Schweitzer wanted his listeners to change their conduct and behave according to "the laws of God," but, as he comments in his sermon of 13 July 1930, "Our wicked heart never wants to forgive, but always wants to have palavers with men."

There were some kinds of behavior that Schweitzer could not abide: lying, stealing, adultery. He railed against these things and was convinced that palavers only encouraged immorality:

> It often happens that people do not tell the truth in the palavers. There are people who are innocent and there are those who are guilty. You all know about these palavers where people who have not stolen are accused as if they had stolen, or as if they had committed adultery, and where people who have not killed are accused as if they had committed murder or even poisoned someone. . . . This is the reason why there is a lot of injustice in the world—because people in the palavers do not tell the truth. (30 March 1930)

According to Schweitzer, palavers encourage lying and bickering and solve nothing. They allow the innocent to suffer while the guilty are exonerated. Palavers not only allow immorality to flourish but are deadly to those who are unable to defend themselves from false accusations.

Schweitzer did not use the specific phrase *reverence for life* in his Lambaréné sermons, but his philosophy of life does appear in his strong exhortation against the wanton destruction of life. He was adamant about the commandment of God that says, "You shall not kill."

On 9 February 1930, he was in the midst of a series of sermons on the Ten Commandments, specifically the commandment prohibiting murder or killing. Schweitzer knew that everyone in Lambaréné lived in constant fear of a violent death—someone might kill them at any time. Tribal rivalries made life dangerous for everyone. Those who kill others, Schweitzer said, will answer to God for their actions, and those who are planning to kill someone ought to reconsider their murderous intentions. Everyone has both good and bad thoughts in their hearts, he declared; when we allow bad thoughts to triumph in the human heart, we commit all kinds of evil, including murder. We must pay attention to our hearts, he said, to monitor our emotions and keep our passions within due bounds. How is this to be accomplished? With the law of God that forbids killing.

Schweitzer did not preach against killing in order to condemn behavior, but rather to change it. He wanted those in his audience to control their aggressive behavior. You must think before you act, he said, and act in light of the biblical commandments.

In the sermon of 2 March 1930, Schweitzer in effect explains his philosophy of Reverence for Life without naming it. He says that only when we are hungry or in danger may we take the life of an animal, because all animals are children of God; they are not to be mistreated. It is up to those who hear this message to "tell everybody in the villages that it is not necessary to kill animals."

Evolution of Schweitzer's Preaching Style

Over the years, the sermons reveal an evolution of Schweitzer's vision. As he learned his role, he relaxed. The sermons uniquely reflect these changes, giving us fascinating glimpses of Schweitzer's maturation on the job.

Schweitzer followed the calendar of the Church year, but he did not use a lectionary. He enjoyed preaching about the significance of Advent, Christmas, Holy Week, Easter, and Pentecost, and took the opportunity to do so whenever it presented itself. Otherwise, most of his African sermons were topical. He did not spend time explicating texts but chose his themes from the great storehouse of well-worn topics used by generations of Protestant clergymen: the Ten Commandments, the Lord's Prayer, the Sermon on the Mount, the parables of Jesus, the coming of the Holy Spirit, and the biographies of the apostles.

Schweitzer used the Bible in the time-honored Protestant fashion. It was his holy book of faith and practice: "the Word of God." All of his sermons were based upon Scripture.

In 1913, he was thirty-eight and new to Africa. The request of the local missionaries that he preach had released him from his pledge to the Paris

Missionary Society to be "mute as a carp."[13] Nevertheless, he was mindful of the society's suspicions concerning his theological orthodoxy. Its members knew he was liberal in his theological opinions, so they listened closely as he preached for the very first time in Lambaréné. It was their job to save African souls. They did not believe this was Schweitzer's primary objective, and they were right. Schweitzer had other plans—he wished to save African bodies—but he was in Lambaréné by the permission of the Paris Missionary Society. Thus in 1913, Schweitzer spoke cautiously and used traditional theological style. He had to be sure that the missionary society would not find fault with him. He needed their approval. Perhaps that is why he wrote out the 1913–14 sermons completely, to make certain he followed orthodox Christian doctrine.

In 1913–14, Schweitzer was just beginning to learn his way around, and he did not know the African people very well. His first Lambaréné sermons were modest and simple, unlike the highly developed and philosophically complex sermons he had once preached (in German) at St. Nicholas Church in Strasbourg. There he had preached to an educated European congregation. Here in Lambaréné his audience was neither educated nor sophisticated; in fact, it was not a Western audience at all. His listeners had no centuries of Christian belief to draw on, no tradition of abstract thinking. The people of Lambaréné were animists. Tribal bickering was the order of the day. It was only in 1890 that the French had officially colonized Gabon, and Schweitzer arrived there in 1913.

Compared with his European sermons, therefore, Schweitzer's Lambaréné sermons are brief. His words had to be translated, line for line, into two native languages, even as he spoke them. Accordingly, he had to pause after every sentence or two. He was obliged to express himself in simple language, directly and clearly; long, complex sentences and abstract expressions weren't useful here.

The translators were indispensable. On one occasion during a later sojourn in Africa, Schweitzer had to break off his sermon before he had completed even one sentence; because of a mix-up, the native translators hadn't shown up, and it was impossible to proceed without them (20 June 1930).

13. Some of the local missionaries were affiliated with the Paris Missionary Society and were aware of Schweitzer's "liberal" theological views. However, after they got to know him personally, this knowledge did not prevent them from asking him to preach.

In his very first sermon (20 April 1913), Schweitzer announced a great plan to the people of Lambaréné. It was his statement of purpose, his "mission" to them. He had come, he said, in imitation of the Lord Jesus Christ, the great healer, and, like the Lord himself, would bring healing to the people of Lambaréné. He had come to establish a site for the Kingdom of God in such an extraordinary location because Lambaréné was a favored place in the heart of Jesus. By his fourth sermon (28 September 1913), Schweitzer was admonishing his audience to live good lives, as befitted the children of a loving father. He declared that they must cease from drunkenness, lying, stealing, covetousness, murder, hatred, and adultery—sins that grieve the Holy Spirit. It was because of these sins that many of them were dying and others were suffering from diseases of all kinds.

Schweitzer began his African preaching career as a moralist. These sermons often admonished the Africans, giving them "the Law." No liberties were taken with Scripture; the Paris Missionary Society was listening.

His first residency in Lambaréné ended abruptly in 1914. Schweitzer and his wife Hélène had arrived at Lambaréné on 16 April 1913. On 5 August 1914, at the outbreak of the First World War, they were arrested by the French authorities and detained as enemy German nationals. They were confined in Lambaréné for four months and forbidden to work. At that point, because the local people complained that they needed the Schweitzers' medical services, the officials reluctantly gave the Schweitzers permission to continue their medical work. This state of affairs did not last long, however; in the fall of 1917, Albert and Hélène were removed to France as prisoners of war.

In 1918, Schweitzer became seriously ill. The following year, Hélène gave birth to Rhena, their only child. During the 1920s, Schweitzer developed a new profession—peripatetic lecturer and concertizer. Several of his books were published. He was now famous and had collected enough money to continue his hospital. Schweitzer returned to Africa in 1924 and lived there until 1927.

He was no longer beholden to the Paris Missionary Society because early in 1927 he moved his hospital from the mission station to a larger site two miles upstream (Schweitzer 1990, 210), on 170 acres given him to use by the Gabonese government (Brabazon 2000, 335). Henceforth the hospital would receive private funding through the generosity of many people and organizations throughout the world. "The land remained the government's, but any building or development would be Schweitzer's property" (Brabazon 2000, 335).

Before Schweitzer left for his second sojourn in Africa (1924–27), an organization, L'Association des Amis de l'Hôpital Schweitzer, had been set up in Strasbourg for this very purpose (Miller, interview with author, 1992). He spent most of the 1924–27 period building his new hospital, and no sermons from that era survive.

In the summer of 1927, Schweitzer returned to Europe. The arrangements for Lambaréné were now in the hands of Mme. Emmy Martin at "the new house at Günsbach" (Schweitzer 1990, 213). He returned to Lambaréné in the autumn of 1929 and remained until 1932.

The sermons from 1930–31 are therefore from his third residency in Lambaréné. In 1930, Schweitzer had every reason to be pleased with his mission in Lambaréné. He was free from the missionary society's supervision; he had earned not only the respect of the villagers but also the admiration of the entire world; and he was older and wiser. Schweitzer had become an authority on native customs and habits and was now thoroughly at home in Equatorial Africa. Sixteen years had passed since his internment—sixteen years of life-changing events and experiences.

The 1930–31 sermons reflect this maturation and freedom. Now literally preaching off the front porch of his home, he was much more relaxed. He had become comfortable with the African people. Accordingly, the 1930–31 sermons contain spontaneous and colloquial elements not found in the earlier sermons, especially those from 1913–14 and those he preached in the spring of 1930 on the Ten Commandments. Schweitzer's 1931 article describing a typical service (translated in its entirety on pages xxxi–xxxiv of this book) illustrates his new approach.[14] In the earlier sermons, Schweitzer used strong moralistic language, urging the Africans to stop lying, stealing, and committing other grievous sins. It is only after Easter 1930 that his sermons change from being exhortations to the Africans requesting that they change their behavior to nonmoralistic themes that "seek to awaken, in hearts, the desire to be at peace with God" (Schweitzer 1931). In his 1931 article he states: "I avoid speaking solely of the Law. Those who preach to pagans are too tempted to use it in this way, by way of preparation for the declaration of the Gospel" (Schweitzer

14. See note 7 for details of Schweitzer's 1931 article.

1931). One wonders what catalyst of self-awareness caused Schweitzer to stop moralizing. Perhaps it was the act of writing the 1931 article.

In his later sermons, Schweitzer presented his biblical texts imaginatively. Making generous use of illustrations from African village life, he invented his own paraphrases of Scripture so that his African audience could more easily understand the biblical stories and moral teaching. Other techniques also helped to make the sermons from 1930–31 livlier and more memorable than Schweitzer's earlier sermons. Sometimes he asked questions of his audience and waited for their responses. And he didn't hesitate to depart from his sermon momentarily for a short digression on decorum if something or someone disturbed the worship service. Later we will examine these aspects of Schweitzer's style in more detail.

In Schweitzer's 1933 and 1935 sermons, during his fourth and fifth stays in Lambaréné, we see another shift. The extemporaneous interjections have ceased. No longer does he depart from his sermon text and comment on the audience's activities. Audience participation seems to be nonexistent. Although a different person transcribed these later sermons, and it is possible that she simply may have omitted offhand remarks, the sermons themselves reflect a more pensive Schweitzer.[15] His fanciful rewriting of biblical material almost ceases, except for his last African sermon, dated 5 May 1935. Most moralisms are gone.

In his sermon of 30 April 1933, the first after his return that year, he shows his genuine gratitude for the gifts of money that ensured the survival of the hospital. We don't often get him speaking his feelings out loud so strongly. These last sermons are quiet musings on the spirit of love, the king of hearts, peace, gentleness, giving thanks, and doing good for others.

After 1935, the transcription of sermons ceased. Although there are some indications that Schweitzer preached sermons to the Africans in 1937 and 1940, no further transcriptions of such sermons have been found.

Ulrich Neuenschwander, the editor of *Strassburger Predigten*, a collection of sermons preached by Schweitzer at St. Nicholas in Strasbourg

15. Schweitzer was just back from Europe, which, like the rest of the world, was suffering from the effects of the Great Depression; and in Europe there were already signs that another war might be on the horizon. In several sermons from this period he speaks of such matters, sometimes referring to the devastation of the First World War or mentioning the bad news he sees in newspapers he gets from Europe.

during the first two decades of the twentieth century, says that the characteristics of Schweitzer's preaching there may be summed up in five points. These points, identified by Neuenschwander in his "Editor's Postscript: Albert Schweitzer as Preacher," may also be applied to the Lambaréné sermons, almost without change.

1. Schweitzer mainly uses the New Testament texts and only rarely a text from the Old Testament. . . . Within the New Testament, Schweitzer obviously preferred the Synoptics (Matthew, Mark, and Luke) and the writings of Paul. . . . But his piety centered entirely on Jesus himself.

2. Schweitzer generally chose short texts, usually a saying [of Jesus'] full of meaning. He did not preach homilies. . . , paraphrasing whole chapters verse by verse. . . . Rather, his method was to be moved and led by the saying, and to explore it. . . .

3. Schweitzer never preached doctrinal or teaching sermons. Nor was he moralistic. Rather, he was concerned with the souls of his flock. . . .

4. The language of his sermons is *very simple*. Schweitzer avoids learned phrases; at the same time, he deliberately addresses simple folk without speaking down to them. . . .

This simple sermon language is made extremely colorful and vivid by its wealth of comparison and illustrations. His language is never abstract but filled to the brim with concrete illustrations. . . . He is a close observer, and his pictures become parables. It would not be wrong to conclude that he modeled his sermons on the picturesque language of the parables of Jesus.

5. In his sermons, especially those of Advent, Christmas, and Passiontide, the pervasion of an almost mystical nearness of Jesus is noticeable. Only rarely does Schweitzer speak of Jesus in dogmatic terms. Everything is rooted in a blessed experience of community of will and life with the Lord. . . . (Schweitzer 1969, 149–52)

These points generally hold true of his Lambaréné sermons, but with two provisos: first, Schweitzer did give a number of sermons on the Old Testament (the Ten Commandments in particular); and second, he did moralize when speaking to the African people. However, Neuenschwander's point about Schweitzer's colorful language and concrete examples is very important, as we shall see.

Biblical Themes in African Dress

The preacher needs to know his audience. By 1930, Schweitzer knew his audience well. After all, it was composed of his African patients and their families. He knew that few in his audience could read. Moreover, unlike a European congregation familiar with Bible stories from early childhood, many in Schweitzer's African flock were hearing them for the first time. As he retold the stories and passages from the Bible, therefore, Schweitzer felt free to modify them for his listeners, either to make them more accessible or to emphasize a particular point he wanted to make. This free style of preaching not only reveals Schweitzer's deepest convictions but also provides us with fascinating insights into village life at Lambaréné.

One of Schweitzer's favorite tools was figurative language. Drawing on African daily life, he added concrete details or altered those in the original Bible stories to enable his listeners to make the imaginative leap from the familiar to the unfamiliar, from the description in his analogy to the biblical concept he sought to convey. Schweitzer relied particularly on the simile. I have already discussed one striking example from the sermon of 9 February 1930, on the injunction against killing (one of a series of sermons on the Ten Commandments), in which Schweitzer warned his listeners that in its passions the human heart is like a monkey. The monkey may first appear to be "sweet and nice," but then it "jumps on you and bites you." Human hearts, like monkeys, need to be restrained, argued Schweitzer; only the law of God is sufficient to bind the hearts of men.

Schweitzer used a similar analogy to bring home to his audience the biblical commandment to work. "The laws of God are like the nut of a palm tree," he explained in a sermon given 9 March 1930. "When one breaks it, there is another inside. So within this law, 'You shall not steal,' there is the other law, 'You must work.' "

In a Pentecost sermon delivered on 15 June 1930, Schweitzer used similes from nature to explain the reality of the "Spirit of God." Asking "What is a spirit?" he compares the spirit of God with clouds that give rain. Just as we cannot touch a cloud, so we cannot touch the spirit that is in a human being, and just as a blade of grass sprouts up without our understanding why, so no one is able to explain the spirit and the thoughts that are in the human heart. "God speaks so that no one can hear. Only the heart understands it." As the light of the sun illuminates the world, so the spirit of God illuminates our hearts, he concludes.

In a sermon from 16 March 1930, he describes the necessity for truthfulness. One must be truthful because a man who tells the truth "is like a man who walks into the lake and cannot drown, and he remains clean, while the other is the one who walks into the swamp." In Schweitzer's theology, cleanliness and truth-telling go together.

Schweitzer also used other sorts of comparisons to help his audience get a sense of things outside their own experience. Knowing that Damascus was much larger than anything his audience was familiar with, for example, Schweitzer said in a sermon delivered on 18 May 1930, "Libreville and Brazzaville are small villages compared to Damascus.[16] There were a lot of houses, all in stone, and beautiful churches, and very rich people." In another sermon, dated 5 May 1935, he described the Sea of Galilee as "a lake almost as big as Lake Azingo."

In his efforts to help his audience understand the Bible lessons he was telling, Schweitzer did more than create comparisons; often, he modified or added details to bring the stories alive. In discussing the burning of ancient Rome, for example, Schweitzer comments that "a large part of this city was burned during the dry season" (4 May 1930). The Bible text makes no mention of a "dry season" in its account of the burning of Rome, but Schweitzer knew that such a reference would make sense to people living in equatorial Africa, where fires occur frequently during the dry season. Schweitzer similarly modified details of the martyrdom of early Christians, saying that the captives were killed, not by the sword—a weapon unknown in Gabon—but by "the machete," or were "given up to be eaten by leopards," familiar animals roaming the jungle around Lambaréné. Likewise, in Acts 2, the Bible states that when the Apostles received the Holy Spirit, they were accused of having drunk "new wine"; in Schweitzer's version, dated 8 June 1930, the "new wine" becomes "palm tree wine." Another biblical passage, Acts 17:17, tells how the apostle Paul would position himself in the marketplace and begin to speak when he visited a city on one of his missionary journeys. Again, Schweitzer adds homely details from

16. Libreville is in Gabon, Brazzaville in Congo. Both cities are river ports.

Gabonese village life, defining a market as a place "where they sold pista-chios and loincloths and everything else" (4 May 1930).

Schweitzer also speculated on the martyrdom of Peter and Paul, com-menting that "probably they were burned. The resin was placed on the body as for a torch, and then they were lit. It is probably like this that they died." No scriptural information recounts any of this; Schweitzer added these details of African village life himself so that his audience could easily follow the stories.

Schweitzer's retelling of the tale of Paul's escape from Damascus in a basket (Acts 9:23–25), given in a sermon on 18 May 1931, likewise adds de-tails intended to make the story more vivid for his listeners. We learn to our surprise that the house where Paul was staying was a "hut," that the rope used to lower the basket was made from "creepers," or vines, and that Paul's friends put "something for him to eat and some water" into the bas-ket. We are also informed that it rained heavily that night. The original Bible story is only three verses long: "When many days had passed, the Jews plotted to kill him, but their plot became known to Saul. They were watching the gates day and night, to kill him; but his disciples took him by night and let him down over the wall, lowering him in a basket." It makes no mention of the composition of the rope, the weather, or of food and drink for Paul.

A second sermon on Paul, delivered on 1 June 1930, draws even more fully on village life. In Lambaréné, the local population was accustomed to wearing little more than loincloths; only the rich could afford fancy cloth-ing. Accordingly, Schweitzer tells his audience that the Apostle Paul had himself been the object of derision for wearing a frayed loincloth: "Then they said, 'What does he want, this pauper who doesn't even have a decent loincloth?' " Needless to say, nowhere in the Bible does Paul ever appear in a loincloth, much less is he criticized for wearing a frayed one. Schweitzer also changes Paul's livelihood from a "maker of tents" (Acts 18:33) to a "maker of mats." The inhabitants of Lambaréné knew nothing of tents, which were virtually useless in Gabon because they would quickly rot in the moist jungle atmosphere. On the other hand, mats, which they used for flooring in their huts, were perfectly familiar. Schweitzer's versions are imaginative amplifications of the text designed to bring the stories to life for Gabonese listeners.

Schweitzer also added details to the Bible stories in order to make a specific point or to stress a lesson he felt particularly strongly about. Common themes in his sermons were the evils of theft and the need for industry and cleanliness.

Schweitzer particularly deplored stealing, a pervasive problem in Lambaréné. Everyone stole from everyone else and showed no regret; hospital patients were particularly vulnerable. "There are some days at the Protestant Mission when a child is admitted for surgery and men have stolen things of value from that child," Schweitzer lamented in a sermon on 2 March 1930. Medicines, food, and equipment also disappeared routinely. Complaining that it was impossible to run a hospital under these conditions, Schweitzer went on the offensive, preaching against theft over and over, warning that all thieves will have to answer to God for their actions, and working the theme into the Bible lessons themselves.

In one rather astonishing sermon delivered on 13 July 1930, Schweitzer recast the Bible story from Matthew 18, touching on both the problem of theft and the need for forgiveness, in terms designed to bring the lesson home. St. Peter, seeking to go fishing in the evening, "looked for his flashlight, but his flashlight (or torch) was no longer there." It appears to have been stolen, along with his canoe. Peter flies into a rage and threatens to go to the thief's hut and "tear apart his mosquito netting. 'I am going to rip up everything in his hut,' " he says. Fortunately for the robber, Peter has second thoughts. Reminding himself that he is still a disciple of Jesus, he refrains from taking revenge and forgives the man.

Schweitzer similarly amplifies on a Bible lesson in which St. Peter and his fellow disciples go fishing in the Sea of Galilee to condemn the sin of sloth. In a sermon dated 5 May 1935, he stated that Peter and his fellows were not "lazy fishermen like you—fishermen who come to ask for line, fishermen who come to ask for hooks, fishermen who come to ask for advances and afterwards do not bring any fish, fishermen who sleep the whole night long in their huts instead of going fishing." Jesus, he pronounced, much prefers hard-working fishermen who have "stayed outside all night long to catch fish and to bring them to those who had given them advances." Obviously, the original Bible passage makes no mention of Jesus giving cash advances to his disciples as an incentive to fish; Schweitzer was scolding the ne'er-do-wells in his audience who were given equipment and cash advances and made no return. They should be good fishermen, the kind Jesus likes.

The need for cleanliness also prompted Schweitzer to expand on Bible descriptions of Jesus. In a sermon delivered on 20 April 1930, he told his audience that Jesus wore a loincloth—a clean one. "You need not imagine that in Jesus' country people were dirty like you—you who wear dirty loincloths. In Jesus' country everyone washed their own loincloths and mended them. Thus Jesus always had a clean and well-mended loincloth." What are we to make of this? That Jesus and his people were cleaner than Schweitzer's audience? Precisely. The people of Lambaréné were not well-scrubbed Europeans, nor did they wish to be; they were not troubled by Western ideas of cleanliness. But Schweitzer wistfully hoped that they would at least pay more attention to the sanitary condition of their loincloths.

The liberties Schweitzer took with the Bible lessons occasionally led to errors as well as deliberate modifications. In telling of Paul's trial before the "tribune" in Acts 23, for example, he stated that thirty men accused Paul (1 June 1930); according to the Bible, "there were more than forty who made this conspiracy" (Acts 23:16). Similarly, he stated that "the son of the brother of Saint Paul came to the captain's house" to inform him of the "thirty chiefs" who were conspiring against him. The biblical account declares that it was "the son of Paul's sister" who did this (Acts 23:16). In most cases, however, discrepancies between an original Bible lesson and Schweiter's account of it were intentional.

On occasions when a biblical text did not fit Schweitzer's need, he followed Jesus' example and created his own parables, some drawn from life and some invented to make a point. For his sermon of 2 March 1930, once again emphasizing the evils of theft, he created an imaginative story about "a country very far from here, very cold, where there is always fire in the huts."[17] There are many poor people in this land, Schweitzer explained, but they are all very honest. In this land, someone could leave his valuable possessions lying about and they would not be taken. Unfortunately, he added, this is not true in Lambaréné. The only way to pass from thievery to honesty is to have a heart "completely changed by the Word of God." Happiness, he concluded, comes from hearing and heeding God's commandment: "You shall not steal!"

17. The country Schweitzer mentions is probably his own native land, or somewhere else in Europe. Cf. the sermon of 26 October 1913.

In a sermon designed to illustrate the importance of compassion and self-sacrifice, Schweitzer used a similar technique. Asking "Do you know what it is to die for others?" he answered his own question with an imaginative tale: "Say there is a canoe, and there is a man in the canoe who doesn't know how to swim, and in the canoe there is someone else who does. Then it overturns and the swimmer throws himself into the water and searches underneath the canoe, and then he pulls the drowning man into the canoe, but he himself doesn't have the strength to hold on and he slips and goes down. He it is who has died for another" (20 April 1930).

The man who searches for his drowning companion is Jesus himself, the One who gives his life for another. In Schweitzer's tale, there is a canoe rather than a boat. In Lambaréné canoes (or pirogues) were commonly used by the people for personal transportation; boats were motorized.

Parables were a particularly useful tool for explaining intangibles. In one sermon, for example, Schweitzer discussed the concept of spirit in terms of trees. "There is the spirit of man and the Spirit of God; and between the spirit of man and the Spirit of God there is the same difference that there is between trees" (8 June 1930). In an elaborate analogy, Schweitzer compares the hardy but barren trees that grow wild in the jungle with more delicate, cultivated trees that do bear fruit, warning that the former will soon overpower the cultivated, nonnative trees if they are not carefully watched: "Look here! We have planted good trees so that the sick can eat the oranges and tangerines that they bear. But what will become of these trees if we leave and do not continue to clear the bush away? So it is with the Spirit of God—exactly the same thing."

These fruit-bearing trees are like human beings, Schweitzer continued, in constant threat from "the bad thoughts of the heart" that may overwhelm them. Each good fruit-bearing tree is like a word from Jesus, and each of his words contains the Spirit of God. The bad thoughts of the heart are like weeds that must be constantly removed. "Without doing this, the trees of the Spirit of God cannot grow. When you see Christian whites or blacks who are not better than other people, these are Christians who have not cleansed their hearts."

Schweitzer makes the important point that there is no distinction between the races on the subject of a clean heart. It makes no difference to God or man, he said, whether or not they call themselves Christian. The only people who are better are those who have cleansed their hearts: "For those who have the courage to cleanse their hearts, there is no longer any need to explain about the Spirit of God, because the Spirit of God grows in them like tiny palm trees, and they will bear the fruit of the Spirit of God."

Another technique Schweitzer used to bring immediacy to his message was that of incorporating the incidental into his sermons. The passage of an animal or a glimpse of activity in the audience became new material for his sermon: "You see this goat that is going by? Does the goat understand what is going on in your head? No! Because it is a goat, and you, you are men. Because you are men, you have other, far higher thoughts than a goat. Isn't that true? As with men, so with God. We cannot understand all the thought of God" (20 April 1930). By such an analogy, Schweitzer could translate into local terms the meaning of a well-known passage from Isaiah (Isaiah 55:8–9): "For my thoughts are not your thoughts, neither are your ways my ways, says the Lord. For as the heavens are higher than the earth, so are my ways higher than your ways."

During another Sunday service, Schweitzer saw a little sheep wandering by. As with the goat, he spontaneously employed it to illustrate the difference between God and humanity. "Look at this little sheep over there! Can this little sheep understand the thoughts in a man's head? No! Isn't this true? Well, then! The difference between a sheep and a man is not as big as the difference between a man and God. So it is clear that a poor man cannot understand God" (20 July 1930).

Even on those occasions when Schweitzer couldn't incorporate immediate village events into his outdoor sermons, he did not allow them to inhibit or halt his transmission of God's Word. One Sunday morning, while Schweitzer was preaching, a man came up from the river with some fish to sell and began to advertise his wares. Schweitzer's response, as recorded verbatim by the transcriber, was to voice his objection and return to his lesson immediately: "Then Saint John said to his disciples—Don't leave! The man who sells carp can wait!—Saint John told his disciples, 'Go to the place where Jesus is and ask him if he is the king of hearts whom God said to send' " (29 June 1930).

Despite Schweitzer's reproach, the fish-seller was back with a companion the following Sunday to sell his catch, and several people got up to buy fish. This time, Schweitzer used the interruption as an opportunity to teach his audience appropriate behavior at a religious service. Schweitzer was telling his congregation about how John the Baptist was executed and how the queen's little daughter danced before the king when he had prepared a great dinner for the rulers. "You two men! You do not leave when the Word of God is being preached! You leave only because you want to go to the toilet or to urinate—not to buy fish! Then the king said to the little girl, 'You can ask whatever you want" (6 July 1930).

Such reproaches were not uncommon. Yet another Sunday, Schweitzer had just begun to preach about Jesus delivering the Sermon on the Mount when a man got up to go. Schweitzer interrupted his train of thought to exclaim, "There is a man over there who wants to leave. He ought to come here. He ought to be ashamed" (3 August 1930). Women, too, were chastised if they acted inappropriately. Once, when his eye caught the movement of two women walking about during the sermon, Schweitzer said, "You don't walk around when the Word of God is being preached!" (17 August 1930).

Only when technical difficulties prevented his audience from understanding him would Schweitzer delay or end a sermon. On one occasion, Schweitzer's sermon was cancelled because the people who translated his words into the local languages did not arrive. We read the following comment in German for Sunday, 22 June 1930: "The female doctors had excused the Sunday service assistants without permission, and so the translation did not take place like the others." There may have been some emergency or some great event taking place nearby at the Catholic mission, because the transcriber also records Schweitzer's first sentence, just before he broke off: "Today you have heard the bell of the Catholic mission ringing for a long time . . ." There is a blank sheet of paper after these comments.

A final technique employed by Schweitzer to engage his audience was to ask them for an oral response to a question. "You are all seated," he said one Sunday. "Now those who have never stolen even an egg, even a piece of cassava, let that one stand up. Ah! There is only one person who is standing. . . . I knew quite well that nobody would dare to say that he has never stolen" (2 March 1930). This little exercise showed that nearly everyone had stolen something at one time or another, and that no one was blameless.

Schweitzer went on to say that a recent famine had been caused by the fact that newly planted crops had been stolen right out of the ground. Only a shipment of rice from Europe prevented disaster. The only way to stop stealing, he stated, is to have a change of heart, a change brought about by an adherence to the Word of God. Stealing does not bring happiness; only carrying out the Word of God does so.

To Schweitzer, the idea of the kingdom of God was central. Not only did he believe it to be coming into existence in Lambaréné, but he also believed that it could be present in the human heart for those who would receive it. Schweitzer, seeking to be sure his audience understood this, asked them outright: "Do you truly want the Kingdom of God to come into your heart? Answer truthfully!" In reaction to the disheartening mutter he received in response to his query, he commented, "Ah! They are afraid already" (24 August 1930).

One transcription, which recorded audience responses in parentheses, gives the overall flavor of such exchanges. Schweitzer was telling the story of the good Samaritan: "And he passed by the side of the poor unfortunate man without even touching or even looking at him." Seeking to know if his audience was listening and understanding, he asked, "Well, was that a good thing to do?" (9 November 1930). Here the response was recorded as "General murmur." Later in the sermon, another question—"Now I ask you all, did the man from the same tribe do good to the poor unfortunate fellow, or was it the man from the other tribe?"—elicited "Murmurs, various movements." Schweitzer then comments, "You see, those who are 'savages' answer best," teaching them that someone from an enemy tribe—even a despised foreigner who knows nothing of Christianity—may be quite capable of doing God's will better than one of them.

Conclusion

These seventy sermons give a unique glimpse of the remarkable person who was Albert Schweitzer. We hear his actual words, as he spoke them to his audience, rather than later recollections, either by himself or by others. We see him establishing a beachhead for the kingdom of God in Lambaréné. We see his understanding of Christianity as love in action and love by service to others. His purpose was not to convert the Africans to his own particular brand of Christianity or moral outlook but rather to be an example of love.

Although he carried with him the paternalistic attitudes and language of his day, his intention, as revealed by his actions, was to love and care for the Africans. The way he ran his hospital allowed them to continue their cultural practices. He healed their bodies while leaving their society alone. Only when certain practices interfered with the rights of others did he seek to change behavior.

When outsiders attacked him for allowing the African cultural traditions to continue, he chose to ignore their criticisms and calmly continued to serve the Africans with dignity. He did not allow those who were critical of his methods to have power in his hospital. He protected his vision of the hospital as a beachhead for the Kingdom of God.

In the sermons we can observe how Schweitzer changed over time, becoming quieter, more mellow, and less moralistic. The sermons exhibit his concept of practical eschatology. Schweitzer intended for Lambaréné to be an example of the Kingdom of God on earth.

PART ONE

The 1913 Sermons

1. Sunday, 20 April 1913 [1]

Why I Have Come to Lambaréné

I was a pastor and a doctor in a large European city. Its church is one of the biggest in the world, a hundred times as big as that of the Catholic Mission in Lambaréné. In this city there are many people who think of the pagans in Africa and who pray to God, that he send people to them in order to preach the gospel so that they will be converted and no longer be ignorant and bad pagans. And the people of this city read in a missions journal that, on the rivers of the Ogooué, there are Galoas and Pahouins, and that dear missionaries preach the gospel to them. They have also learned that there are Galoas and Pahouins who are converted—who have been baptized and hear the Word of God.

But the people of this city are astonished. "How," they say, "does one preach the gospel to all the Galoas and to all the Pahouins? In all the villages they learn from the missionaries and the catechists that God has sent the Lord Jesus Christ to bring the good news and to save us, and also to save the Galoas and the Pahouins, and they are not all converted?" And the people of this city were sad that the Galoas and the Pahouins close their ears to the good news and do not wish to believe that God and the Lord Jesus Christ love all men. Then they learned that Pahouins and Galoas suffer from many diseases, wounds, and many pains, and that their little children die in great numbers, and that there was no doctor to take care of

---

1. Rhena Schweitzer Miller personally transcribed sermons numbered 1–6 into typewritten French from her father's handwritten manuscripts. The originals remain with her.

them—neither at N'Gomo, nor at Lambaréné, nor at Samkita, nor at Talagouga—no doctor who knows all the medicines of the whites, that very wise men have found in order to cure diseases, close wounds, and eliminate pain.

Then the people of this city said, "We are going to show these Galoas and these Pahouins, whom we do not know, that we know that God and the Lord Jesus Christ love them and that we love them also, because the Lord Jesus Christ said that all men must love one another. We are going to send them a learned doctor who knows all medicines." And I said to them, "I am a doctor; send me." And they said, "Go in our name. Take all the good medicines. Take a great amount. Put them in boxes and carry them on a large oceangoing ship and then onto a boat on the Ogooué. Go to Lambaréné where the missionaries live. Let the Galoas and the Pahouins, those who are ill and those who have wounds, come to your home. You will give them medicines and take care of them. And you will say to them that we send you and that you come so that they may believe that God loves them and that the Lord Jesus Christ calls them and that he wishes them to be healed, as he himself cured the diseases of his people. And if you care for their bodies, tell them that their souls are well rather than sick and that the soul is more precious than the body, as the Lord Jesus has said. And though there are many good medicines for the body, there is only one thing—only one—for the cure of the soul. This medicine is the gospel that was preached to them for years and that many have rejected and no longer listen to."

And so I have come with my wife, who also knows all the medicines and knows how to treat illnesses, and we are here among you. May God give us grace to relieve you of your illnesses and to help the dear missionaries, our brothers, to open your ears to the good news of the gospel and the love of our Lord Jesus Christ. So may it be. Amen.

2. Pentecost, 11 May 1913

Pentecost 1913

Ephesians 4:30, "And grieve not the holy Spirit of God"

You know that the great day we celebrate today is Pentecost. It is a Jewish festival that we celebrate fifty days after Easter. This Jewish festival has become a Christian festival because on that day, in the morning, while the Jews went to the temple, the disciples began to preach the good news of our Lord Jesus. The Spirit of God revealed itself in their midst, and they were empowered to proclaim to the world that Jesus was the Messiah and our Lord.

This is the day that they founded the Christian church that has lasted so long and of which we are a part. Right now, when we are gathered together here to celebrate this festival, in innumerable cities and countless towns of Europe, Asia, and America, in all the corners of the world, Christians are assembled and are celebrating Pentecost. And we think of the parents and friends of those who have come to bring you the gospel, and feel united with them in the Spirit of God, and are happy that here also we are celebrating this lovely festival.

What are they going to do in the temple on this day, at this hour? They come to give thanks to God, who has placed his Spirit within human beings. God is good; his Spirit is holy and pure. And he looks at miserable human beings and sinners and says to himself, "I want to save them. I want to let my Spirit live in them, so that it will purify their spirit and those of my disciples." The prophets proclaimed this. His Spirit spoke through their mouths. And in our Lord Jesus Christ his Spirit came to dwell in the midst of humanity; he became human. And this is the Spirit that was experienced by the disciples when they were sad that the Lord was no longer with them. It is this Spirit that gave them the power to found the church. It is this Spirit that gave courage to those who had suffered persecution and death for Jesus. It is this Spirit that shows itself along the road of life to all those who are pious. It is this Spirit that said to the Christians of Europe, "Go into all the world, leave your cities, your parents, your friends, and proclaim the gospel to those who have not yet heard of Jesus Christ." It is this Spirit that is in our midst—with us together, all of us who are here at Lambaréné under this roof—uniting us with Christians throughout the entire world.

And I ask you in this hour, "Have you come with your heart full of gratitude toward God, who has sent his Spirit to poor human beings, to you [. . .]?" We here are only a small assembly. We are not gathered in a beautiful temple, but only under a poor roof. But if our true praises show forth living in our hearts, if only there are twenty true Christians in the midst of us who thank God from the bottom of their hearts, who say to him, "We thank thee, O God; thou art good; I have been a poor soul, ignorant of the right way of life, ignorant of true goodness, and thou hast given thy Spirit which illuminates me, which lifts up my life, as the sun rises after the night and lifts up the day": if it is thus that we give thanks, then God hears in this hour, in the midst of the praises of the whole world, our poor praises, the praises of Christians of Lambaréné, and he blesses us and sends peace into our hearts.

What is the Spirit of God, the Holy Spirit? No one can describe or explain it. But each of us knows it because we feel it. The Spirit of God is a fire which burns in our heart when once we have heard and understood the words of Christ. It is a fire which can consume evil thoughts, as a fire destroys trees and vines when one wishes to make a plantation with trees that bear good fruit. But people say, "Oh, this fire burns too strongly." They would rather that he not destroy their evil thoughts. They would rather keep them, because they seem pleasant enough. They are as those people who would like to plant coconut palms and other precious trees without destroying the wicked forest. They do not know that in acting that way they are slowly chasing away the Spirit of God, which can no longer live in our hearts along with evil thoughts.

It is for this reason that I have chosen this text from the apostle Paul. "Do not grieve the Holy Spirit." I place it before you. Carry it away with you. Let it stir you up in your hearts. It has been written for each of you. And if you make evil schemes, or do so while speaking, you may think to yourself, "It is nothing; no one will know." Then immediately you must think of this text that we are bringing to this service of Pentecost, and you must say to yourself, "I have grieved the Spirit of God, the Spirit that he has placed in my heart." And then you will come to feel sadness.

To conclude, I am going to speak of two ways of grieving the Holy Spirit—you must pay particular attention to this. The first way is to lack the courage to make a confession to our Lord Jesus Christ. The Holy Spirit is the courage to speak of Jesus and to live for him. Look at the disciples. They were afraid. They hid themselves when the Lord had died. They did not dare to speak of him. That is because they still had not received the Holy Spirit. But at Pentecost, from the time that they felt the Spirit among them, they had courage, and fear and cowardice no longer reigned in their hearts.

And so you, on the day of Pentecost, you must ask yourselves, "Do we also have the courage to confess our Lord before others, to speak to them and to show them? Here he is, with his words. He is my master. It is he that I want to obey. It is he who gives me happiness."

If you do not have this courage, you grieve the Spirit of God, and it is in vain that you celebrate Pentecost, for the Spirit of God cannot live within the hearts of those who are not courageous for Jesus.

The other action by which, thoughtlessly, you grieve the Holy Spirit, is by lying. God is Truth. His Spirit is the spirit of Truth. Truth cannot live with lying. And the reason the Spirit of God dwells so feebly in human beings is because time and again we injure ourselves by lying. And it is for this very reason that I am preaching to you about the Spirit of God on Pentecost, in order to speak to men and to tell them again, "Pay attention and do not fall into lying. Do not grieve the Spirit of God, as you do so easily."

And there are among you certain people who in this hour will say: "I suppose this is the Holy Spirit; I sense a little bit of it in me. But it seems so feeble. I would like to feel it strongly, as strongly as the apostles did." To those here, I tell them, "Go, and each time that you want to lie, let the words of the apostle Paul, 'Do not grieve the Holy Spirit,' confront you and touch your heart, so that you will quit lying, so that you will even be afraid to lie." And then, when Pentecost comes once again, you will feel it, and you will know the Holy Spirit better, and you will be better able to thank God, something that you were not able to do today. Do not forget: the Spirit of God is the spirit of Truth. So may it be.

3. Sunday, 18 August 1913

The Light of the Gospel of God

Matthew 5:14–16, "You are the light of the world"

I returned yesterday evening by pirogue. The sun had already gone down; night had fallen. And then, far away, I saw some lights on the hill, which sent their rays onto the river. I said to myself, "Here is the missionary station of Andende, which resembles the city situated on the mountain spoken of by the Lord. Its lights are also those that he speaks of." Just as these lights come at night and are visible to men who are far away on the river and on the banks, so the light of the gospel must spread from here throughout the countryside. And it is for this reason that I have chosen these words of the Lord in order to speak with you today.

First of all, so that we can all rejoice together, we recall that God has wanted to establish the light of his gospel on these hills, and here he founded the town toward which all eyes are turned. I want us to be completely happy here at this station where the Word of God reigns. I also wish that those of you who have come here have come, above all else, to find work and to experience the goodness of life here among us—at the home of those whites who are not seeking to make money, but who have come to bring you something and to help you.

But I ask, for those who live around it, is this station truly the city on the mountain and the light that gives light? I would say to you that I experienced a certain kind of sadness on my arrival. In Europe I imagined a missionary station as a holy place or as those people who have united in order to live according to the law of God and who give an example to all the people of the area, who say of them, "Here is the beginning of the rule of God in our country; we want to imitate them." And on my arrival I heard lying talk, talk of stealing and of adultery. I saw people who work without pleasure. I heard the bell call for the Sunday service, and there were natives who did not follow its sound but remained in their huts. This mocks the true love of the gospel.

I tell you my sadness. And believe me that many of those who give money in Europe for the work of God on the Ogooué and who think of this work and pray for it, they will be sad to see the indifference that reigns among the natives at the station and round about.

No! This is not the city on the mountain and the light that gives light, spoken of by our Lord. It is a poor little flame that has hardly any brightness and that wavers in the wind. But it must become a big light—it *must*, do you hear? And it is for this reason that I ask you to fight against sin. This station must become a pure and holy place in this country, so that those who live in its vicinity notice that those who live here are struggling to become better; struggling to get rid of ideas of covetousness, lying, and adultery; struggling to be good and to forgive those who have done evil to them. What makes this station beautiful and powerful cannot be only the Word spoken by the missionaries, but the struggles that take place in your hearts, the victories won over evil thoughts. Then the people of the area will see the power of the gospel. They will see that those who live here are happier than they—richer, even if they do not earn as much money—and they will say to themselves, "We want to be as happy and as rich as they are," and they will come to seek the Word of God. And when the bell of this station rings on Sunday, not just a few will come, but many, and the landing will be full of pirogues.

This is the main idea: that one day, with the grace of God, this little torch will be a light that will enlighten the surrounding country. This will give our missionaries the power to live here and to start each day's work afresh. And you, you must help this come to pass, in order that God will also inscribe your names in the book of life and that all of us together will be called by him to the life eternal.

4. Sunday, 28 September 1913

Jesus Heals by Forgiveness

Matthew 9:1–8, "Your sins are forgiven"

The story that has been read to you from the Bible tells that Jesus healed a man while saying to him, "Your sins are forgiven." The men who were present did not understand that sins had caused the sickness and they were surprised that the Lord said to him, "Your sins are forgiven," instead of announcing to him, "You are healed." You resemble these people. You do not fully understand that sins have caused sickness. This is why I am speaking to you.

When I am sitting up there in my little hut and one sick person after another enters my house, I always see these two things together—sin and sickness. These are two sisters who walk together and hold hands. When I listen with my instrument to the beating of the heart and the breathing of the lungs, I look to see what is sick in the body. And before the man even opens his mouth to tell me what is the matter, I know it already: "There are sins which have made him sick."

The wounds and the pains inform me that this man or woman leads a wicked and adulterous life. This is why sickness is destroying that person's body and has entered the blood.

In other words, while listening to a man's lungs and while hearing about his suffering, I say to myself, "Here is a man who drinks or who has drunk a lot of palm wine." He used to be robust and in good health but then he became a drunk. It is the palm wine that is consuming his chest and his heart and making him feeble, giving him pains throughout his body.

Still others are sick in mind and spirit. After a few years at the mission, having learned about goodness, they say to themselves, "I want to lead a good life and do God's work." And they follow the good life for some time. But then they fall into vice and shame. These are they who feel sick everywhere, whose hearts are full of anguish and who hardly have any power to live.

Some of these sicknesses I see every day. If Jesus was up there [2] with his healing power, he would not be saying "Your sins are forgiven" only once, but five or ten times in one morning in order to be able to heal the natives. And he would be able to see far better than me the sin in their hearts. But Jesus himself could not heal them, because they do not realize that their own sins have made them sick. The man spoken of in the Bible knew this instantly. That is why he understood who Jesus was and that Jesus was able to heal. But among those who come to my house, many do not know even this.

---

2. Schweitzer is probably pointing to the medical buildings, which were on higher ground.

Don't you see? Medicine isn't the only thing that is necessary for healing. Certainly it is God who has given us medicine and who wants us to use it to heal others and to give him thanks. But in order to really heal, something more is required. You must say to yourself when you are sick, "What is this sickness telling me? Why has God allowed me to be sick?" And you should consider this and humble yourself before God and be thankful, like the man who came to Jesus. You all have many sins that need to be forgiven, and you ought to know that, despite all the medicines, you will not be healed completely without first having heard the voice of Jesus, who says to you, "Your sins are forgiven." Pray to God to forgive you, and be repentant before him.

A life healed of sickness does not mean only being delivered from pains and feebleness of body. To be healed means to become a new man, who in the midst of his sickness has felt the hand of Jesus drawing toward him. To heal means to have not only a body without wounds and without pain, but to have found, by means of the sickness itself, a new soul; to have found not only health of body but eternal life.

And those who come to me in this way, in order to be truly healed of their sickness, of their sins, these I am able to heal far better than all the others, with the help of the one who is able to heal bodies and souls, our Lord Jesus Christ. Amen.

5. Sunday, 26 October 1913[3]

"Seek His Kingdom"

Matthew 6:33, "But seek first his Kingdom"

You are well aware, when I speak to you of the gospel, that I still do not know you as well as the old missionaries who have lived among you for

---

3. Rhena Schweitzer Miller notes: "I thought first that this sermon was from the year 1914, as the date was very difficult to make out. But it is from 1913 as I found out from the content and from knowing that in October 1914 my father was a prisoner."

many years. But slowly I am learning to know you, and during the Sundays when I will preach to you, I am going to speak of those things that have struck and surprised me about you, and I will explain the gospel to you based on these observations.

First of all, and for today, I will speak to you about something that has astonished me very much and that makes me afraid for you and your souls. This is that you love wages and money too much. Now you understand why certain passages from the gospel were read to you and why I have chosen for my sermon the saying, "Seek first his Kingdom and his righteousness, and all these things shall be yours as well."

When, in Europe, I would preach on this saying, I had before me people who lived in a big city and who were obliged to work hard in order to earn what they needed to live. For doubtless you know that in Europe one pays dearly for the house in which one lives and for each piece of fruit that one eats. You also know that it is very cold there and that it is necessary to buy wood to make a fire, and that those who cannot earn this money become ill because of the cold and may even die of the cold.

Then, when I preached on the saying "Seek first the Kingdom of heaven," I would say to myself, "Oh, how difficult it is for them to have this saying enter their hearts, because they must consider, before everything, how to earn money so that they do not die of hunger or cold."

And when I was coming to your place, I rejoiced. I had learned that this is a country that feeds its inhabitants well, that there are bananas and lots of other fruits, and that it isn't cold. I said to myself, "It is going to be easy to tell them, 'Seek first the Kingdom of heaven,' for one will be able to tell them, 'See! The good Lord gives you every fruit all year long and makes life easy for you with only a little work on your part, so that you have time to think about the Kingdom of heaven and your own soul before all else.' "

But from the very first day that I arrived, I have seen everywhere, with astonishment and sadness, that the natives (or almost all of the natives) think about earning a lot of money, the most possible, instead of reflecting on the Kingdom of God and how to enter it. They go to do hard work in which a lot of them lose their strength and health while cutting down trees in order to sell them. And what do they do with this money? They buy bad things like alcohol, which eats up their hearts. Recently a woodcutter, after I listened to his heart, confessed that he drinks fifty francs worth of alcohol a month! Thus most days he has worked solely to buy this poison and to become very ill. You buy useless things in the factories and yet you want to earn still more money.

Tell me, does the money that the natives pursue so hard return riches to your tribes and your villages? The young people go to cut wood and drive the timber-rafts to Cape Lopez and return in lovely white clothing— and the cabins fall into ruins, the plantations are abandoned, the people no longer have pirogues because no one can carve them any more, finding that this no longer brings in enough money.

Look, this thirst for money makes your villages poor. You will be much richer if your men say, "We wish to work and earn our living. We want to take good care of our plantations, to plant and cultivate trees, cocoa, and others, and sell their fruit, to learn the carpenter trade and other trades, but we no longer want to run about the earth in order to cut down trees and earn money that we spend badly."

Is the day near or far when the natives will understand this truth? I only know that they do not understand that they are perishing and becoming even poorer and sicker. I would also like you to know this, you who are here, the adults who know life already, and also the children.

You know quite well what the Lord Jesus has said: "What is the body and all its needs, all its worries and all the joys of life? The body dies and is buried. But the soul does not die. It is eternal. And because of this it is necessary to first think about the soul."

There was a time when the whites, who still did not know the natives very well, used to say, "The natives do not have souls like the whites." But the missionaries who know you well know that you have a soul, and the Lord Jesus said that all men have a soul and that God loves everyone as his children. And we come to tell you, "Pay attention, and take care that you do not forget to guard your soul because of the money that you wish to earn!" For the Lord Jesus has said, "If a man loses his own soul he can no longer buy it back." Amen.

6. **First Sunday in Advent, 30 November 1913**

Preparing for the Kingdom of God

You will remember that I wanted to tell you everything that surprised me about you. I spoke to you about your thirst for money. I also told you that you do not know enough to really celebrate Sunday and to participate in the service, as it should be when you present yourself before God. Today I am, once again, going to speak to you about something that struck me. This will be the last time; later I will start again when I know you better. The thing that struck me is just this. When we hear missions spoken about in Europe, we imagine that those who are converted have truly undertaken the work of God and go to a lot of trouble to help in the conversion of those natives who are still pagans. We imagine that practically all those who leave school want to become catechists and that all of you think of only one thing: what can we do to bring the Kingdom of God to our home, that it may be extended everywhere, in order that every native may become a child of God?

There are missions in Africa where this is so. But in your country it is not so. Otherwise the whole Ogooué and the N'Ggounié would be already converted to Christianity and your missionaries would not be discouraged as often as they are. They would have no need to ask you for money for the church of the Ogooué, for you would bring it yourselves. They would not look with worry at those boys who leave school so young, and they would not say to themselves, "Our catechists are old and we have no young ones, because the young ones are only thinking how to make a lot of money with what they have learned." All would be otherwise and all must become otherwise.

And this Sunday, when I say this to you, is not a Sunday like the others, but a very special Sunday. It is the first Sunday of the Sundays of Advent. You know that we have four Sundays and then it will be Christmas. And these four Sundays are called in the church "the Sundays" that anticipate what must come! These are the Sundays when we ready ourselves to celebrate the birth of our Lord and to celebrate what he brings to us. And during these Sundays we think of that which must come. And that which must come is the Kingdom of God and of our Lord. And we must think about this very thing with all our soul's power.

And you know that those who first thought about the Kingdom of God were the prophets. It was God who put this thought into their hearts. And the greatest of all the prophets was Isaiah. And it was read to you today how he proclaimed this to the men who lived in his time. One day God will send the Lord in whom his spirit will live, the Lord who will save the world, who will be the King of all men, who will reign in their hearts. And when the prophets announced this good news to them, the men of his time were sad, for they said to themselves, "How far away it still is! We shall die and our children shall die and we will still not have seen the Lord." And those men still await the one who must come, whom the prophets proclaimed.

And we, we know that the Lord has come, that he has saved us, and that the Kingdom of God has begun on this earth. But during the four Sundays before Christmas we are thinking of that which is still to come, that the Lord must become King in the hearts of all men, black and white, and that the Kingdom of God must come everywhere, as far as the last native village of Africa.

We often lose courage. We see those whites, who in their youth learned the gospel, coming to bring you not what is good, but what is bad, in order to make money from alcohol, and that the natives prefer what is bad over what is good. We see how weak you are and how you always fall back into your sins. If we believed only what we see with the eyes in our heads, we would say, "The Kingdom of God will never come here. Jesus will never be King of their hearts." But we believe what we see with the eyes of our hearts. It is for that reason we are certain that the Kingdom of God will one day come here, as it will over all the earth, and that the spirit of God will reign and that Jesus will be King. And because we believe this, we have the courage and the power to be far away from our families and to labor among you. And you believe with us and work with us. And during these Sundays before Christmas, during these Sundays of Advent, think with us of what must come and pray that God will send it soon.

PART TWO

The 1914 Sermons

7. Sunday after New Year's Day, 4 January 1914

Humble Yourself[1]

Romans 8:28

1. A new year, 1914. Happy New Year! Listening to the whites. Also doing. But let me also tell you, "Happy New Year!" In a deeper sense [ ] the others [ ] that the year may be good; that you have everything that you want: all pleasures, all that your heart desires. And we know, nevertheless, that our wishes do not change anything.

2. But in this hour I wish you a happy new year: How to make the year good for you and for us. Because you know that happiness does not come from external things, which make us succeed or not succeed: but all happiness comes from the heart. Whatever may happen to make us more or less pleasant, we will be worth more to men. To wish a heart that can be happy.

3. Happy New Year! 1914. Why 1914? According to Jesus. The Jews counted the years according to the years since the Creation; the great peoples according to the great kings; the Romans according to their great city. All that is far away. It remains a fallen and reconstructed city. Immense fallen stone houses, kings are dead; the earth will be destroyed one day, too.

---

1. Sermons 7, 8 (both notes and full sermon), and 9 come from Schweitzer's handwritten manuscripts, which remain in the possession of his daughter, Rhena Schweitzer Miller. Photocopies were given to Dr. Melamed from Rhena Schweitzer Miller's private collection. Subsequently they were transcribed into typewritten French by Mme. Poteau-Müller. Sermons 10–12 were transcribed into typewritten French by Rhena Schweitzer Miller from her father's handwritten manuscripts for Dr. Melamed. She retains the originals.

But Jesus is eternal. And more, he can help us. 1914: The year of his birth. Jesus loves us. By thine example, by thy words, by thy spirit fill our hearts! In thy name we want to begin the year.

4. And a word to listen to, a good feeling. Perfume bottles. Useless. Also seen at the shopkeepers'. But this Word is as a gourd of water that one carries across the virgin forest. Look ahead! As in a fog when one does not see mountains. What can await us? The injustice of men. To tell wicked things, lies, what we are not ready to give back to them. We make a palaver if they have wronged us. To steal. If that happens to you, you are inclined to be angry. To be [ ] shameful, vengeful, to retaliate. Then pull out the Word and look at it from all sides. "To those who love God all these things serve [ ] to those who have been called." All things: and injustices. Bear it and endure it with meekness. These things are not from men but from God. All things. In pain, goodness, as a coconut in a very hard shell. Look back at my life. All things [ ] when our heart is good [ ] and what we say. It is good. Often a great misfortune. A great happiness. God calls us to him . . .

5. [ ]: all misfortunes. Bad luck: Sickness. Man goes. Tomorrow he writhes with pain and sees the face of death. These days here: Mrs. Christol.[2] One loses others. To lose friends . . . And [ ] is very [ ]. Why God sends us that. When I have preached to whites, [ ] to console a man struck with great misfortune. Always repeated: why does God send this to me? Why me? What have I done? Because God has sent goodness to you, or not. It is beyond understanding. But then others: it is true. When in the greatest misfortune, since they are misfortunate: and happiness belongs to God. A man carving stones. Every Sunday afternoon for ten years. Stone crushed. Suffered and no physician helped him. And poor. Then what is a happy man? I have seen very rich people, very happy . . .

One day if God sends me a lot of misfortune. And if it is still death for me: to those who love God. When 1914 is past, it is probable that all of us will be at a place further on in life. Listen. God will send death to seek such or such. And we whites: on this great boat to return, to see friends again. But perhaps: at the small cemetery a new stone beside others. And one will speak of such misfortune. But we know that only one thing is necessary: to be ready . . . and if God calls us, it is because we love him and because it is good this way. And when we want to carry this Word with us, and perhaps

2. Sonja Poteau-Müller has identified Mrs. Christol as the wife of a missionary.

when the year will be ended, each of us will tell how it helped. And tell it also to those who have not been here.

8. 8 February 1914

Sermon Given in Talagouga for the Assembly of the Synod[3]

Matthew 13:31–32: "The Kingdom of heaven is like a mustard seed"

Sermon Notes

Special Sunday. All members of the church of the Ogooué are assembled. The elders who have seen its beginnings and the young boys of all the schools who one day must continue the work.

And our thoughts reach out toward those who have founded it. There are many there who rest in their graves.[4] Others are still living who can no longer work at their positions but who are with us in thought . . . to name names: Dr. Nau, Mr. Allegret, and Mr. Teisserès.[5]

And we think of the dead and the living and we thank God who has given such faithful servants for his work.

And this day has yet another special meaning because, for the first

---

3. This sermon was preserved in two forms: as sermon notes (incomplete, with omissions indicated) and as a transcription of the full sermon, which here follows the notes. Schweitzer drew up the notes on 2 February 1914, for a sermon delivered at the Assembly of the Synod at Talagouga on 8 February 1914. The notes come from a copy of Schweitzer's handwritten notes, given to Dr. Melamed by Rhena Schweitzer Miller from her private collection, which were subsequently transcribed into typewritten French by Mme. Poteau-Müller. Schweitzer indicates time markings for two services. Mr. Wouare-Bilne was the Gabonese translator for the full sermon given at the 8:30 service. We do not know who translated the 10:30 service. Schweitzer always preached in French and his words were translated orally into the two local languages by Gabonese nationals who stood near him.

4. Schweitzer has a marginal note here: "Vernier." At least two additional names are illegible followed by "Gabon."

5. These were missionaries. Schweitzer has named a few of them. The others remain unknown to us.

time, the church of Baraka is represented at the synod. Two of our elders are in our midst. It is necessary that they know how much the church of the Ogooué is happy to be united with the church of Baraka and that they tell this to their members when they return.

I am one of the last to come onto the Mission field of the Ogooué who must speak the Word of God to you today. When the missionaries chose me I was afraid, and I said to myself, "This should have been done by one of the older missionaries."

. . . .[6]

May fervent evangelists be lifted up in your midst, and may we be aware with you that you say as we do, and as we do among ourselves, "It is necessary that our church be like a tiny grain of mustard that becomes a great tree."

While I am saying this, I am looking at the children who have been brought here from all our schools. It is upon them that we must count. Do not be students who sit and learn and say to themselves, "When I leave school I will have learned how to earn money, I will be able to become a hospital worker, an interpreter . . . if these are your thoughts, poor students! But you know that the most precious thing to carry away from our schools is the thirst for the Kingdom of God and his justice, and that each of you must one day be an assistant for the church of the Ogooué and spread the gospel, if he is a catechist or not.

I am going to tell you a parable to conclude.[7]

Full Sermon[8]

We are celebrating a great festival today. All the elders of the church of the Ogooué are assembled. We see in this temple these friends, some of whom are still assisting us from the first beginnings of this work. We see boys from all our schools, who will one day have to continue it.

And our thoughts are directed to those who have founded this church.

---

6. There are two pages of illegible and damaged manuscript in the original here. They defy reconstruction.

7. The final portion of these sermon notes is missing.

8. What follows is the transcription of the actual sermon that Schweitzer preached to the synod.

Many of them are resting in their graves, here or in the cemetery of their country. Others are still alive, but, to their great regret, can no longer work in our midst. I pronounce the names that ring as great bells in your ears: Dr. Nassau, Mr. Allegret, Mr. Bon, Mr. Teisserès, Mr. Bifalche, and Mr. Venier.[9]

We think of the dead and of the living, and we thank God for having given faithful servants for his work.

This day has still another special meaning. For the first time the church of Baraka, the church of Gabon, is represented at the synod. We are anxious that the old churches report how much the church of the Ogooué is happy to be united to that of Baraka, and we pray they will repeat this to the Christians over there when they return.

For our meditation together I have taken from the gospel the parable of the small grain that takes root and grows and becomes a very tall tree. You know that Jesus is speaking of the Kingdom of God. And you know what the Kingdom of God means: the land where men do the will of God all together. The Christian churches of the whole world are parts of the Kingdom of God. The Kingdom of God is still imperfect, but it must always grow and develop to become more nearly the perfect Kingdom of God.

By setting this parable before your eyes, I put to you a question of the heart. Does our church resemble a seed that is developing? Has the beautiful parable of our Lord come true for it?

When the missionaries chose me to speak to you today, I was overcome with fear. I said that this should have been one of those who have known you for a long time, in order to speak to you today about the church that the synod here assembled represents. He would have been able to tell you what it is and about the defects that it has.

And I believe that he would have had harsh words to say to you. He would have had to observe that there are a lot of Christians in name only, rather than in truth, by life and actions, and that you all do not have the love and ardor that you must have for your church.

When I have been with you for a long time, I will be able to tell you all

---

9. The names of missionaries listed above are those who were sent from the Paris Missionary Society. There may have been others. Schweitzer provides no additional information about any of them.

the harsh words that have to be pronounced. But today allow me, first of all, to express my joy to be at the first meeting of the synod of this church of the Ogooué that I loved before ever meeting it. And it seems to me that I am bringing a message to you in this hour, as a message from a lot of European whites with whom I have spoken about this church, and who love it as I do, without ever having the joy of seeing it. But I want that [ ].

The little seed has sprouted. It is like a cocoa tree some years old that has branches and leaves and from which one waits for the first fruit. But you know that this is when the planter begins to look at his trees with concern, because now the danger begins. Are all the branches remaining green? Will they have leaves? Will they bear fruit? Or will he see dry branches appear? Will he see the life of this tree threatened by insects that sting it, dryness that takes its strength, and diseases that damage it?

You know the look of these cocoa trees that are half dead, half alive. You have often seen them in plantations. Your church has been like this, as well as your Christianity. God has planted this symbol before your eyes so that you may see yourselves reflected there, and so that you will be afraid to resemble those trees that no longer renew themselves but slowly wither year after year.

Certainly believe that those who lead you, the missionaries, have this fear for you, not from time to time, but often. When you see them tired, this is not only the work or the fever that has rendered them thus, but also the worrisome thoughts causing them to ask themselves over again: What will become of this church?

There is an infallible sign to recognize if a tree is alive or if it is in the process of perishing. One has only to see if it is growing. Is the church of the Ogooué growing? Is it spreading?

A few steps away from us flow the waters of the Ogooué. They pass before Talagouga, Samkita, Lambaréné, and N'Gomo. Can you hear anything else in the sounds of these running waters? Do they not come from afar, and have they not seen the plains and mountains where your brothers live? These brothers still do not know the work of God. Do you not hear in the sound of the voice that says that it is necessary to bring them the light that already illuminates you, so that what we call today the church of the Ogooué truly becomes this—becomes the church of all the great land that this river crosses, with all of the rivers that flow into it?

We celebrate today the union between the church of the Ogooué and that of Gabon. Do you know what that means? There is a great land between the waters of the Ogooué and the waters of Gabon. The union between the two churches means that they must get up, walk, and evangelize all this land that is between them, and someday meet and touch.

When I was still in Europe, I looked at the map where the lands of the earth are drawn and I said to myself, "How big the land of the Ogooué is, and that country behind and around Talagouga! Why is this station the last? Why aren't there any more further on in the interior of the land?" Today I understand. It is not the missionaries who are missing the opportunity for the church of the Ogooué to grow; it is you who do not want to grow. I believed I had found in you a burning desire to bring the light that has been placed in your hands to your brothers who live all around you, and I see with astonishment that there is nothing there at all. I believed that each indigenous Christian did the work of a catechist in order to convert others, and I learn that one does not even find enough catechists to put them at the head of the villages.

The tree does not grow; it grows hardly at all. Judge for yourself if the life that is in it is good and if there is no danger that it is not beginning to die slowly.

Our synod remains at Talagouga. Do not look to the sea, look to the land in the direction of the sun that rises, and say in our hearts that it must happen someday, a day that we will still see, where the synod will not be held here but in the farthest station inland.

My gaze is resting on the children of all the schools who are gathered here. And I am telling them something that they must keep in their hearts: Do not be schoolboys who say, "We want to learn to read, to write, to calculate, to be able to earn a lot money when we are big, to become interpreters and attending physicians, and everything that will make us rich." If your thoughts are there, you are poor schoolboys and your hearts will be poor all your life. I want you to know that it is important to bring the school nearer to the source of all knowledge; it is the thirst for the Kingdom of God and its justice and the thirst for taking the work of God and announcing its truth wherever you will be. One day it will be up to you if this church will grow or perish.

May God bless us all, those who are old and those who are small, God who puts in our hearts the love of the gospel and the love of the church, so that his truth may shine among us like a great fire and illuminate this land that is still in the darkness of ignorance and far from God. Amen.

Saturday evening.[10]

9. Palm Sunday, 5 April 1914[11]

Sermon Given at Lambaréné, Palm Sunday 1914

Matthew 21:1–15

1. The triumphal entry [of Jesus into Jerusalem]. Meaning of Sunday. The people cut down branches. Stories of the journey. All the Jews several days before Easter at Jerusalem. Jericho. Significance of the city. A small passage between mountains. It is through there that the people of Israel had walked toward Jerusalem. It is through there that Jesus comes.

2. He entered as a King. The people who accompanied him when the great city appeared on the mountain, they felt that what prophets had said about the great King of goodness, the men had to accomplish and could not do otherwise. Jesus on the donkey. Zachariah 10:9. It is as if this Sunday we were able to be among the people to then see his figure, his eyes . . . Here is our King. Blessed is he who comes in the name of the Lord.

3. In each country, in each city, in each village today: he is our King. Blessed is he who comes to the name of the Lord. In my country a beautiful song is sung today. "How must I receive thee? How do I go to thee, O Savior of the world, O friend of my heart? . . ."[12] I believe I hear him speaking to you from afar; and all Christians of the Ogooué should think

10. Schweitzer wrote "Saturday evening" probably to indicate that he completed his sermon the night before he delivered it.

11. These sermon notes come from photocopies of Schweitzer's handwritten manuscript from Rhena Schweitzer Miller's private collection. They were then transcribed into typewritten French for Dr. Melamed by Mme. Poteau-Müller.

12. The French reads, "Comment dois-je te recevoir? Comment vais-je vers toi, O Sauveur du monde, O ami de mon coeur . . ." With this ellipsis Schweitzer indicated he has omitted reciting the rest of the hymn.

today: Here is this great land. It is also necessary that Jesus comes there, that he may be King. It is necessary that its residents can sing to him. Blessed is he who comes in the name of the Lord.

4. You have rulers, you have administrators, you have ministers in Paris, and you have the president. These are they who govern the country. And they can do much good if they seek to be just. But the only things they can do are those things that are external to the Law: build roads and bridges, judge the wicked, help to prosecute them.[13] And they die. But to make the country happy, it is necessary that the King be Jesus. Obey him because it is necessary . . . because one senses that he brings happiness to the land . . . A sad country if one does not accept him . . .

5. When the people of Jerusalem saw Jesus accompanied by the people of Galilee, and when they heard these shouts, they smiled and they mocked him. They had already seen a lot of kings enter the city, in beautiful outfits, escorted and carried by their warriors. And here is a man, dressed as a poor man, seated on a poor ass . . . And this was a king. And they did not want to believe it. And nevertheless they would have laughed if they had been told: The kings that you have seen enter, they will be forgotten one day and their names will no longer be known, but the name of this one will be known and it will be said that he is a king still, many years after, when a lot of men and their children and children's children are dead, and always it will be said that he is a king.

6. And today again you will [say] here: Oh no, Jesus is not a king; the whites mock him and also the blacks . . . but nevertheless [he is] a king, the King of this country . . . he governs it already more than those who have the power to command. Because one proclaims his law and there are people who obey him and he will always have more of them. He is the King, because he commands far more than the others. I already know you well enough to know that you do not like the tax. But nevertheless this is not a lot that they are asking you for: five francs not to steal, not to kill, and to settle the major disagreements of the Post Office . . . [14] For the rest you can do what you want. Those who govern ask of you only a little bit. But the King: the tax: it is paid once and then it is finished . . . the heart. It commands all the time. You have a bad thought: a bad word, a lie, etc. . . . He

13. In the margin, Schweitzer wrote, "To change the country."
14. The reference is obscure.

does not forbid only: he orders you: to love, to forgive . . . He asks a lot, a lot . . .

7. Then the men: he is too hard, we do not want him. And today when one proclaims to them: Oh yes, rejoice you are the King; but then to obey . . . Say with words thou art the King and do not want to obey him. Who bear the name of Christians. Jesus withdraws; he does not want to hear their songs, their praises. And you people of Lambaréné, what do you think today? Do you want Jesus to be your King? Open to him the doors of your hearts, as one would open the doors of Jerusalem. Sing in your heart: Blessed is he who comes in the name of God . . . [15] And when you say that, do not make them just pleasing words, but a promise to Jesus that he will be King, that we want to obey him . . . Then you have understood the beautiful story that has been read to you today. Amen.

10. First Sunday of Passiontide,—April 1914

The Son of Man Must Die

Matthew 17:22–23, "Jesus said to them, 'The son of the man is to be delivered into the hands of men.' "

Today we begin those Sundays that we call the "Sundays of the Passion." We call them this because we are nearing Good Friday, the day of the death of our Lord. In those days he announced to his disciples, at the lake of Gennesaret, that he must die in Jerusalem; and, during those days, he readied himself to go with them to the big city where he had to die. During these Sundays we follow him in thought and we reflect on the words that he spoke before his death.

In the text from which I am going to preach, he announces to his disciples that he must die. Notice that he says this in simple words. "The son of man"—that means the Savior—"has to die." This is all that he tells them. He "has to die"; this means it is the will of God. Jesus knew that he had to

---

15. Schweitzer uses "Dieu" here. Normally he uses "Seigneur."

die in order that all men might be saved. He might have asked himself if God, who is omnipotent, would not have been able to save them otherwise. He might have said, "Is it necessary that I, who have never done evil, be delivered up to wicked men so that they will make me suffer and kill me?" But he does not say anything like this. He knows that it is the will of God. So it is for good.

For us it is also the will of God that each of us must have misfortune and that we must suffer in life. But a lot of men have far too much sorrow to understand this. When a misfortune happens, which knocks them down, they say, "Why has God done this to me?" But we ought not to propose such questions within our hearts, because we have all done wicked things in life, through bad actions and bad thoughts. We could say, "God sends us misfortune in order to give us penance." He punishes us as a father punishes his child. However, a lot of men think about those misfortunes that come to them as if they come by chance, those afflictions that strike them. You see, then, that they are disconsolate and there is no comfort in their hearts. But we, we need to turn and look to our Lord Jesus. Like him, we want to learn to take everything that happens to us from those unhappy things in life and to accept them from the hand of God, and say, "It is God who sends it; we want to bear it as his children. He knows why he sends it to us." But yet our Lord teaches us something else. He also takes the pain, which was done to him by men, as if it were sent to him from the hand of God.

Jesus was a very good man. He loved his people and wanted to do good to everyone. He spoke the Word of God to them and healed many invalids. However, he knew that they would return evil for good. They pursued him and hurled insults at him. He knew that one day they were going to demand that he be crucified, and that they would mock him on the cross. But you see that Jesus was neither surprised nor angered by what the people did to him. He says that this also comes from the hand of God. We also receive evil from those men to whom we wish to do good. Certainly, you have already noticed that we meet more enemies when we want to do good than when we do not want to do good. We know how wrong is done to someone. We go and say that it is evil, and we defend him. And so it is that we have enemies that we would not have had if we had been silent. And perhaps even the one whom we helped will not be grateful to us and will also become our enemy.

Or, again, we know that someone has had a misfortune. He is not from our family. We could say that he doesn't care about us. But we help him; we lend him money. The time comes when he could render us a service. We remind him that we helped him in his misfortune. But he is ungrateful and claims that this is not true. And he becomes more wicked towards us, as much as an old enemy, and he tells lies against us.

And if that happens you become heartbroken and you become angry with men. You do not understand why they have done you evil for good. Why do them good? You say to yourself, "No, I will not do the good that I wished to do." I have met a lot of men in life who have met with tremendous ingratitude and so have become hard and wicked. They have an injury in their hearts, which always bleed. I tell you that, among yourselves, there are men who suffer in the very same way.

But look at Jesus. He does not cease to do good to men who are wicked toward him. Because, he says, God has sent me this misfortune from men. And you also, when men do you much evil, do not be surprised, do not be overcome. But tell yourself, "This thing comes from the hand of God. I want to carry it like Jesus and to persist in goodness toward men my whole life long."

11. Sunday, 10 May 1914

"Peace Be unto You"

Luke: 24:36; *Matthew*: 13:44–50: "Peace be unto you."

When Jesus went away, his disciples were sad. There was no one to come back to teach them the truth and to guide them. You are also aware that they were afraid of the people and hid themselves. In one of our last Sunday school classes you learned how two disciples were overjoyed to meet Jesus at Emmaus, and then how he appeared to all the eleven. And when he was in their midst he spoke only a few words and saluted them with the words, "Peace be unto you."

I would like you to repeat this saying, in these days after Easter, as if

Jesus were also here to say to us, "Peace be unto you." What does this saying mean?

First of all, a question. Do you feel a need for peace? Perhaps at this very moment there are among you those who are upset by the hard events of their lives, or their hearts are shaken. You have lost someone who is very dear to you; you have concerns for your health, and you have been given a diagnosis. And if some of these persons are here among us, their hearts are prepared to understand this saying, "Peace be unto you," because they need something to hang on to. They are like those who have gone in a canoe. The canoe has overturned and now they, no longer able to be rescued, seek for the root of a tree on the riverbank so that they will not sink into the river and be swept away. And those who are drowning in their sad thoughts and fears say to themselves, "Ah, how beautiful it must be to have peace! The peace of God which makes you serene in all sufferings and anxieties." We all seek peace.

But certainly God often sends misfortune to people to awake in them the desire for peace. And afterward, when they have found it, they say, "The misfortune was good, because otherwise we would have lived all our lives without seeking peace." But those of you who are at this moment living an easy life do not say, "We live carelessly, as carelessly as when we allow our canoe to flow with the current whenever we go down the river without paddling." Because those who can live this way are far from God, and they do not see that there is no peace in their soul. They think for a moment and then close their eyes. They consider their sin and everything that they have done, and everything that they are going to do, and all that is in their conscience. Then they open the lid of the corner of their heart where all the bad thoughts are, which stir like wicked snakes—these thoughts with which they awake, with which they live the whole day, and with which they go to sleep. And they reflect upon what they are doing in their lives. Are they useful for something? Are they living for God, for Jesus, for their neighbor? Or are they not able to fulfill their lives by the pleasures that they desire? God wants us to be faithful in our lives, so that we do not live only for ourselves.

If peace is still in your hearts, close your eyes and dare to reflect on all these stories. Oh no! A man who is true to himself, who knows himself and understands his life as it truly is, cannot have peace; and he sees that those who believe they can have real peace deceive themselves. I am certain that those who understand the things of God feel that way, and they know that our whole life is vanity, because they do not have the peace of God. And by telling you this saying that entered as a light into the hearts of the apostles, "Peace be unto you," I tell you this: Feel that you do not have peace, even if everything now happening in your life is just as you want it to be, and even if you have internal happiness. Be thirsty for peace!

And what is this peace? It is to feel that we love God and Jesus above everything else in the world and that we want, before everything else, this one thing—to remain fastened to God and to know that all the other things of life are as nothing, neither the good things nor the bad things, if only we feel closer God. (Story of the Titanic)[16]

12. Second Sunday of Pentecost, 24 May 1914

"The Temple of the Holy Spirit"

1 Corinthians 6:19: "Do you not know that your body is the temple of the Holy Spirit within you, which you have from God?"

Today is the eighth day of Pentecost. Pentecost means fifty days after Easter. The feast of Pentecost is the feast of the Holy Spirit, because on this day the disciples of Christ felt the Holy Spirit in them, urging them to preach the news of Jesus to all Jews and to all the people of that time. And to prepare us for this feast I would like us to think together about what the Holy Spirit is.

First of all, what is the Spirit? I know as well as you that the pagans of old, along with your relatives, believed in spirits, and that pagans of today still do. They believe that spirits are in the air and that they can do either evil or good to men. But we know that these are the lies of witch doctors

---

16. The transcriber has added a puzzling phrase at the end of the text of this sermon. It is possible that Schweitzer concluded his remarks by telling his listeners the story of the sinking of the ocean liner *Titanic* in 1912.

and that these spirits do not exist. We whites do not understand how natives can be so deceived by their [ ].

But what then is Spirit? Spirit is something that is and that exists without anyone being able to see it. And of course there is only one Spirit—God. But when we say, "God is a Spirit, the eternal Spirit of the world," we know that we cannot explain everything. This means that God is invisible, eternal, and everywhere. It is the Spirit of God that has created the earth. It is he that has given light to the sun and stars. It is he that gives life to the grass and trees. The Spirit of God is the power of all that lives. It is what the most learned men of the world have always recognized as true, and this is also written in the Bible. But in the Bible we still speak of the Spirit of Jesus and of the Holy Spirit. What does this mean?

When I came up the Ogooué from Cape Lopez to come here, seeing sometimes two and three rivers, one beside the other, that surprised me, and I said to myself, "Is this really the Ogooué?" But then I understood that the river had separated into several rivers to give water to the whole country, and so there is only one Ogooué River, of which several currents of water have been born and are found in it. It is the same with God, who is Spirit. He has revealed himself in many forms of the Spirit to come close to the hearts of men, but nevertheless he is always the same Spirit.

First of all, there is the Spirit of God, and this Spirit spoke in the hearts of the prophets who proclaimed that one day God would send the Savior who would be filled with the Spirit of God. And this Savior came in Jesus. And then they knew the Spirit of God in Jesus. And when Jesus had left the world, God left his Spirit in the hearts of the disciples, and this was the Holy Spirit that awoke in them on the day of Pentecost, and which gave them power and courage to announce the good news to men. This means that since the time of Jesus, God has once again put more of his Spirit into the hearts of men who truly want to belong to him. And if you read the books of all the first Christians, you will find on each page words of joy in which they tell how happy they are to know the Spirit, the Spirit of God, the Spirit of the Christ within them. And the one who has written the most beautiful words about the Spirit is the apostle Paul, who wrote to the first Christians the text that has been read to you, the text in which he tells that we are like temples in which resides the Holy Spirit. "Do you not know that your body is the temple of the Holy Spirit within you, which you have from God?"

PART THREE

The 1930 Sermons

13. [1]Sunday, 9 February 1930; 8:30 in the morning[2]

"You Shall Not Kill"

Part of a series of sermons on the Ten Commandments

Exodus 20:13

Last time I told you about God's laws, which he gave to his people on a high mountain. There were ten laws just as one has ten fingers. Two of these laws I have already explained to you. I repeat to you again these two laws.[3]

---

1. Sermons 13–18 are part of a series of sermons on the Ten Commandments. However, since the sermons from earlier in 1930 are missing, we have no way of knowing how many sermons there were or how many were preached on the Commandments; we do not have a sermon for every commandment.

The extent 1930 sermons have the following sources: Sermons 13–25 come from copies of typewritten transcriptions of notes handwritten during Schweitzer's oral delivery by European secretaries and nurses. Copies of the typewritten transcriptions of sermons 13–25 were given to Dr. Melamed by Rhena Schweitzer Miller. Sermons 26–39 are from copies of typewritten French transcriptions from the special collections library at Syracuse University that were originally provided to the university by Rhena Schweitzer Miller. Sermons 40–44 come from typewritten transcriptions located at the archives of the Maison Albert Schweitzer in Günsbach, France, courtesy of Mme. Poteau-Müller and Professor Jean-Paul Sorg.

2. The notation "8:30 in the morning" is by Schweitzer himself.

3. It would appear the "two laws" considered by Schweitzer were "You shall have no other gods before me" and "You shall not make for yourself a graven image." He has combined the first two commandments as a single commandment.

Today I am explaining to you a third law. This law is very short: "You shall not kill." This law is written in the hearts of men, because when a man hears that another is killed, it frightens him and he thinks, "This is terrible." Isn't this true? Nevertheless, this law is often forgotten, and especially by poor pagan people. You had chiefs who killed men. And you had chiefs who sold men as slaves in America, and you know that many slaves died during the trip. Even today, if you go to the place where men are completely savage, you know that often they still kill men. And when the patients from here return to their villages, they do not want to go alone, because they are afraid they will be killed. Because this is so, it is necessary to hear the law of God. And this law says, "YOU SHALL NOT KILL."

It is a major law that is true for blacks and for whites. There are whites that say, "I am very strong, and I have a gun. I intend to kill those who are less strong." But when he is dead, God will have a big palaver with him. And God will summon all the men whom the man has killed, and the man will be judged by God. And as for the chiefs who have killed men, God will summon them to a big palaver when they are dead. But now we do not want to speak about whites and chiefs; we want to speak about us. Perhaps there is someone among us who has already killed a man, and we do not know who he is, and nobody has a palaver with him, and he is not judged by men. But God knows whom he has killed, and God will have a conference with him when he is dead. Perhaps someone among you goes from the hospital to return to his village, and he proceeds to have a big palaver with someone, and he thinks, "I am going to kill this other one." Then he must think of this Sunday and of the law of God: "You shall not kill." And for this reason always remember the law, so that when you have a big palaver with someone, you do not become angry enough to kill.

Here is still another reason why one man kills another. He kills him to get his money. A man comes into another's village with a lot of crates. Then the second man thinks in his heart, "Here is a rich man with all these crates, and I am poor. I want to find this man and kill him. Then I will be able to take all his crates." It is for this reason that each man has to pay attention to his heart. In the heart there are bad and good thoughts. The heart of a man is like a monkey. The monkey is perhaps sweet and nice, and all of a sudden it jumps on you and bites you. So the heart of a man is perhaps quite peaceful, and all of a sudden bad thoughts come there and tell him, "Go and kill a man." And if he does not pay attention to his heart, he goes and he kills the man. What does one do with monkeys who bite? One ties them up. (I do not speak of Mrs. Canada's small monkeys because I do not speak of the hearts of small children.[4] The hearts of small children do not yet contain bad thoughts, and Mrs. Canada's small monkeys are not wicked.) One ties up monkeys that bite with a chain. With what does one bind the hearts of men? The Law of God. So it is necessary that you always pay attention to your hearts so that no wicked thoughts enter there.

Men also kill because they detest someone. Someone has insulted your mother or you. He becomes your enemy, and you say, "I detest him, and I will be happy only when I will have killed him." Isn't it true? In this way, a man comes to kill someone. Because he has neglected his heart, he does not have God's law there.

14. Sunday, 2 March 1930

"You Shall Not Steal"

Part of a series of sermons on the Ten Commandments

Exodus 20:15

[ ] until now I have explained to you two laws. The first law is that God is the only God and that there is no other God, and that there are no idols; and the second law is "You shall not kill." I have spoken a great deal about this law. First, I told you that there is no need to kill men. In order that men not be killed, we must be very careful of the wicked thoughts of the heart, since it is because of these bad thoughts that a man does such a terrible thing as to kill a man. [ ] who made the idol and who poisoned it? [ ] and the native medicine man says that it is such or such a man, but the native medicine man is a liar if he says that a man is the cause of the death. If another man has killed a man, it is God who will punish him, and God is a good judge.

4. For information about "Mrs. Canada" and her monkeys, see footnote 1 to the Textual Notes in the front matter.

I have explained that the law is not only "You shall not kill men," but "THOU SHALT NOT KILL." Because all animals are children of God, just as men are, God does not want us to kill an animal unnecessarily. God allows us to kill an animal when we are very hungry, or when a beast is harmful, like a snake. [ ] but we need not kill a poor small bird, because a poor small bird has not killed a man. It is not necessary to kill all the poor little animals that creep upon the earth. You need not kill them. Do you all understand? Tell everybody in the villages that it is not necessary to kill animals. We whites are terribly upset to see how badly you treat animals. We think of the palaver that God is going to have with you. [ ] and when God says, "[ ] if you kill [ ] I am going to punish you [ ]." It is for this reason that we speak the word of God to you. You must say to the others in the villages, "I have heard the word of the doctor, and this is what he says [ ]." When you sit beside the fire to drink *bitzi* [a native potion], you must say this instead of telling foolish stories. I have still many more things to say about the law "You shall not kill," but I will tell you later.

Today I will tell you a new law, which is in the book of God, and this law says, "YOU SHALL NOT STEAL." You shall not steal! So you say, "This is a good law! Ah, if people would not steal! They have already stolen my canoe." Then someone else says to me, "They have stolen my bananas." Each of you could tell about someone who stole from you. It is terrible how you natives steal from one another. [ ] the poor people at the hospital steal things, and you know that at this time [ ] because there are natives near the post office who stole eighteen thousand francs from a white while he was sick. They stole twenty thousand C.F.A. [Communauté financière africaine] francs.[5] Yesterday I saw a family who had not slept because someone stole everything they had earned for their children and their fathers and mothers in Europe. Now they write, "Everything that we earned for our children's food and for our parents, the blacks have stolen from us." There are some days at the Protestant Mission when a child is admitted for surgery and men have stolen things of value from that child. They have also taught a small child to steal [ ]. And all these people believe, "They have not discovered us. This is good. We have earned a lot of loincloths,

---

5. Schweitzer gives us no further information about this incident. The C.F.A. was the African Financial Community, the central banking authority for the French colonies in West Africa.

wine, [ ]." Perhaps they will never find them out. Then they will say, "Oh! I am happy, and they have not found us out." But there is someone who knows it [ ]. When this man is dead, God will say to him, "It is you who have stolen from Mr. and Mrs. Lépine, from Mr. Schatzmann [ ], who entered the Mission shop and stole a lot of things." He will not be able to say, "No one has seen me." He will be obliged to keep quiet, and then he will be punished by God far more severely than by men.

I have spoken to you about thefts that have been committed, and I have told you that it is very bad to steal. You are all seated. Now those who have never stolen even an egg, even a piece of cassava, let that one stand up. Ah! There is only one person who is standing up! Why? If all of you have already stolen [ ]. I knew quite well that nobody would dare to say that he has never stolen. [ ] that if there was a liar here [ ]. Well! I want you to say in your hearts, "It is sad that I have already stolen," and that you know quite well [ ] that it is only because God protects you. I want you to think in your heart [ ]. Now we are going to reflect. Why does God protect someone who takes something that belongs to another? Some say, "Oh, this man is rich, and I am poor, and [ ]." So it is that people come to steal. They say, "The rich have a lot of goods, and I have only taken a smattering of the whole." But God does not allow this [ ] when we think about this. [ ] but he wants each of us to leave the other that which is his, even if that someone else is rich and we have practically nothing.

There are people here who believe that the doctor is rich and who want [ ] boxes for medicines. [ ] Do you know that in Europe the doctor bought a beautiful box like that [ ] twenty francs? There are men who say, "The doctor is rich, he can buy a lot of rice and cassavas and oil of palm tree [ ]. If there is a system [ ] we are going to cut [ ]." I know that there are many who say, "Soon the moon will rise and then we are going to cut nuts from the palm tree!" I know [ ]. And you laugh. But I am sad because I am not rich, and I spend all my money for your sake, and I have planted everything for you [ ] so that you should not think that one can steal from a rich man [ ] because I know that your hearts are not so wicked.

I know that there are many among you who would never steal from a poor man. They would say, "This is a poor man; I do not want to steal his cassava," and I am happy that there are many like this, but I know that there are a lot who say, "If he is rich, I will steal a little bit from him, because that does not affect him at all." I apologize for you when whites are very angry, and I say, "It is because they believe that all whites are rich." Isn't this true? Now, why does God want people to work? How can a man say, "This is mine"? Men do not make trees. Men have not made fruit to grow. Then how can a man say, "These are my trees?" Because he has paid money for the business. But how does he have this money? Did he find it while asleep? No! [ ] earned this money by working. Therefore, because he earned this money by working and bought the business, it is his even if God grew the trees. Why? "These trees are mine," [ ]. It is not I who grew them, it is the good Lord. Have you seen a man who can grow trees? Men can make machines, but nobody ever grew a tree. Isn't this true? But the good Lord gives everything that he has grown to those who work. Permit me to say, "It is mine," because it is I who have cleared the land; it is I who have pruned the palm trees so that they bear nuts; it is I who have paid for the machetes and axes of which so many have been lost and stolen; it is I who have given the food allotment to men who work; it is I who have given the gift. It is I who have [ ]. The good Lord said to a native woman when she cleared and planted and harvested the cassava, "It is hers." When a man has carved a paddle, it is his. When he has earned money with his work and given a cooking pot to his wife, the pot is hers; nobody ought to take it. When a man has worked to give her a flatiron, this flatiron is hers. Then God said, "Do not take what another has earned by his work." If God said, "You shall not steal," he says by the same mouth, "YOU SHALL WORK!" God wants you to work. Why?

Haven't you already thought of the difference between a monkey and a man? The monkey has a figure a bit like a man. It walks like a man, but what is the difference between you and a monkey? Don't you see? The difference is that the monkey strolls through the trees and takes all that it sees— spiders, fruit, birds—but it does not work. No! It is because of this that the monkey is only a poor animal, and you would all be like monkeys if you did not work. There would be a lot of you who would die of hunger [ ] tornado [ ] fire to cook [ ] cooking pot. A man is truly a man who is able to think only when he works, who wants to work even if others steal from him.

Then, when I was in Europe, they said to me, "But it isn't possible that there was a famine and that you were required to make a lot of rice to feed them! Why don't they plant bananas? Are they that idle?" I know that you are not that idle. You are a little idle—especially the men, not so much the women. The women would always want to plant things. "Why don't they want to plant things?" When they ask me that, I say, "Come a little closer! I am going to tell you the real reason, for your ears only, and don't repeat it, because it is too sad. It is because everything that was planted was stolen. [ ] People dying of hunger, thousands who don't have the spirit to plant things, because the whole world steals." Isn't this true? It is because of this that the government is so severe and punishes [ ].

If things are going to be the best that they can be, a change within the heart is necessary, and this change cannot be brought about through punishment, but only though the Word of God. This law is, "You shall not steal! You shall never steal! You shall steal nothing!" Because [ ]. It is when people steal that people do not have the spirit to work. There are palavers, there is weary misery, and there is famine. Everywhere it is the same thing. Because there are so many thieves in your country, nobody works with pleasure. Many say, "What can change the hearts of men?" It is the Word of God. I have traveled a lot in countries where nobody steals. How do these people do that? Because they have obeyed the word of God.

I am going to tell you a story. There is a country very far from here, very cold, where there is always fire in the huts, where, during several months the trees have no leaves because they fall from the cold, where one can plant things only during the months there is no snow. It is a big country where there are a lot of poor people, but it is an honorable country, a famous country, because it has the fewest thieves of all the countries in the world. A man arrives in his canoe. It has perhaps four canteens, and it is evening, then night, and the village is far away, and his wife says, "How can we carry these four canteens?" And the man says, "We will leave them here at the wharf, and we will go to the village, and we will tell our friends, "Come help us!" And in the morning they get up and they know that the canteens are still there. Isn't this true? But how would that be in your country? Would you believe that the canteens would still be there in the morning? No! They would say, "There are some canteens! I am going to take them! This man has forgotten his canteens, I am going to take them!" So these men in this country have become completely indifferent to the word of God.

So it is that your hearts must become completely changed by the Word of God. You should reflect upon this, that this is not from men, it is from God. Because this is the Word of God: "You shall not steal!" And all of you here will not be happy until you have understood this Word.

15. Sunday, 9 March 1930

The Laws of God

Part of a series of sermons on the Ten Commandments

Exodus 20:1–17

Many years have passed since these laws were made for all mankind, for whites as well as for blacks. There are ten of them. I have spoken to you about the law, "There is only one God and there are no idols." Then another law: "You shall be good to your parents, and to all old people." Then the fifth law, "You shall not kill, you shall never kill! You shall never kill other men, and you shall never unnecessarily kill animals, but you must have a good heart toward all men and all animals."[6]

Last Sunday I spoke of a new law, "You shall not steal," and you know that this law is very necessary for everyone. When I asked, "Is it wicked to steal?" you replied, "Yes, it is very wicked!" Isn't this true? Then, when I said to you that whoever has never stolen must stand up, nobody dared to stand up. Isn't this true? Now, I would like everyone to have in his or her heart the thought, "I have already stolen, but now I no longer want to steal. I do not want to steal at the hospital even if the doctor does not know that I steal. I did not want to steal the machete from the table the evening that Mrs. Canada forgot it." You want to steal because your heart has told you, "Here is a machete that someone has forgotten—take it!" Isn't this true? Then you must say, "Oh wicked heart! Hush up! I am going to take this machete and to give it to a nurse." It is the same thing when you find a paddle. You shouldn't say, "Here is a paddle that belongs to someone. I am going to take it." But you should tell a nurse, "Here is a paddle that I have found." And then you are inside, and someone who has a small canteen with a key has gone out. It has been quite awhile since the doctor gave him medicine, and you say, "Here is a key! I am going to see what there is inside." Perhaps it hasn't been completely shut, or perhaps it can be opened with some wood. If you know the law of God you say, "Well!

6. Schweitzer seems to indicate that he may have given another set of sermons on the Ten Commandments that have not been preserved.

Never!" You say to your heart, "You speak like a wicked man. This doesn't belong to me, I never want to open it, and even if is left unlocked, I will not do it."

I will tell you a story. When we come here, we all are advised that everything must be locked up. When a new nurse arrives she is given twelve keys, and she says, "Why all these keys?" They tell her, "This is the key for this cupboard, and this is for this door. It is necessary that you have the key." Then she says, "What a curious country! Why do I have to carry all these keys? Why not leave the key in the lock of the door of the cupboard? That is how I do it in Europe." But she is told, "One can't do that here. It is not possible. These are poor black people, and their wicked hearts are often stronger than their good hearts. They say, 'The white is not there, he will not see me.' " "What?" she says, "Is this how it is with the blacks?" She is very sad, and we are all sad that we are not able to have a lot of confidence in many blacks and that it is necessary to lock everything up.

I know that there are blacks who never take anything. Do you know Oyembo, who was at the Protestant Mission? Once, on a big boat, I heard the whites speaking and they said how sad they were because so many blacks want to steal. And then one said, "I know a black who never steals. It is Oyembo." And that pleased me. Here as well there is a black who never steals and whom I love very much as a brother; nevertheless I am angered about other things. It is Aloÿse. In the morning I often find him at the carpenter's, where he tells stories instead of paying attention to his fire. But the doctor likes him nevertheless because he can leave everything opened. I could give a lot of petrol to Aloÿse, and he would never take some for his lantern without asking me. I could give him a lot of grease, and he never would take some for his kitchen. I could give him a lot of flour to make bread. With another I would be obliged to place the bread on the scale, but with Aloÿse I have no need to get out the scale. He will not take anything, neither avocados nor oranges. And I tell you this so that you hear how happy we are to find a black who never steals. This one knows God's law, which says, "I will never steal, but I want to work in order to have everything which I need." We say that the beginning of thievery is laziness. All those who steal are lazy.

And then the other reason why someone steals is that they want to have things that are unnecessary. There are people who steal because they want to smoke. How many men want to have money to buy tobacco! If someone wants to smoke, he has to work. But he doesn't need to smoke. When the doctor was young, he smoked, but one day he said, "It is pointless to smoke. I no longer will smoke! I will put this money aside." And so, for the same reason, the doctor does not smoke, because of you, in order to have money to buy medicines. Be like me and say, "It is pointless to smoke."

There are others who have taken it into their heads to have beautiful clothes, and if someone earns the money he can have fine clothing, but he must see if his old parents have enough to eat, and, if there are poor people in his village who haven't enough to eat, he must give them something to eat. Then God will be happy, and when he is dead God will say to him, "You have had a good heart, and you have given food to your parents and to these old poor people," and this man will be happy in the house of the good Lord. But if he has allowed his parents and old people to go hungry and has bought beautiful clothes, then the good Lord will say, "Get thee hence!" The man will say, "What? I have never done evil, I have never killed anyone, and I have only stolen just a little bit." And the good Lord will tell him, "This is not for that, but I have seen you stroll on Sundays in beautiful white outfits, and your wife has a beautiful loincoth and overblouse [ ], while in your village there were old people dying of hunger." Then the poor black who made *faro* [unknown word] here will be frightened, and he will say, "I never thought of that. I thought that the money I earned was for me." But the good Lord will punish him.

So that this does not happen to you, say, "God wants us to work so that we do not become thieves. God wants each one to do a lot of work in order to have food for himself and to give [some] to his parents and to the poor who can no longer work." For this reason I say that the laws of God are like the nut of a palm tree; when one breaks it, there is another inside. So within this law, "You shall not steal," there is the other law, "You must work."

We who love you, we think that the time will come when one will be able find a lot of villages with pretty cabins and pretty plantations, where each one will have his plantation next to that of another man, just as it is in our country, where each one knows that this tree belongs to that man there. Around my village there are many trees—far more than those at the Catholic Mission—which bear fruit, but when the fruit is ripe it is not necessary to place guards, since everyone knows that this tree belongs to that one there, and this tree here is mine, and I want to take only the fruit of trees that are mine. People are happy like this. And you can be happier, because in this country you have more sun. We have no avocados, oranges, and tangerines, and you have everything that the doctor has planted.

Go into the villages of the Pahouins and the Galoas. All these villages have a lot of trees, but it is not like that here. Why not? Why do people dare not plant? Why do they not plant? Who can tell me this? Go ahead! Nobody speaks! Why does one not plant trees? You do not plant trees because you say, "The thief will eat the fruit." That's the reason why. So I continue to plant fruit trees. Perhaps, when my trees bear fruit, the blacks will not steal from me because they have heard the Word of God. When you have pretty huts and these trees around the villages and, when you will have these villages, no administrator will come to say that the village must be altered. When he sees these pretty huts and these trees and this fruit, he will say, "This village must stay."

God has created trees, which bear fruit so that men may work the earth. He wants men who work with their hands. Oh, how angry I get with those merchants who become commercial exploiters of the forest instead of working the earth, and who do a lot of trading! Real happiness is to work the earth, to know friendship, and to earn just what is necessary in order to live, and to have no debts.

I have told you about two laws that are like the pit of a palm tree nut. The nut of the palm tree is the law "You shall not steal." And the pit is the law "You shall work." And so, tomorrow morning, when those who must work are called, they shouldn't say, "Oh, why don't they leave us in peace here?" And when a machete is handed out, which we don't do like this, and then [ ] the file [ ], and that when Mrs. Canada has left, they immediately relax.[7]

One can work solely because one is forced. Do you work for me? No! You work for yourselves and for the other sick people here, so that we may have palm oil for those who come and bananas for those who cannot eat rice. So it is [ ] not to work as slaves but as men who have a good heart [ ], if there are one or two or three who understand that work is a law of God. And if there are only some, Mrs. Canada and I will be happy to know that the law of God has already entered the hearts of some men. Also, the good Lord will be pleased.

7. The text is fragmentary here. The sense seems to be that when Mrs. Canada stopped supervising the work of the local men, no further work was accomplished.

16. Sunday, 16 March 1930

"You Shall Not Lie"

Part of a series of sermons on the Ten Commandments

Exodus 20:16

[ ] and I believe that there are people who fear God, because there are people who [ ]. And, when you are dead, the good Lord is going to have a palaver with you. You are going to say, "I did not know," like a woman who sets a fire where she should not, and says to the doctor, "I did not know." And he says, "You would have known if you had wanted to." So then the good Lord will say, "You had the knowledge. Weren't you at the hospital when the doctor explained the laws of God?" Then you will not be able to say, "I didn't know." You will be obliged to say, "Yes," because the good Lord knows all. You will be ashamed. The good Lord will say, "Because of a little piece of fish, you sat on your rear end!"[8] And he will punish you. He will have reason to punish you. Isn't this true?

There are men who stay in their huts because they fear the law that I am going to speak about today. They should be far more afraid of the law, "You shall not steal," because this is a law that offends a lot of men. The law says, "You shall not lie." The good Lord knows how many misfortunes have happened on account of lying, because all evil begins with lying. When a husband and a wife are miserable, this begins with lying. When a child acts naughty toward its parents, this begins with lying. And when people who were good friends make a palaver and become enemies, this also begins with lying. Isn't that so? Now, one can say that a man steals in order to have something, but it is not the same thing as lying. Often one lies for nothing. One tells things that are not true simply for the pleasure of telling these things. And we, we whites, are very sad to know how much natives lie. Isn't this true? If you knew how to work as well as how to lie, you would be masters of the world, and we whites would be obliged to obey you!

8. A colloquial expression for "you did nothing at all."

It has become a habit in your country to lie. Each one says, "If the other lies, I lie also. Everyone lies. This man about whom everyone says, 'He is a very good man,' I know that he lies. So I will lie also." And when little children see how much lying is done, they lie also. And this is the way you live, everywhere wallowing in lies as in a swamp. If I told you, "Go, walk in the swamp there!" you would say, "No, it is dirty. When one goes in there, one becomes black as an elephant. One cannot swim in the swamp. I prefer to throw myself in the river than to go into the swamp." But in your life you are always walking in the swamp. You are as dirty as the filthy pig, which lives in the swamp. That is to say, you are dirty in your heart, because every day you walk in the swamp of lying. And it is because of this that God says, "You shall not lie." He says this from the very first, because from lying come all the palavers and all the misfortunes that overturn men.

You see this sheep? It is a poor sheep, but it has a better heart than all of you because it has never lied. Isn't this true? And every time that you see a sheep you will think of the doctor, who said that the sheep has a better heart. It is because of this that the good Lord has not permitted animals to speak, because if they knew how to speak, they would lie as you do, and the good Lord would no longer like them. But when the good Lord made men he said, "I will make them speak," and now man is in great danger of lying, and because of this it is necessary to pay attention.

In the country of the whites there are large companies of men who live in a big house and who never speak.[9] Everyone who enters the house promises never to speak. Only the leader has the right to speak so as to give orders; the others do not speak. I know of a house like that, far larger than the hospital. There are a lot of men in the house, which is not far from my village. Why do these men say, "We will not speak?" In order not to lie. And so, because we have speech, we are always in danger of lying, and all the palavers in the country of men come about through lying; and, what is still more harmful, the heart of man becomes evil through lying, because everyone, even the poor native, knows that lying is bad.

9. It is probable that Schweitzer refers to a European monastery. He says that there is a monastery near his village, but he does not identify it for us.

See this woman there? She is carrying banana leaves. She must come here! It is the young woman who [ ]. One does not look for banana leaves at my house [ ].[10]

Therefore, lying makes the heart sick. A man can say, "Then lying makes my heart wicked." Then he says, "I am wicked. If I am more or less wicked, that is all right!" And, in this way, this man becomes thoroughly wicked. He could have remained good if he had not lied. It is because of this that it is necessary to struggle against lying. Every day it is necessary to say, "I do not want to lie, so that my heart has peace, and so that my heart does not become wicked."

You have heard of the big war that there was in Europe where so many men died, and also about the poor native people who were forced to be soldiers or to become porters in Cameroon where [ ].[11] You still remember [ ]. How did this war come about? Because in the country of the whites there were a lot of great leaders who told lies, and from these lies came a big palaver and then the war. In the struggle against lying it is necessary to begin by saying, "I do not want to speak a pointless word."

Look at a child. It lies only to tell things that are not true. Isn't this so? Well then! A lot of men remain like children. They lie only to tell something. They want to tell something, and so they enter the homes of others [ ]. Then they say something completely different, merely in order to speak, just to be men who know some big news. You yourselves have acted in this way. It is because of this that it is always necessary to pay attention in order not to tell pointless things.

In the Word of God it is said, "Watch your mouth, because God will one day have a palaver with men for all the words that have left their mouths." There are many people who lie in order to do evil. They have someone who is their enemy. They do not kill him with weapons; they kill him with words when they are seated near the fire and say, "Oh, I know a lot of stories about this man. You know the things that have been stolen? They have never found the thief, but I know. It is this man!" And in this way they lie to cause this man pain. They speak about a woman. They say, "Everyone thinks that she is a good woman, but I know things! And I can-

---

10. This aside by Schweitzer, in which he interrupts his own sermon, is the first of several such occurrences recorded by the transcribers. How fortunate for the reader that the transcriber has included Schweitzer's extemporaneous comments.

11. We do not know to which incident in World War I Schweitzer was referring.

not say any more." They say this, and they know that it is lies. Thus men lie to be wicked toward those they detest. And God will punish them. He will punish also those who have not killed men. You will ask the good Lord, "Why are these men, who have not killed, in the heavenly prison?" And the good Lord will say, "They have not killed with the machete, they have not killed with the ax, but they have killed by lying. By their lies they have made as much pain as a man who kills others with the machete." And men will say, "God, you are just!" And you will be afraid that God will say, "You are a man like that."

There are also men who lie through fear. They have done something that they were not supposed to do, and now they are having a palaver. Perhaps it is a small thing. They have found a fishhook or a machete, and they have kept it for themselves. Then another says, "You have taken my fishhook," or "You have taken my machete." Then the men say to themselves, "He cannot prove it. I am going to lie." And he begins to lie. Every day you see men in this hospital telling lies for no reason at all. A man cuts a bunch of bananas, and I ask, "Why have you cut this bunch?" He replies with a lie. I tell you that he is afraid to be punished because he fears punishment. It is not necessary to be afraid. If you have done something, do not lie but take your punishment, and you will see that everyone likes a man who does not lie because of fear. Myself, if [ ] and he tells the truth, I forgive him because I know that his heart is good. And you yourselves, you are like this. If someone has taken things [ ] and he says, "It is true, I have taken [ ]; tell me what to do," you no longer seek to do him harm. Isn't it true? Because you are pleased that this man does not lie, you have pity on him, and this is the way it must be.

God has given you speech, which he has not given to the animals. Because he has given us speech, we have the ability to lie. Therefore it is necessary to hold a palaver within your heart, and say to it every day, "I do not want you to lie," and then to refrain from lying through pointless words, or to harm someone, or through fear because you have done something wicked. It is always necessary to hold to the truth, and the one who does so is like the man who walks into the lake and cannot drown and remains clean, while the liar is the one who walks into the swamp. He becomes dirty, and perhaps he drowns and disappears into the swamp, entangled in the roots. So then, you must always think, "I do not want my heart to be in the swamp."

You can recognize those men who lie and those who don't lie. When you see a certain man, you say, "He is a liar!" He has the eyes of a liar: he does not look at men because he has fear in his eyes; he looks here and he looks there. You can also recognize men who do not lie; their faces show it, and all the world likes these men. Men like them, and the good Lord likes them too. So then, become masters of your hearts. Become true men, because a man that lies cannot be the child of God.

17. Sunday, 23 March 1930

"You Shall Not Commit Adultery"

Part of a series of sermons on the Ten Commandments

Exodus 20:14

You have already learned several laws of the good Lord. These you have learned from me: the law that it is necessary to have one God only; the law that it is necessary not to kill; the law that it is necessary to be good toward parents and old people; the law that one must not steal; and the law that one must not lie. Today I will tell you a new law: the law, "You must not commit adultery." Men also have this law in their hearts. When a man takes the wife of another, he knows that it is wicked. The greatest savage knows that it is wrong; he knows that he will have a palaver, and that if he is judged and convicted in the palaver, it will be just. Isn't this true? But a lot of men believe, "This is the law of men. If I can commit adultery and nobody knows it, and I am not condemned, that's fine." This is why many natives commit adultery, because they believe that there will be no punishment.

We Europeans are very sad to see all the misfortunes in your country that are due to adultery. We do not mean that white men are better than black men, but if you came to our country you would see that in our villages there aren't disputes over women the way there are here. That is to say, this is not only a law of men; it is a law of God. God wants a man and a woman to be together as two in their dwelling place and work together to feed their children. God said it this way, by creating the world with a man and a woman. Because the good Lord likes order and peace, God will punish those who, with a light heart, commit adultery and make palavers.

I am sure that in your country there are many who think that adultery is a small thing, those who tell themselves, "Oh, there are a lot of people who commit adultery, why can't I do that too? If there is a palaver, I will cope with it, and I will say, 'This is not true,' and perhaps they will not condemn me." This is the way men and women think here, and this is why the Word of God is proclaimed to you, the word that says, "YOU SHALL NOT COMMIT ADULTERY!" Keep this law fully, in your heart! And when the thought of committing adultery enters your heart, think of God.

Now I am going to tell you why there is so much adultery among you: because there are so many men who have no wives. Isn't this true? Is it totally true? [ ] and gives a present to a woman to have adultery with her. Why are there so many men who are not married in your country? Because, from the beginning, instead of putting the money aside to buy a woman, they buy stupidities. Look at all those who are doing this! Why have they left their villages to gamble instead of making plantations in their own community? They said, "I want to earn money in order to buy a wife." Isn't this true? There are many who are committed to buying a wife, and many who have not bought one. Why? Because when they earn the money, and see foolish things, they say, "I am going to buy that!"

When they return to their villages, they have nothing left and cannot buy a wife. Then this village is full of men who want to commit adultery. Isn't this true? You see, I know you! And this is a big misfortune for your community. It is for this reason that I say to you, "Instead of buying stupidities, put your money aside to buy a wife so that this major sin, which exists in every cabin, will no longer thrive in the villages."

But there is another reason why men have not married. It is because women are so expensive, and this is a big shame. When a native has a girl to give in marriage, he doesn't know how much to sell her for. Formerly one asked two to three hundred francs; later, a thousand francs; and now, two thousand francs. For a native woman who is ugly, who is wicked, who is silly, one pays two thousand francs, because the family wants the money. Everybody in the family wants the money, and I tell you, it is a shame! I tell you all! As long as a woman is something for which one goes to market, and for which one asks more than a poor man can pay in this way, and for which they ask so much money, there will be adultery. I tell you that the good

Lord will be sad as he looks at this, and he will say, "Here are even more cabins where adultery is always being committed!" It is because of these very sad things that I tell you, "Look here! I have come to the community of the blacks because I love them, and because God said to come and help you," but when I see all your dealings and palavers concerning women I am angered, and I say, "It would be better if all of you were slaves, working day and night as prisoners until you were sensible, until you learned reason and no longer had palavers in your community."

Isn't it true that all the misfortunes in your community are due to these dealings about women? This is sad. Now don't tell me, "This is the way it is! It can't be changed." Everything can be changed. Formerly this was the forest, the bush: there were only trees that did not bear fruit, and there were snakes. Now it is changed. There are huts, there are roads, there are trees that bear fruit, and there are young goats. So your community can also be changed if only you want to, and if everyone has the law of God in their hearts, not only the law of men.

When you are in your villages and your hearts have these thoughts, I want you to think of this Sunday morning and the law of God. Someday I would like all this talk of adultery to disappear from every single cabin.

Let us pray! Oh God, who art the father of men, place good thoughts in our hearts! Tear out wicked thoughts from the hearts of men and women in all villages, so that they may live before the law as children with good hearts, and so that all these ugly palavers cease in the villages, and peace may reign in our villages. Amen.

18. Sunday, 30 March 1930

"You Shall Not Bear False Witness"

Part of a series on the Ten Commandments; second sermon on lying

Exodus 20:16

These past Sundays I have spoken to you about all the laws that God has given to men—to whites as well as to blacks—and that are written in the book of the words of God. You know that there are ten of them, and, in order that you do not forget, I will tell you once more about the laws that God has given to men. The first law is "There is only one God, and there are no idols." Then, "You must be good to your relatives and to all old people," "You must not kill," "You must not lie," "You must not commit adultery." These are the laws that you have already heard about, and today, once again, we have a law that tells us something new. This law says, "YOU SHALL NOT GIVE A FALSE TESTIMONY."

Do you know what a testimony is? When there is a palaver and someone says that a man has stolen something, someone then asks, "Who has seen this man steal?" and then someone says, "[ ]" and these people give their testimony—the people who tell what has happened. And in the palavers you know that there are people who do not tell the truth.

A man has stolen. Others know it, but then, when there is the palaver, someone says [ ], "I know that he is innocent, because he was at his wife's house at the plantation." A man has been killed, and it is such or such a man who killed him. Then some of his friends come to the palaver and say, "Oh no! He was at our house in the village. He did not kill." Isn't it true that it is just like this in the palavers? Now, the good Lord has spoken the law, "You shall not lie," but to show how terrible it is to lie in the palaver, he has added a law that says, "You shall not bear false witness." Even though there are many men who do not lie very much, they lie in the palaver. They lie to help their friends. They say to themselves, "Perhaps someone is going to denounce my friend, but I will lie so that he will not be judged." And it is for this reason that the good Lord gave us a special law, "You shall not give a false testimony." If you have to speak in a palaver, you should tell only what you have seen. When you have not seen anything, you say, "I have not seen anything." When you have seen something, you say, "I have seen this thing."

Often people lie in the palaver because of fear. I know this is true. Because of their fear these men say, "It is he who has killed," or "It is he who has committed adultery." This often happens. Then these people say, "Because I was afraid, I have not told the truth. I am not wicked, I lied only because I was afraid" [ ] and so it is that many people give false testimony. And because the good Lord knows this, he has given us an entirely special law, which says, "You must not bear false witness."

It often happens that people do not tell the truth in the palavers. There are people who are innocent and there are those who are guilty. You know about these palavers where people who have not stolen are accused as if they had stolen, or as if they had committed adultery, and where people who have not killed are accused as if they had committed murder or even poisoned someone. And why are they charged? Because there were people there who did not dare to tell the truth because they were afraid. Perhaps each of you can be accused like that, because there are people who do not tell the truth. It's true, isn't it? This is the reason why there is a lot of injustice in the world—because people in the palavers do not tell the truth. And because of this the good Lord says, "You shall not give false testimony against men." But the law of God says something far more. The law says in addition: "You shall not say wicked things about another man. You shall pay attention to your tongue, and be aware of what it is saying."

I will tell you why there are so many palavers in your country: because your women speak so foolishly. There are three women. One of them begins to speak. She says [ ] she does not know if everything is true, but she says so anyway. Why does she do this? Because it gives her pleasure to tell wicked things. Then another woman says, "I also know things!" Then she tells wicked things about other women. She does not know if this is true, but only that she has heard it from someone else. Then the third says, "I am also going to tell something. Listen closely! I know that such or such a man has done something." She does not know the whole story. She has only heard these women who tell wicked things, and these things are told in the village. There are a lot of villages where it is exactly like this.

What is so sad is that there are a lot of men who act just like women; they also speak foolishly when they are sitting together around the fire. And then suddenly a man who hasn't done anything says, "This man is a thief," or "This man has committed adultery." Oh, I know it! How distressing it is in your villages because someone tells things that are not true. Someone tells something only because [ ] and each has heard it from another. And someone says, "I wasn't the first to say it." And he has not actually lied; it's not he who was the first to discover this lie. It is a false testimony because he has told something which he didn't really know. And the good Lord will be angered with him as if he were a liar, and he will put him in the same prison with the other liars.

It is for this reason that the good Lord does not want a man to tell on others without knowing whether or not it is true. This law means, "You shall not repeat what others tell, but you shall always examine it to see if it is really true." Ah! If men had a bit more fear of their wicked tongues! If you hear wicked speech, do not repeat it; say, "I do not tell it because I do not know if it is true."

A man has to know how to be silent. He must not repeat useless things, because he should be afraid to tell lies, to bear false witness. Everyone gives false testimony before God if they tell something that they have not seen, something that they do not know. It is possible that you know that it is true that a man has done such or such a thing. But nevertheless you do not have to repeat it. It is not necessary to tell wicked things, even if one knows that it is true. God knows everything—those who have lied, those who have stolen, those who have killed, those who have committed adultery—and it is he who will punish them. It is not necessary for men to speak foolish things about this. God [ ] to pay attention to your language, and when your wicked heart wants to make you tell wicked things about others, then do not say these things, because those who do not tell wicked things with their tongue are the true children of God.

19. Palm Sunday, 13 April 1930

Palm Sunday

Today is a special Sunday. It is the Sunday in which Jesus our master entered the city of Jerusalem, the major city of the Jewish people. For this reason I am not speaking about God's laws but telling this story, the story that today is being told in all the churches of the whites.

You know that God had a favorite people, this Jewish people. It is to this people, because he liked them the most, that he sent people to speak the truths of God, and these persons were called prophets, and all the prophets announced that God would send, at the end, someone who would have his Spirit completely, so that we could say that he was the Son of God. They did not know the name of this man [ ] and this man was called Jesus. All of you who are listening to me have already heard this name, because all

Christians say that Jesus is their chief and their master. And we have, in the last pages of the Bible, all the words that Jesus spoke.

Jesus was a man who was not rich. He was poor, and men who walked with him, who recognized that Jesus was the man that God had promised, were also poor people. At that time Jesus was not an important chief, because God did not want him to be important among men, but only important by the spirit and the heart, because of all the knowledge and the truths that God had written in his heart. Isn't it just like this when an important chief like the governor comes here who has no need of handsome clothing? The doctor's cook goes about in lovely clothing, but the governor has no need of lovely clothing. The governor can stroll about even in khaki trousers. Isn't this so? On Sundays you may see people who are far better dressed than the doctor. This morning I have seen natives going to mass wearing white trousers, collars, ties, dressed entirely as Europeans. Even so, they are not the doctor.

So it is that the good Lord God sent his Son into the world, and he said, "I do not want him to be a rich man, but a completely poor man. Nevertheless is it he who will be the King of the whole world, the King according to truth, thought, and the heart." Then all the Jewish people who had heard the speech of the prophets were awaiting this Son of God to be the great King of the world. In this way they had understood the words of prophets. And then, when they saw Jesus as a poor man in his loincloth, eating like the others, without a beautiful outfit, they said, "It is impossible that this man has come to govern the hearts of men." And the important chiefs laughed at him. They said, "Who would want this man? He has no militiamen, no one obeys him, yet it is he who says that he is the King of hearts whom God has sent!" They forgot that it is one thing to obey with the body or with the arm, and quite another to obey with the heart. It is not possible to be an important chief without enough soldiers, with power [ ] there is nevertheless [ ] when he says, "I want to move this village," and the village is moved. When he asks for a hundred kids, a hundred kids are brought to him, because ultimately he can make men obey him. But there is another way to obey. It is to make hearts obey, and this we cannot do with external force, with militiamen. You see it yourselves. It is possible to have an administrator who makes everyone obey with militiamen. Everyone fears him, and when we hear that he is going to come into a village, all streets are cleaned and all men are seated in their huts. And when he comes they smile and pay their respects. There is still another administrator [ ] he seldom has militiamen. He does not [ ] a lot, but the whole world knows that he is just; the whole world knows that he is good, and that he has compassion for the poor. When there is a village that cannot pay taxes because there are no bananas, he says, "Well! I decline these taxes." When he has condemned a man, and he sees that the man regrets what he has done, he says, "Well! I want to forgive him!" And when people come to his place, he always has time to listen to them. This administrator governs according to the heart. Which of the two administrators is the greatest? The one who governs by militiamen, by force, or the one who governs by the heart? Speak up! It is the one who governs by the heart, because men love him. Isn't this true? So God, when he sent the Lord Jesus Christ, did not send him as a supreme chief with a lot of power, but he said, "Thou, thou wilt govern according to the heart."

But the people at that time did not understand, and they mocked Jesus. At that time Jesus had not been in the capital city of the Jewish people; he had lived in villages. Every Sunday he preached in the villages. He had gone into plantations to speak with the women who worked there; he had sought to put the truth into their hearts. He had spoken the Word of God to the little children whom he had taken on his knees, he had spoken the Word of God, and these people loved him. Then when the major festival of the city of Jerusalem drew nigh, Jesus said, "Now I am going into this city." And those who loved him said, "Do not go there! In that place there are big chiefs with soldiers, and when they hear that you are the grand chief of hearts, the governor of God on earth, they will kill you!" They said, "What does he want, this poor man?" But Jesus, who knew that God wished him to die for the sins of men, [ ] he was not afraid and told his friends, "Now we will go to the big city where the important chiefs are who will not want to hear the truth that God has sent to govern the hearts of men. They are going to kill me, but this is the will of God, because God wishes me to die for all the sins of men." And so Jesus went to Jerusalem. Jerusalem is the major city of the Jewish people, and because Boulinghi[12] is not Jewish he

12. Someone well known to the Lambaréné community. The second half of this sentence does not flow logically from the first half. Why Schweitzer introduces the name of a man who cannot pronounce *Jerusalem* eludes us. There may be some explanatory text missing here, but we have no way of knowing what is missing.

cannot say this word *Je-ru-sa-lem*. It is a city on a large mountain. Before arriving there, Jesus healed a man who was blind, a poor man who sat beside the road. He shouted, "If thou art the Son of God, thou canst heal me!" And Jesus healed him. And then all the men who were with Jesus said, [ ] because he healed a man who was blind, "This is the true King! He it is who has the Spirit of God, and this [ ] today." And then, when they approached the city, they cut branches of palm trees. They put them on the road. They also took their loincloths and threw them on the road to give honor to Jesus. And Jesus did not walk; because the prophets had announced that the King would come seated on an ass, his friends sought an ass.

You know that we have two sorts of animals to sit on. There is the horse—you have seen horses before. I remember that there was once a horse on the "Faadji" [name of a ship] brought by an officer who rode beside the river. And you have all seen horses in pictures. This is a large beast that runs far more rapidly than a gazelle and that obeys men. Only rich men ride horses. The doctor has no horse in Europe. And then there is another beast that is far smaller: the ass. This is a beast that has large ears. There was one once at the Samkita plantation. Perhaps those who are old remember seeing these asses. Asses do not walk rapidly, but quite slowly, and poor people, when they are old or tired, are seated on an ass.

In order to announce that Jesus was the King of hearts, the prophets declared that he would enter seated upon an ass. And so it is that today, many years have passed since Jesus entered Jerusalem riding on an ass. All the men who were with him sang hymns in order to proclaim, "God has sent us a King! May God be praised!" And then, when the chiefs heard that the people sang, "God has sent us a King!" they were surprised. And the following day, Jesus spoke the truths of God before all the people of Jerusalem, and all the people who heard him said, "How powerful and strong his voice is! Truly he has the Spirit of God. Truly he is the King of hearts!" But the chiefs said, "We do not wish there to be any king other than ourselves. We are going to kill him." Then Jesus preached in Jerusalem Monday, Tuesday, Wednesday, and Thursday. And Thursday evening he was taken prisoner at night. He was killed on the cross Friday morning. All of this happened during this week, and for this reason this week is called Holy Week in Europe. People work, but in the evenings there is church. There they preach the words of Jesus, and we who work among you this week, we live with the thought that this week is holy, and we think of all God's words told in those days, and we think of his death. And on Holy Friday we speak of his death.

I wanted you to know what kind of Sunday this is, and tell you to think during this week of our Lord Jesus, who is the King of hearts, and also of your hearts, because he is the King of all men.

Now let us pray! God, our Father, we thank thee that thou has sent us the Lord Jesus, who bore in his heart thy Spirit, and who died for us, for our sins, in order that thou, thou wilt forgive us. We thank thee for sending [ ] and that we are thy children. Grant that in our hearts we obey [ ] the spirit [ ] more [ ] of men [ ] the spirit of our heart.

20. Sunday, 20 April 1930

Easter Sunday 1930

Last Sunday I told you that all this week would be a big celebration for Christians because it was the week of the death of our Lord Jesus Christ. I have explained who Jesus Christ was. I told you that he was the King of the hearts of men, whom God had sent; and because he was not a king like other kings who hire soldiers, God sent Jesus as a poor man into the world. When he came this way, people said, "He is a poor man. He doesn't wear clothes. He wears a loincloth." But it was a clean loincloth. You needn't imagine that in Jesus' country people were dirty like you—you who wear dirty loin-cloths. In Jesus' country everyone washed their own loincloths and mended them. Thus Jesus always had a clean and well-mended loincloth.

Jesus went from village to village announcing the Word of God; he spoke words far stronger than a man can speak because God had put his Spirit into the heart of Jesus. Jesus was the Son of God, the Son of God by the Spirit. When Jesus had finished announcing the Word of God in the villages, he said, "As the King of hearts, I am going to announce the Word of God in Jerusalem." Jerusalem was the big city of the Jewish people. I told you how Jesus had entered the city. I have also told you what the rulers said, "This is a poor man. He wants to be more than us; he wants to be the

King of hearts." They said this because they knew that it was a greater thing to be the King of hearts rather than to be rulers like them. Then, every day, Jesus preached the Word of God before all the people, and all his words are written down. Later I will tell you his words. During the day no one dared to touch him. But Jesus had twelve disciples about him, men who always walked with him, whom we call apostles. You know already who the chief of the apostles was. It was Saint Peter. Later I will tell you names of all these disciples.

In the evening Jesus went into a small village near a large city to rest. Then the rulers said to one of the apostles, "You can betray him to us when evening comes, and then we can take him and kill him." The apostle who betrayed him was called Judas. All Christians pronounce this name with sadness. The rulers gave a lot of money to this apostle. Then, Jesus left the city in the evening, having had his last supper with his disciples. This last supper, which Christians still celebrate every Sunday, is called Holy Communion. Then, when he went out to a little forest, the disciple who betrayed him came with the soldiers. It was very dark. Judas told the rulers that the one to whom he would say, "Greetings, my dear Lord," was the one they must take. Then the soldiers knew whom to take. They knew that it was Jesus, and they took him and led him before their rulers. All the rulers were seated in a large room, and there they began to have a palaver with him, just as you have palavers in your country, and they decided to kill him. You know that there are many unjust palavers. In these palavers they do not seek the truth, only evil. And so they condemned him to death. They asked him, "Are you truly the King of hearts, the Son of God?" "Yes." And then they said, "You, a poor man in a poor loincloth, you cannot be the Son of God; you cannot be the King of hearts. You are a liar, and we are going to kill you." They said this while it was night. And in the morning they led him to a small mountain, and there they put him on a cross.

Do you know what a cross is? It is formed from a piece of wood, which is like this, and another which is like that. This is why there is a cross on the church of the Catholic Mission. Here at the hospital, where we place those who have died, there is a cross on each tomb. Because Jesus died on a cross, we Christians place the cross everywhere, and that's why we put a cross on tombs of the dead and on churches. You see Catholics wearing a small cross over their hearts. We Protestants do not wear a cross over our hearts. We say it is necessary to have the cross in our hearts and that we must always think of the cross where Jesus died.

This was a terrible death. They fastened Jesus to the cross with nails in his hands and feet, and with terrible sufferings he slowly died. The rulers and the soldiers and the people were standing below the cross, and they laughed. They said, "If you are the Son of God, you can come down from this cross." But Jesus did not say a word, because Jesus knew that his death was in accord with the will of God. He knew that these men could place him on the cross only because it was the will of God that he die for sins of other men.

There had already been men of God, prophets, who announced that a man would die for the sins of others according to the will of God. We know that we all have many sins. If God held a palaver for our sins we would all be lost. We would all be dead, according to justice. He would be obliged to put us in prison. A man fears death. However, God has decided to forgive men, but only if his Son wishes to die for others.

Do you know what it is to die for others? Say there is a canoe, and there is a man in the canoe who does not know how to swim, and in the canoe there is someone else who does. Then it overturns, and the swimmer throws himself into the water and searches underneath the canoe, and then he pulls the drowning man into the canoe, but he himself doesn't have the strength to hold on, and he slips and goes down. Thus he has died for another. (In Europe we are acquainted with another story in which a man was condemned to death and someone else came and said, "I am his friend. Allow me to die for him!")[13]

So Jesus received God's permission to die for men so that God would forgive them their sins. And Jesus died for men, for Christians and pagans. In their villages the pagans know nothing of this, but it is true nevertheless because it is written down in the Word of God, in a large book. It is extraordinary that there is a Jesus, the Son of God, who died for men so that God forgives them their sins when they are dead. No one can explain this, because it is a thought of God.

You see this goat that is going by? Does the goat understand what is going on in your head? No! Because it is a goat, and you, you are men. Because you are men you have other, far higher thoughts than a goat. Isn't

13. Reference unclear.

that true? As with men, so with God. We cannot understand all the thoughts of God. Jesus died on the cross knowing that he was dying for all the sins of men. It was morning when he died, but the whole sky became just as dark as if it were night. The rulers were afraid when they saw this strange thing, and those who were in charge of the soldiers said, "Oh, this Jesus was truly the King of hearts!" While Jesus still lived, he said, "But I will come back again." We all think that when we are dead, we do not remain dead, but that there is something in us that cannot die. Jesus had told his disciples, "When I am dead, you will see me again." On Sunday the disciples went to his tomb and saw that the tomb was empty. At the same time they saw Jesus. Because they were very frightened, they did not tell their story very well, but they were certain they had seen Jesus. They were certain that he still lived and that he was the King of hearts. When we are dead, God gives us a new life. This also is very difficult to understand, but it is certain. And because the disciples saw Jesus alive on Sunday morning, we celebrate the festival of Easter.

As God has given a new life to Jesus, he will also give us a new life when we are dead. Nobody knows how, but we know that God gives us a new life, and so we believe it, and it is for this reason that we celebrate Easter, and that you are celebrating this Feast with us. Amen.

Let us pray! O God, the Father of all men, we thank thee for sending our Lord Jesus Christ, Jesus, our Master! We thank thee that thou didst die on the cross for us all, die for our sins. May we never forget what thou hast done for us. Be the King of our hearts, so that we may truly be with thee as sons of God.

21. Sunday, 4 May 1930

The Apostles

Last time I spoke to you of our Lord Jesus, of when the rulers of the Jewish people killed him on a Friday, because he had said that he was the King of hearts whom God had sent to the earth; Jesus told men that if he was dead he would return alive. And the Sunday after his death, the men who had been with him, the apostles, saw him. They did not see him again as a man is when he is alive naturally, but they saw him as a man is when God has given him eternal life. And so we all know that God, after our death, is going to give us eternal life: eternal life where there is no longer evil, eternal life where one needs no longer to eat and to drink, eternal life where our heart no longer has wicked thoughts, but eternal life where we are truly children of God.

Now, what happened after the death of Jesus? I told you that Jesus chose twelve men, and he said, "These are my students, and these men are called apostles." And these apostles, they were twelve; therefore we say, "there are twelve apostles." And you know that one of these apostles, called Judas, betrayed the Master. It is he who told to the rulers of the Jewish people where they could find him to capture him. And you know that this Judas who betrayed the Master hanged himself, killed himself. Then there were only eleven apostles.

Now, what did the first Christians do after the death of Jesus? They were frightened. They said to themselves, "The rulers have killed the Lord Jesus, and we who were his men, they are going to kill us also." And so they remained hidden in the big city of Jerusalem in order not to be killed. And after some weeks, after fifty days, suddenly the Spirit of God came into their hearts, and they made speeches that Jesus was truly the King of hearts. All this is written in a book of the Bible called "What the Apostles Did." And the day on which the disciples, the apostles, began to preach the Word of God, is called Pentecost. You know this holiday, and you know that there is also a second holiday, the Monday of Pentecost, when Christians do not ordinarily work. I will tell you all about this holiday another time, but today I am still going to tell you about the apostles.

You know the names of some apostles. The apostles are called saints, because they led the kind of life that God required. The best-known apostle is Saint Peter. All of you have already heard this name, which is known to Protestants, Catholics, and even Pagans. It is Jesus who gave a name to this apostle. He said, "You are like a rock, so strong, and so you are [ ]." Then there is another apostle, Saint John. You also all know Saint John, don't you? And you know that this apostle, Saint John, also has a holiday. It will be soon. It comes at the beginning of the dry season. I will name the other apostles. There was an apostle named Philip; there was an apostle named Andrew; there was an apostle named James. These are the best-known apostles. In addition there was a great apostle named Paul—Saint Paul. You have all heard this name. True? Even the pagans [ ]. This apostle was formerly an enemy of Jesus, but when he was converted he became an apostle of Jesus. I will tell you about this another time. And this apostle, Saint Paul, traveled all the time; he went throughout the entire known world. He traveled by land and by sea, and he worked to earn his bread. When Christians told him, "You are our father. We want to work for you," he replied, "No! I wish to earn my bread myself." And when he was in a village and preached, he appointed Christian rulers. This is called the beginning of the Christian church—the beginning, that is to say, when something begins.

The Church is all the Christians in the world together. Isn't this what today is called the Christian Church? It is the Christians of Paris, of Lambaréné, the Christians of the village of Mrs. Russell, the Christians of the village of Miss Marie—all Christians together.[14] Formerly there were Christians only in Jerusalem. And then the apostle Paul began to educate Christians in all the large cities of the world. He made long trips, and when he came into a city, he stood in the town square and said, "I want to speak." He stood in the market place where people conducted their businesses— where they sold pistachios and loincloths and everything else—and he began to speak. There were men who stopped and said, "Here is one who wants to speak!" And then he said, "I tell you great news that you do not know. I announce to you the King of the hearts of men! I announce to you that after our death God gives us eternal life." Then, very often, people became angry with him. They said, "What is this man telling us, this man who is dressed like a pauper? He wants to proclaim a new religion to us. Who is this Sir Jesus? No one knows him, and it is he who is to be our king, the King of our hearts!" And then, often, they were angered.

Often, poor apostle Paul was put in prison. Often wicked people beat him. Often they threw stones at him so that he lay as if dead. But he endured all that. And he preached the Word of Jesus throughout the entire known world. And when he left a city, in order to repeat the words, which

14. Mrs. Russell is Mrs. C. E. B. (Lillian) Russell, known at the hospital as "Mrs. Canada." See explanatory footnote 1 to to the Textual Notes in the front matter. Miss Marie is Marie Secrétan, a laboratory technician who transcribed the sermons from 1930–31. She later became Mrs. Gustav Woytt, wife of Schweitzer's nephew.

he had said, he wrote letters, and we still have these letters. It has been a long time since these letters were written, but Christians have preserved them, and so we have these letters in the Bible, and I will speak to you about these letters. I will read you the words of these letters.

And now the end of the apostles! They all died captives. The apostle Peter went into the city of Rome to preach the gospel. You know that the city of Rome was then the largest city of the whole world, and the emperor who ruled the whole world was there. He was called the emperor of the Romans. He did not want to hear anything about a King of hearts, and so he made a captive of Saint Peter when he was at Rome. Then the apostle Paul was made captive in Jerusalem, and from Jerusalem he was put in a boat and transported to Rome, and he arrived at the same time that the apostle Peter was already captive. And one day at Rome there was a huge fire. You know how it is when a village burns, but when a great city burns it is far greater. And then a large part of this city was burned during the dry season, and the people were very miserable. Wicked people said, "It is the Christians who have set fire to the city." Then all the Christians were made captive. They were killed. They were slaughtered with the machete. Their heads were cut off. Others were sent to be devoured by leopards. And one day, when the emperor gave a great feast, he killed the two apostles Peter and Paul. Probably they were burned. The resin was placed on the body as for a torch, and then they were lit. It is probably like this that they died. And this is the beginning of the Christian Church. And you see how much men have suffered in order for the Word of God to remain in this world, and for this reason we all must recognize the apostles who died for the Word of God, because, if they had not been courageous, the truth of God would have been extinguished from the world, like a fire that is smothered. Amen.

Let us pray! O God, we thank thee that thou hast sent the Lord Jesus into the world. God, we thank thee that thou hast sent apostles to preach the Word of God. We thank thee for having given them the power to suffer for the truth, and we pray thee that this truth is in our hearts and remains in our hearts, and that we know that it is the most precious thing in this world. Amen.

22. Sunday, 18 May 1930

The Apostle Paul

First of two sermons on St. Paul

[ ] that Jesus was dead [ ] that there were [ ] apostles who continued to preach about the Kingdom of God, and I told you that there were twelve apostles, and among these apostles I have told you the most famous names. I named Saint Peter. I named Saint John. All those who are called John are called with the same name as the apostle John. John Mendoum is called John because the apostle John is the one for whom he was named, and he must be as wise as the apostle John because he has the same name, and each time that he acts headstrong he must remind himself that he carries the name of the apostle John.[15] Then there is yet another important apostle who is called Paul—Saint Paul—and there are many people who are called Paul. The doctor's brother is called Paul. And I am going to tell you about the life of Saint Paul, too. It is told in the book of the apostles of God. When Jesus was dead, there were 120 men who said, "Jesus is the King of hearts." And the rulers of the Jews said that it was necessary to kill those men who said that Jesus was the King of the world. There were many Jews who said that it was necessary to kill these men. And among these men was one called Saul.

Saul was a very learned man. And he was the one who was the enemy of these 120 men who believed in Jesus. Among these men there was one who was called Stephen, and this Stephen was a very good and learned Christian. And then enemies of the Christians said, "This one must be killed first." They made him a prisoner and dragged him before the rulers, and told lies against him. They told the lie that he said that it was necessary to destroy the large church that was in Jerusalem. The Jews—the Jewish people—had large churches like the Christians, large churches in stone like the church of the Catholic Mission, but far larger, much larger. This church was very tall, and everyone was very proud. Liars then said that

15. From the context, we would guess the John Mendoum was present in the congregation or at least known to those who were. Schweitzer has not told us anything else about him.

Stephen had said that it was necessary to destroy this church, and all the people who were at this palaver believed this. They said, "He must be killed!" They took him outside the city and everyone threw a stone until he was dead. This was the first Christian who died for the Lord Jesus; such Christians who died for the Lord Jesus are called martyrs. And the one who stood before all the men in order to throw stones was called Saul. And then, when this man was killed, he said to the rulers, "Now, give me a document so that I may go into every city and seek out those who say that Jesus is the King of hearts, and kill them." And the rulers said, "This is good," and they gave him this document to tell the cities, "Help him to seek them out. He must have the right to kill them." Then Saul took the men and the soldiers and went throughout this country into all the villages and asked everywhere, "Are there any Christians?" He went into the huts and asked, "Are there any Christians?" And everyone was afraid of him. Then, finally, he went into the large city, which was called Damascus. This city of Damascus was far larger than Libreville and Brazzaville.

Libreville and Brazzaville are small villages compared to Damascus. There were a lot of houses, all in stone, and beautiful churches, and very rich people. There was a large wall in stone all around the city. To enter the city one passed through the doors that were in this wall in order to keep thieves out. And at night these doors were closed. They were doors of iron. And behind the doors there were soldiers and militiamen to guard the city. And it was to this large and rich city that Saul walked with his soldiers to seek out the Christians. Having searched the city, Saul then said, "We are going to find the Christians, and we are going to kill them," because he believed that God did not like the Christians. This was because Saul was a very pious man, as pious as the Jewish people. And then suddenly those who walked with Saul saw him fall down. They listened, and then a voice was heard from heaven above, saying, "Saul, Saul! Why do you persecute me?" All the men were frightened, and then Saul asked, "Who is it that speaks?" Then the voice replied, "I am Jesus Christ." When Saul got up he was blind; he no longer saw anything. And the men who accompanied him were obliged to lead him, and he walked as a blind man, and they came into the city. Then Saul asked, "Where are the Christians here?" But he did not ask to kill them; instead he asked to hear the Word of God and Jesus Christ. "There is an old man who is a Christian," he was told, and then this old catechist taught Saul the Word of God, and after that he baptized him.

You know that all Christians are baptized, and that one puts a little water on the head so as to wash away all sins, and to give them a pure heart. And thus Saul was baptized.

And now, listen! When this Saul was baptized, he was no longer called Saul but Paul, and he became the apostle Saint Paul. And this is the way that Saint Paul started out: by seeking and killing Christians. And this also happened in your pagan land. When the first missionaries arrived in your community with the Word of God, there were chiefs who said, "It is necessary to kill all Christians!" And you know also that here in Gabon the first Christians were often killed by the chiefs. This was the time when there were no Europeans other than missionaries, and as it was in your country, so it was throughout the whole world. And thus there were many people who died for the Lord Jesus, and blacks also who became martyrs just like the whites. Then sometimes the wickedest chiefs who opposed the Christians became Christians themselves; and they ceased to be chiefs and became humble catechists. And there were quite a few who died for the Lord Jesus like the apostle Saint Paul.

Now the apostle Saint Paul was in this city, and everyone learned that the most important leader who came from Jerusalem to kill Christians is now himself a Christian. And then the chiefs of this city said, "It is impossible! Now it is necessary to kill Paul!" Then Paul was obliged to hide. He went to the Christian community to hide himself in their huts. Then the militiamen arrived and said, "Is Paul here?" But he had already been put into another hut. Then someone asked the Christians to tell Paul, "You can no longer remain; if you remain, the militiamen [ ]. You must leave the city!" But it was difficult to exit the city.

I have told you that there was a large wall of stone around the city. There were only a few doors, and there they put militiamen and people who knew Saint Paul, and they said to them, "If he wants to leave, he must be captured and killed." Then everyone was very sad. Nevertheless, Paul exited the city! How? The women made a large basket, and the men made a good rope with vines, and then at night they went with the basket onto the wall, probably during a night when it rained hard, like thieves in your community come at night when there is a lot rain. And then they put Paul into the basket. They also put in it something for him to eat and some water, and then they let Saint Paul descend the wall in the basket, and this is the way he was saved from that city. And everything that he did after that,

I will tell you next Sunday. But today you know about the one who is called Saint Paul, and that he was called Saul when he was not yet a Christian, and it was he who had been killing the Christians.

Let us pray! God our Father, we thank thee for having empowered the apostles to preach thy Word. We thank thee for having given courage to the first Christians to die for the Word of God. We pray thee to make us thankful for all thy goodness to us, so that we can be Christians without having to die or to suffer, and we pray that we can be thankful for the power to live according to thy Word and to be Christians. Amen.

23. Sunday, 1 June 1930

The Apostle Paul

Second of two sermons on St. Paul

Do you recall the man whose story I told you last time and what his name was? Say the name! "The apostle Paul, Saint Paul." I told you how he wanted to kill all Christians, and how he heard the voice of Jesus from heaven, and how he became a Christian. [ ] and that they said, "No! We do not want to look at you, because it is you who have killed the Christians," and they were afraid of him. He went into his own country, which was far from Jerusalem, and there he found some Christians. From that time on he began to proclaim the Word of God throughout the entire world.

First, he walked by foot for many, many years, going from one village to another. Then, after he earned some money by making mats, he went by boat to some other cities. So he traveled for years and years. Sometimes people were good to him. They said, "This man tells the truth!" They said to him, "Come into our hut! Eat with us!" At other times they were wicked toward him. Then they said, "What does he want, this pauper who doesn't even have a decent loincoth? He wants to preach us the truth!" So they took stones and threw them at him, and, in this way, several times, they almost killed him.

Finally they brought him to the house of the chief of the city. They said, "This fellow who is going around here is a foreigner. We don't want to listen to him. He is a wicked man. He must be punished!" Then they bound him and beat him. Also, they often put him in prison. He often went hungry in the forest and in the desert. He had nothing to eat. Several times the boat in which he traveled sank, and he was obliged to swim. So he led this kind of life for years and years.

Then he learned that there was a famine among the Jewish people at Jerusalem, and that Christian poor people had nothing to eat. So he said to all the other Christians in the world, "Give me some money for the Christian poor in Jerusalem." At that time there was no money like we have here, which we can put into a pocket, but only money made of metal, as was once used around here. He had some small cases [for the money] and some men who carried these cases. Thus he arrived in Jerusalem. This is as far as I told you. Today I am going to tell you the conclusion.

When he had arrived, the Christian poor were overjoyed, but the other Jews, those who were not Christian, those who had remained Jewish, were very bad toward him, and they said, "We want to kill this man!" Saint Paul knew this because already, during his trip, some men had told him, "Do not go up there! There are men who want to kill you." Saint Paul said, "I am going up, nevertheless, because God is in heaven, and if he wants me to be killed, I will be killed, and if he does not want me to be killed, I will not be killed. Men will not kill me, only God."

At Jerusalem they were in the great church of the Jews, because Christians also went into the great church of the Jewish people in order to worship God. When he was there the Jews saw him. They called for some wicked young people, some palaverers, and they said to them, "Here he is—Saint Paul! Seize him! Drag him outside! We are going to kill him with stones." They seized him, and everyone shouted. It was festival time and everyone was there. Then the captain, who was there with some soldiers, heard a lot noise. He came up and asked, "What's going on here?" The Jews said, "We want to kill this man!" Then the captain said, "No! No one is killed here without having been brought before the commander." Then he said to the soldiers, "Take Saint Paul! Guard him!" And they brought him into the big hut that was there on the mountain. There were walls all around it and all the soldiers, too. And there was Saint Paul.

Those who spoke against him came in the morning. Then the captain said, "Well! Conduct the palaver! If this man has done something wicked he will be beaten, he will be imprisoned, and he will be killed; but if he has done nothing, I will do nothing to him." You see, he was a good captain. Then the chiefs of the Jewish people began to speak. The captain said, "This man has not done anything wrong!" The captain was not a Jew; he was a pagan, but a pagan who had a good heart. The following day the son of the brother of Saint Paul came to the captain's house and said to him, "This man is my uncle. I want to speak to you about him because there are thirty chiefs of the Jewish people who say that they will neither eat nor drink until they have killed Saint Paul. They have a small knife hidden in a loincoth. They will ask to take him to the palaver. Then, when they have led him through the streets to the chief's hut, they will kill him." The captain said, "You have spoken well about this matter." He told the soldiers, "Now take Saint Paul, and go with him to the home of the chief commander."

The chief commander resided in a city that was next to the sea. You know that at that time all Europe was under the rule of a major chief who was called the emperor of the Romans. This emperor, with his administrators, ruled all the cities. These emperors were chiefs as have never been seen since. Everyone belonged to them. Then, when Saint Paul came before the administrator, the latter listened to the palaver and he said, "He has done nothing wrong. I am going to free him." Then the major Jewish chiefs at Jerusalem [ ]. It was already done as the [] today. He was kept captive. Then, when there was a new administrator, he said, "Here is a prisoner. You can do with him as you wish." Then he asked Saint Paul, "What did you do?" He called the chiefs of the Jewish people to hold a palaver again, and when he had listened to them he said, "No, I cannot kill this man. I am going to send him to the emperor, to the place of the great chief at Rome." Then he gave him to a lieutenant who was going to Rome with some militiamen, and he wrote a long letter in which he told everything to the great chief in Rome. Then the lieutenant and militiamen took Saint Paul and went on a large boat with him.

It was the beginning of rainy season and the boat was not able to go forward because there were tornadoes all the time. They were at sea for weeks and weeks. The wind blew at them all the time, and everyone was afraid. There were more than a hundred men on the boat: militiamen, prisoners, administrators, and merchants. Then Saint Paul got up and told them, "I have listened to the Word of God in my heart this night, and it has told me that none of the men on this boat will die." They recognized that this was a man of God, and they were very happy. Everyone's appetite began to improve. They had not eaten for several days because of their fear. Then, in the morning, someone saw land far off. They tried to reach this land, which was an island, with the boat, but before they reached land, the boat hit a rock.

Those who have seen the sea know that before land is reached, there are rocks. When a boat strikes the rocks, it is broken up by the waves that beat upon it. So the boat was destroyed. However, the land was not far off and the men who knew how to swim came to the land. The others caught boards and came with their boards to the land, and none was drowned. Then the people of this island received them and made a big fire to dry them out. Everyone looked for wood to put onto the fire. Saint Paul also looked for wood, and while he was searching in a heap of small branches for some wood, a snake bit him, and the snake attached itself to his hand. Then all the people shouted and said, "He is going to die! God wants this man here to die. He is a wicked man."

Saint Paul was very calm. He was not like you when you see a snake. He did not shout. He did not protect himself, but he took the snake with his other hand and threw it into the fire. When he did not die everyone said, "He is not dead! He is a man of God!" They stayed in this city throughout the entire rainy season.

In the dry season a boat was passing by that was going to the big city of Rome. They took this boat and went to Rome. Saint Paul was put in prison for two years; then he was condemned. He was condemned at the same time as Saint Peter, who was also in Rome, and the two were burned: burned alive! Some torches were prepared with resin and these torches were tied under them and lit. So they died.

All Christians know the name of Saint Paul. This is the reason why I told you about his life, so that you might know how the first Christians suffered to keep the Word of God.

Let us pray! Gracious God, Father of all men, we thank thee that thou hast sent thy Word to us. We thank thee for giving courage to Saint Paul and to many others who were not afraid of being struck down or killed. It is through them that we have this Word. May this Word be truly in our hearts, that it may also enter into the hearts of pagans, and that we may all truly become thy children: to have a good heart and to do that which is good and thy will. Amen.

24. Sunday, 8 June 1930

Pentecost

Acts 2

You know that today is a great feast in the Christian world, and all of you, even the pagans, know the name of this feast. This feast is called Pentecost. You know what Pentecost means. Pentecost means five times ten—fifty. It means that this feast takes place fifty days after Easter. It has been fifty days since we celebrated Easter, and if you take a calendar and count fifty days you will see that this is true. But what does the feast of Pentecost mean? It means the feast of the Spirit of God. I am going to tell you the story [about Pentecost].

For as long as he had been dwelling among men, Jesus had said, "A day will come when you will feel the Spirit of God within you." And even before Jesus, the prophets had announced, "A day will come when the Spirit of God will be with men." Everyone knew these words, which were written in the book of the words of God. Then, when Jesus was dead, the apostles and the other Christians waited for the Spirit of God. They were well aware that they still did not have the Spirit of God, for they were afraid of men. They sat inside huts and hid themselves instead of speaking out and telling everyone that Jesus is the King of hearts. So they remained silent and hid themselves. In this way, fifty days passed by. Then the fiftieth day came. It was a Sunday. Once again they assembled together in a large hut and prayed to God. Then a curious thing happened. Suddenly they felt compelled to speak about Jesus, so they went to the window of the hut and shouted into the street. It was very early in the morning. The people stopped and said, "What's going on inside this hut?" There were some who said, "Oh, probably these are people who have already drunk palm tree wine this morning!" Everyone stopped.

Then the apostle Peter got up. He began to speak and said to them, "You believe that we are full of palm tree wine because we are speaking loudly and we are laughing and happy. This is not true. Something happened to us that we have been waiting for for a long time. What happened is what was written in the Word of God so long ago. What happened is that the Spirit of God has come into our hearts." In this Spirit they began to speak to everyone about Jesus as the King of hearts. The chief people who had killed Jesus were there. There were the militiamen, captains, and lieutenants who had stopped Jesus, and all these men could say, "Oh, these are some Christians! Since they have opened their mouths, we can seize and kill them." Saint Peter and the other Christians should have been afraid, but they had no fear. They could not be afraid because they had the Spirit of God within their hearts.

Then Saint Peter told about Jesus in the Word of God, and they listened. Those who had laughed at first, saying, "They have drunk palm tree wine," now became silent. When Saint Peter finished telling them about Jesus he said, "I am going to tell you something. This Lord Jesus has come for all of you, in order that all of you might become Christians. Come then! Be baptized! Hear the Word of God!" Then there were many persons who came forward and let themselves be baptized. It is written in the Word of God that there were three thousand, three times a thousand persons, who came and said, "We want to be baptized!" Up to this time there had been only one hundred and twenty Christians. This is why we still celebrate this feast in a world in which there are still so many who are not Christian. This feast means: "Come! The Lord has come for you. Be baptized!" This feast means, "Come, and discern the Spirit of God, which is coming into your hearts!"

Now I hear someone who is saying, "Is it true that all Christians have the Spirit of God?" You may be saying this. "We know some whites who say that they are Christians and who have been baptized, but they have exactly the same spirit as other men do." This is sad but true. You also say, "Here are some blacks who have let themselves be baptized, but you do not see that they have another spirit in their hearts." This is also true. I have already explained this to you.

There is the spirit of man and the Spirit of God, and between the spirit of man and the Spirit of God there is the same difference that there is between trees. There are trees of the forest, the bush, and the jungle where savage beasts live. The trees of the bush do not bear fruit that can be eaten. A man who is in the forest can die because there is no fruit to eat, and you know how many men have already died like this in the forest. Then there are trees that can bear fruit: the oil palm, the lemon, the avocado, the banana, the orange, and the tangerine, all of which you may now eat from.

Well! In the past, these fruits did not exist here. There was only the forest. Men who came over the sea to bring the Spirit of God here also brought these precious trees. The other trees grew by themselves. Did the fruit-bearing trees grow all by themselves? No! The jungle consumed the good trees.

A few years ago I planted some small breadfruit trees there, high up near the forest. I am still able to find one or two of them. What happened to the others? The bush ate them, because the space around the trees had not been cleared enough.

Look here! We have planted good trees so that the sick can eat the oranges and tangerines from those trees. But what will become these trees if we leave and do not continue to clear away the bush? So it is with the Spirit of God—exactly the same thing.

In the words of Jesus, there is the Spirit of God, and each of these words is like a tree of the Spirit of God that is planted in the heart. But it is not enough to plant these trees; it is also necessary to maintain the plantation. It is necessary to struggle against the bad thoughts of the heart and to pull them out like weeds. Without doing this, the trees of the Spirit of God cannot grow. When you see Christian whites or blacks who are not better than other people, these are Christians who have not cleansed their hearts. All of you have already heard the words of Jesus, because the words of Jesus are now in your community, like the nuts of the palm tree that the birds take and drop in the forest.

Does this palm tree, which grows up in the forest, bear fruit? No! It remains a poor palm tree, a palm tree covered with vines. You see a lot of these palm trees behind there, but when Mrs. Canada comes with men carrying axes and machetes and makes a clearing, then what becomes of these palm trees? Suddenly they sprout up beautifully, and we see them flower and bear fruit. So the people at the hospital have palm nuts to eat. Thus it is with you.

In the bush of your pagan hearts there are some tiny palm trees of the Spirit of God. What matters is that you have the courage to cleanse your heart. For those who have the courage to cleanse their hearts, there is no longer any need to explain about the Spirit of God, because the Spirit of God grows in them like tiny palm trees, and they will bear the fruit of the Spirit of God.

So this feast of Pentecost means two things. In the first place it means this: "Men, rejoice that God has sent his Spirit into the hearts of men!" The second thing it means is: "Men, cleanse your hearts so that the tree of the Spirit of God can grow in your hearts!" It is with this thought that today everyone must celebrate the feast of Pentecost. Amen.

Let us pray! O God, our Father, we thank thee that thou has sent thy Spirit to men. We thank thee that thou hast sent thy Spirit into the hearts of the apostles Peter and Paul to preach the Word of Jesus. And we pray thee, by thy power, send thy Spirit always into the hearts of men, because when thy Spirit is absent from the heart, all men are miserable. Send also thy Spirit into the spirit of the men of this country: into the hearts of both whites and blacks. Send it into our hearts and give us the power to cleanse our hearts, so that thy Spirit may grow like beautiful palm trees. Amen.

25. Sunday, 15 June 1930

The Spirit of God

Second sermon on Pentecost

We have celebrated a great Christian festival this past Sunday: the Feast of Pentecost. I told you that Pentecost means fifty—five times ten—and that the Feast of Pentecost is the feast of the Spirit of God. On that day, last Sunday, the Spirit came into the hearts of the first Christians and apostles. Today we want to speak about the Spirit of God once more.

What is a spirit? I know that the pagans believe that there are spirits. They believe that there are spirits of the dead, and it is because of this that they do not dare walk over there, where people are buried. They are afraid of the spirits within the forest. Isn't that so? Well then! And the Christians come and say that according to the Word of God, these spirits do not exist; there are no spirits in the forest that stroll about like birds, and men do not have to be afraid of spirits—they have only to fear the bad spirit that is in their hearts. What is the spirit of man and the Spirit of God? The spirit is something that cannot be caught and held or touched like a piece of wood. In each human being there is a spirit. God has put this spirit into everyone, and it is through the spirit that a man can become a child of God—because the spirit is the thought[s] of men.

During the dry season, have you ever seen something white on the water that looked like a little cloud? Well then! This is also water, but it is water that cannot be grasped by the hand. These clouds are made of water, like the clouds we see above us. We know that the rain comes from these clouds, but it is the sort of water that cannot be held in the hand. It is the water in the air. So there is something within man that man cannot touch, that man cannot see. It is the spirit of the man. Is this clear? Now God has given the spirit to men in order that they can understand the Spirit of God. The apostle Paul once said in a letter that no one knows what is in God; only the Spirit of God knows it. This is profoundly true.

I am looking at this man here. I do not see the thoughts that are in his heart. I see that he opens his mouth, that he puts a hand to his head, and that he laughs, but I do not know what he thinks. He himself knows what he thinks. How does he know that he thinks? By his spirit. Isn't this true? Now, pay attention! So the Spirit of God is real. Many men say, "Where is the Spirit of God? I do not see the Spirit of God. I do not hear the Spirit of God. I see the trees, I see the clouds of the sky, I hear birds, I hear the child that shouts, but I do not see the Spirit and I do not hear the Spirit of God." These men seem to be very intelligent, but nevertheless they speak foolishly. It is as if they mean that there is no spirit in this man because they do not see the spirit. Nevertheless, each of us knows that in every man there is the spirit. Isn't this true?

Well then! Why doesn't this man see the Spirit of God in him? Because he does not have the spirit to understand the Spirit of God. It is curious that I know the thoughts of this man when he speaks to me. What does this mean, "to speak"? It means to move the mouth and make sounds with the tongue by which I understand the thoughts of his heart. It is a very curious thing that we understand words of a man by the sounds that he makes with his mouth and tongue. Have you ever thought about that? There are some very curious things around us that we see every day.

When a piece of grass sprouts up, this is a very curious thing that we cannot explain. Isn't this true? Is there anything more curious than seeing how a piece of grass sprouts up? Then there are also flowers and grains. Only God can explain it. Even the most learned of men [cannot explain it]—even those who have read all the books. And so no man can explain how, by the sounds that a man can make with his mouth and by his words, a man is able to explain the spirit and the thoughts in his heart. There is also another curious thing. The Spirit of God speaks to the spirit that is in the hearts of men, and the Spirit of God does not need to speak out loud with words like men do. God speaks so that no one can hear. Only the heart understands.

A man wishes to steal. It is at the moment when he wants to steal that he hears in his heart, "Thou shalt not steal!" He wants to close the ears of his heart so that he will not always hear in his heart the words, "No! Thou shalt not steal!" Well then! Where does this thought in his heart come from, the one that he does not want to think of? It is the Spirit of God that speaks in his heart. It is this way that come all good thoughts, which are within the hearts of men. It is the Spirit of God that has put them within the heart.

All the light that illuminates and heats the world comes from the sun. Isn't this so? Perhaps there are some people who will say, "No, there is still the light that comes from the moon." But learned men in Europe will tell them that this light of the moon also comes from the sun, that all the light that plants need to grow comes from the sun. In this way, all good thoughts come from the Spirit of God, who has spoken within the spirit of men. Since Jesus Christ has come into the world and has [ ], this light is far stronger in our hearts. There is no one who has not heard the Spirit of God in his heart. I am sure that even the most wicked man among us has at one time heard the Word of God in his heart, only he has closed his ears because it is more convenient to proceed according to our bad thoughts than to live according to the good thoughts of God.

Well then! I tell you today, do not close your ears, do not close the ears of your hearts! Do not believe that men who do everything that they want to are happy. Only those men who have the spirit of God in their hearts are happy. Why? Because to be happy means that the heart is at peace. Wicked men do not have a quiet heart. Have you every seen a wicked man who had a tranquil heart? Have you ever seen one of them? No! Isn't this true? When a wicked man wants to be tranquil, his heart suddenly speaks. It speaks to him about all those wicked things that he wanted to forget. He tells it, "I do not want to think about all these things that I have done." Nevertheless, his heart speaks all that to him. His heart is like the Ogooué during the rainy season, when there is a tornado; but the man with the Spirit of God in his heart is like a tranquil river. [ ] the sun. In like manner, to be truly happy, it is necessary to have a peaceful heart.

Do not close off the Word of God that you hear in your heart. Know that the Spirit of God wants to speak to your heart, not only to the hearts of Christians, but also to the hearts of all men—to poor pagan people—to do them good and to gladden them. When the moment to die comes, those who have opened their hearts to the Spirit of God will be tranquil. They know that when they die they will come before God and he will say to them, "I know you. You have heard the words of my Spirit in your heart. You are my child. Come into the beautiful house that I have made for my children. You were sad in the world. You have suffered pain. You will no longer have pain. You are my child. You will be happy, like a child who is with his father."

As long as we are in the world, we are like children who are far from their father, but when we die, we will be like children who are near to our Father. What I tell you is true. Amen.

26. Sunday, 22 June 1930

[Interrupted Sermon]

[In French] Today you have heard the bell of the Catholic mission ringing for a long time . . .

[In German] The [female] doctors had excused those assisting at the Sunday service without permission, and so the translation did not take place like the others.[16]

---

16. The initial sentence fragment in French is all that was preserved of this sermon by Schweitzer. After it breaks off, it is followed by a comment, written in German, apparently by the transcriber. It would seem that the two native translators were given permission to leave. There may have been something unusual happening at the Catholic mission because the bells were ringing longer than customary.

27. Sunday, 29 June 1930

St. John the Baptist

Matthew 3

Last Sunday there was a great holiday for Christians. It was the Feast of Saint John. You all heard about it. Now today I am going to tell you the story of Saint John. Saint John was a man who lived among the Jewish people. Then, when he was old, he heard the voice of God in his heart, which said, "You are going to announce the Word of God to your people." "What must I announce?" he said to God. God told him, "Proclaim that the Kingdom of God is at hand and that the King of hearts is about to come into the world." Then Saint John said, "I will obey."

In the Scriptures, in the great book of God, it is said that when the King of hearts is about to arrive, another will come and announce to the Jewish people that the King of hearts is coming. Then Saint John did not go to a great city to preach the Word of God, but instead went to a place where there was no village, where there was only sand beside a large lake, and there he stayed. He began to preach the news.

He was completely dressed like a poor man. In this place he had nothing to eat. Just like you, he ate the honey that he took from trees. When he was hungry, he even ate grasshoppers, those tiny creatures. At first there were only a few men who passed by and listened to what he said. Soon it was learned in the cities there that there was a man near a lake in a very remote place who was announcing some news, and all the people—there were more men [ ]. At last, for hours and hours, crowds of people came by foot from Jerusalem to hear this man. And what did he preach? First of all, he told them: "Confess that you have committed a great deal of wickedness! You see in your hearts that there are wicked thoughts." To recognize how wicked our hearts are is the beginning of everything. After this he said to them, "Now that you know that your heart is wicked, you know that God is going to judge you, because God does not want men to have wicked thoughts in their hearts."

Then the people were afraid, and they said to him, "Tell us what we have to do so that God will be good to us." He said to them, "Begin by repenting your wickedness and pray to God that he will be good to you." Then he said to them, "Come, I am going to baptize you!" He explained to them that to be baptized means that God is good and that he forgives us our sins. Saint John is the one who baptizes. This Saint John is John the Baptist. There is another Saint John, Saint John the Apostle, who was a disciple of Jesus.

When Saint John baptized those people who came, suddenly he saw a young man, and this man was Jesus, and Jesus had also come to be baptized. A short while after Jesus had been baptized by Saint John, Saint John was taken captive. Why was he taken captive? The king of the Jewish people had taken the wife of his brother, and Saint John had told all the people, "What the king is doing is not good." Then the king was angry, and his wife too, and they said, "What? This beggar, this man who has nothing, dares to speak against the king?" They said to the militiamen, "Seize him and take him prisoner!" Then he was shut up in prison, but his disciples came and brought him something to eat.

When Saint John was taken captive, Jesus began to preach. You know that Jesus, when he preached the Word of God, also healed the sick. Then the disciples of Saint John came and said [ ] Jesus, who preaches the Word of God and heals the sick, who are completely sick [ ]. Then Saint John said to his disciples—*Don't leave! The man who sells carps can wait!*[17]

Saint John told his disciples, "Go to the place where Jesus is and ask him if he is the King of hearts whom God said he would send." They came to Jesus, and when they had come to the place where he was, there were many people around him. In the presence of all these people, they said, "Saint John, who is a prisoner, asks if you are the King who must come to this people?" Then Jesus told them, "Go and tell Saint John that I am proclaiming the Word of God, the good news, and that I am healing the sick."

When John's disciples had gone, Jesus spoke to the people, telling them, "Of all men, John is the greatest. He is greater than all of the prophets who have proclaimed the Word of God up to this time, for it is God who told him, in his heart, that the Kingdom of God has come, and that the King of hearts has come." Then the people were utterly surprised.

---

17. We are fortunate that many of these sermons were written down exactly as they were preached. Here is an unrehearsed and out-of-frame remark. It appears that "the man who sells carp" began to ply his trade just as the sermon was being preached. Schweitzer let it be known that he was not yet through preaching.

Sometime after this, Saint John died. The king [of the Jewish people] killed him.

One day the king made a feast for all the chiefs of the country. They drank a lot of wine and became drunk. When they were drunk, the little daughter of the woman whom the king had married came to dance. She danced very well, and so the king was happy. He said to her, "I am going to give you a gift. Ask what you want for a gift." She went to her mother and said to her, "What must I ask for a gift?" And her mother, a wicked woman who was angry with Saint John for saying that she was a wicked woman, said, "Ask for the head of Saint John on a dish."

When the king heard this from the child, he was frightened. He was not so wicked that he wanted to kill Saint John, and he had meant to say, "The head of a man is not a present for a child!" But he was afraid of the rulers, who were present and had heard him tell the child, "I am going to give you the gift that you ask for." With a heavy heart he told his servants, "Go into the prison and cut off the head of Saint John!" Then, a little while later, his head was brought in on a tray and given to the child, and the child brought it to her mother. The disciples of Saint John came. They prepared a tomb and carried away the body of Saint John.

We who are Christians think about Saint John because he was certainly the first one to hear, from the voice of God, that the Kingdom of God was going to come and that the King of hearts had come. In my native land, Christians light fires on the evening of the Feast of Saint John. You see that we are also lighting a fire on the sand bank here. Amen.

Let us pray unto God! O God, who hast sent Saint John to tell the people to have a good heart, give us the strength to hear thy Word. Open our hearts as thou hast opened the hearts of those who have heard thy Word, who have been close to thee, so that we may become thy children. Make us afraid of those wicked thoughts in our hearts; and, we pray thee, be good to us and forgive us, so that we may no longer seek to repeat our former sins. Amen.

28. Sunday, 6 July 1930

Forgiveness

First of two sermons on forgiveness

Luke 6:37

Last Sunday we spoke about a man whose name I hope you all remember. I know that you all still know this name. This man was called John the Baptist. That means that John [was the one who performed] baptism, since John was the first one to baptize Christians. Do you know how John lived? He lived where there were no villages, beside a lake in the bush, and there he preached and baptized the people who came. Then the king put him in prison because John said, "It is not right that you married the wife of your brother."

You know how John was executed, how the Queen's little daughter danced before the king when he [the king] had prepared a great dinner for the rulers and—

These two men! You do not leave when the Word of God is being preached! You leave only because you want to go to the toilet or to urinate, but not to buy fish![18]

Then the king said to the little girl, "You can ask whatever you want." Then the little girl asked her mother what to ask for from the king, and the mother said, "Ask for the head of John the Baptist!" After that, John was executed.

When Jesus learned that John the Baptist was dead, he went to his own country. He did not go to the great city but, like John the Baptist, he stayed far away from the city and allowed the people to come to his home, and, as he was by a small lake—as big as Lake Asingo—known as Lake Gennesaret, there he preached and there he held morning prayer. People came from cities and villages and brought something to eat so that they could listen to him. They did not know who he was; they did not know that God had sent the King of hearts into the world. They only knew that this was the man who had opened his mouth to speak the Word of God after the

---

18. Here, two men who were known to come to the hospital village in the morning to sell their fish interrupted Schweitzer. The transcriber of this sermon has recorded Schweitzer's spontaneous verbal outburst.

death of John the Baptist. Jesus did not say to them, "I am now the King of hearts, the Messiah whom God has sent in the world." He spoke to them only the Word of God, not about himself.

One day, when there were a lot of men around him, he sat down upon a little mountain with the people around him, just as you are around me here, together with the women and children. He gave them a speech, and his disciples who were with him later remembered each word that Jesus said, and they wrote down all the words of this speech—of this sermon, as it is called. They wrote down all these words in the book of the Word of God, and they called this speech "The Sermon on the Mount."

We know each word of this sermon. In Europe every little child learns the words of this speech when they are very young. During the following Sundays I am going to tell you too about the words that are in this great sermon. Today I want to speak about only one saying that is in this sermon. It is a saying so short and simple that each one can take it to his heart, and if one of you truly takes this saying into his heart, he will be a rich man. If you take this saying to your heart, you will all be as rich, even richer than if I were to put into each of your hands one hundred francs five times over.

How happy you would be if I were to empty out a little bag and say, "I am going to put a hundred francs into each hand!" Immediately, tomorrow morning, you would go to where the stores are to buy loincloths, and I even believe that there are some headstrong individuals among you who would also buy some wine. But would you be happy if you had that? No! A man can have money in his hand and money for his mouth and money for clothing and [ ] and a man will only be happy [ ]. Jesus gives money for the heart, and it is that money of the heart that I give you in this saying.

Now I am going to tell you how this saying goes. This saying is, "If you forgive men what they have done, God will forgive you your sins." It is a very simple saying and a beautiful saying. Since God is just, we all know that when we are face to face with God we are poor men indeed. We have often sinned against him through lies, thefts, and the many things we have done.

Since I am a just man, it is also necessary for me to have a palaver with you. When I know the men who have stolen the canoe of a poor man who is here at the hospital, I have a palaver with them, and when I find the men who burn the doctor's boards and beams [for firewood] even though there is a lot of wood in the forest [to burn], then I have a palaver with them. So, this happened yesterday with the Bendjabis [a group of tribesmen] there. Isn't this true? But God—we have far more sins against God than against a man, even if he is the most righteous of men.

Every man is afraid, if he thoroughly examines his heart. So he asks, "Can God forgive all the sins I have committed?" If you listen carefully to the words of God, each of you must know how wicked his heart is and how necessary it is that God forgives him when he is dead, so that he may be in heaven with the good Lord—even a man of whom men say, "He is a good man who does not steal, who does not tell lies [ ]." There are many wicked things in the heart that are not seen. So each man needs God to forgive him for the many things he has done that other men know nothing about. Isn't this true?

Now everyone is saying to himself, "How can the good Lord forgive me?" Then Jesus says, "I am going to tell you how. If everyone forgives all the men who have done him evil, then God will forgive him everything." This is very strange. You therefore have [to do] two things. First, you must be sorry for all the bad things that you have done and for all your bad thoughts, and you must say to yourself, "I am no longer going to steal; I am no longer going to tell lies [ ]." The second thing that God asks of you is that you forgive all the men who have caused you pain.

It is so simple! Yet those who want to try it see that it is very difficult. It is especially difficult for blacks because, since your childhood, you have heard nothing but palavers. Isn't this true? You think only, "They have done me wrong, therefore I go [ ] to eat [ ]. You are happy that the other is obliged [ ], and to give you a lot for that pain that has been done to you.

When someone has been bad to you, you say, "Oh, I am going to think of that all my life, and I am going to give him pain." You take pleasure in not forgiving. This is in the wicked heart of a man. You say, "I am not going to forgive." God says, "I will forgive you only if you yourself have forgiven [others]." This is why he makes us forgive, so that he himself can forgive. If you see [ ], that of all the sayings of God that you know, only this saying [is crucial]. . . , when one is dead, God will forgive him just as if he were a Christian.[19]

19. Schweitzer's interpretation of the New Testament message of forgiveness suggests that God's forgiveness does not depend on whether the person asking God's forgiveness is a Christian. What does matter with God, says Schweitzer, is that the person in question is able to forgive others.

Now I would like each of you to hear this saying as the greatest of treasures and how you can be sure that God will forgive you. Every day this saying walks next to a person like a very strong man. This very strong man, whom nobody sees [ ], forces him to follow this saying. If this man learns to obey this saying, he will become a happy man, because he will have peace in his heart, peace with men, and peace with God.

Haven't you ever noticed sometimes that when the Doctor has been angry because someone has stolen wood [ ] done wickedness, he goes to punish them [but] then he does not punish them? [They might think], "Oh, the doctor isn't a great chief! He forgives [ ]. Then everyone can do what he likes at this hospital!" Isn't this true? Well then! Do you know why the doctor does this, why he forgives even Boulinghi, when he acted so foolishly?[20] Why does [the doctor] have servants when he knows that they steal, lie, and drink wine; [why does he] keep them nevertheless? Because when the doctor becomes very angry, and he tells himself that he has the right to punish this man, there is something that seizes him like a strong man, and this something is the Word of God pronounced by the mouth of Jesus: "If you forgive men their faults, God will also forgive you your faults." The doctor forgives in order to obey the Word of God, to have peace in his heart, to have peace with men, and, what is far more, peace with God. Amen.

Let us pray! God our Father, thou knowest how wicked are our hearts and how much we need thee to forgive us now and [ ]; and, we pray thee, grant us the strength to forgive men, to forgive them all that they have done against us, so that we may know the joy of forgiving and the joy of having the peace of God in our hearts. Amen.

20. Someone well known to the Lambaréné community. He appears to be rather notorious. There is no further information about him. See also footnote 12 in sermon 19.

29. Sunday, 13 July 1930

Forgiveness

Second of two sermons on forgiveness

Luke 6:37

I spoke to you last Sunday about the sermon that Jesus gave on the mountain near the lake, and I told you about one of the sayings in this sermon. This saying said to you, "If you forgive those people who have been wicked toward you, God will likewise forgive you your sins." I explained this saying to you, and I told you that each man, even a savage, feels in his heart that this saying is true, that God cannot forgive a man who is not able to forgive others. Our wicked hearts never want to forgive, but always want to have palavers with men. I told you that this saying is like a strong man who accompanies us in life; and when a man does not want to forgive, then this saying takes hold of him and obliges him to obey, so that he may acknowledge this saying that is in his heart.

If Jesus had been living in the land where the blacks live, who are greater palaverers than whites, [he might have] seen a greater necessity to forgive. In this same Sermon on the Mount, God taught the people to pray. You know that this is the prayer that all Christians say every day. This prayer begins with the phrase, "Our Father, who art in heaven." In this prayer, which is quite short, there is the saying that we [must] forgive all who have been wicked toward us. In addition, Jesus wants everyone, every day, to consider that God does not forgive the sins of those who are not able to forgive [others].

Once, when Jesus was with his disciples—the apostles—the apostle Saint Peter came and said, "I want to ask you something." Jesus said to him, "Speak!" Then he said, "Is it enough if I forgive my brother seven times a day?"

To forgive seven times a day is already quite a lot. Consider, therefore, if someone came in the morning to insult Saint Peter's mother or his wife, and he did not have a palaver [with him]. Then another man came to steal his food, and he did not have a palaver with him. He said [to himself], "I must forgive." Someone else tore his loincloth. He did not say, "You must give me a new loincloth." He forgave. A different person stole his wood for cooking. He did not have a palaver, nor did he ask, "Who has stolen my wood?" He said, "The Lord Jesus says that it is necessary to forgive." His neighbor's goat came and ate his bananas. He did not run to his neighbor's house to say, "Your goat has eaten my bananas." He said, "Oh, perhaps the goat has eaten only two bananas!" Therefore, before the sun had gone down he would already have forgiven five times. And so he said [to himself], "This is a lot!" I would like to see one of you here, during the course of a day, forgive five times!

Then, toward the evening, Saint Peter wanted to go fishing. It was the dry season. He looked for his torch but his torch was no longer there. Then he saw that his neighbor had a torch just like his. (Pause.)[21]

I told you how Saint Peter's torch was stolen, and that he did not have a palaver over it. He had already forgiven six times. Then, when he came to the wharf, he saw that his canoe was stolen—that it wasn't there. Someone else had taken it and gone fishing. He was very sad and angry and said to himself, "This time I am not going to forgive. I am going to go into the hut of the one who took my canoe and I am going to tear apart his mosquito netting. I am going to rip up everything in his hut, and I am going to tell him [ ], and, if you do not give back all the fish and fifty francs as well, then I am going to the commander." During the time he was so angry, he heard the words of Jesus in his heart: "If you do not forgive the men who have been wicked to you, then God cannot forgive you." So he said, "I am going to forgive one more time." But his heart said, "No, no, no! You have forgiven enough. This is not [ ] this time here." Nevertheless, Saint Peter told his heart, "Listen to what Jesus says: 'You must forgive!' " He forced his heart to forgive.

During the night, he sat on the wharf behind a tree, and there he waited the entire night. Then, in the morning, when the other man returned, Saint Peter was there before him, without warning. When the man saw him, he was afraid. He said to himself, "Saint Peter is a strong man. Now he is going to beat me." He was totally surprised when Saint Peter said to him, "You have had my canoe this night and, if I were not the disciple of Jesus Christ, I would have a palaver with you right now; but because the Lord Jesus wants

---

21. The transcriber has indicated that Schweitzer stopped speaking here, perhaps for dramatic reasons.

it, I forgive you." Then the other man was thoroughly astonished, and he looked it him and said to him, "Saint Peter, I will no longer ever take your canoe, and here is half the fish—it's for you." Then, that morning, Saint Peter went to the place where Jesus was, and asked him, "Is it enough if I forgive seven times a day?" [This was] because he had forgiven seven times, and he thought that Jesus would say, "Have you already forgiven seven times?" and then he would tell Jesus, "Yes, Jesus, yesterday I forgave seven times," and Jesus would say, "How good you are, Saint Peter, to tell me that!" And then [St. Peter] would have told him how he had forgiven [all those who had done bad things to him] and Jesus would then say to everyone, "Oh, how good he is! I want everyone [to be like St. Peter!]" But Jesus never said anything like that. He simply said, "Seven times is a lot, but it is necessary to forgive seven times and seven times and seven times yet again, and still seven times and still much more than seven times a day."

Then Saint Peter, who believed that he was a very good man, was utterly baffled. When Jesus saw that he was quite confused, he said to him, "Sit down! I want to tell you a story." Then he told him the story that I am now going to tell you. It is written in the Bible—in the Word of God. A king had a servant. He had great confidence in this servant, and he had put this man at the head of all his plantations. The man had control of the money from all of the cash boxes [that contained] all of the king's wealth from all of his factories. Then, at the end of the year, the king said, "Now we are going to make an inventory."

Then they began to calculate, and all at once they saw that the servant had taken the money from the king's strongbox. He said that he had paid the workers, and that he had paid many workers more than a thousand [francs]. However, he had kept the money for himself. Similarly, he had collected the taxes and not told the king, but had kept [the tax money] for himself. He had sold the king's goods and kept the money for himself. He sold the king's large and beautiful canoes and kept the money for himself. All this was discovered the day the inventory was made. The servant could not lie and say, "It wasn't me!" He was obliged to tell [everything]. Isn't this so? Then the king said, "Very well. Let the militiamen be called to put you in prison for life.—*Hey! [You there] with the fez! You're not here to stroll around!*[22]

22. Schweitzer interrupts his sermon to speak directly to a man who is walking about in the audience and disturbing the service of worship.

Stay there in prison [because you owe me] so many millions of francs!"
The man knew very well that his wife was poor, and that she could never
pay this. Then he fell to his knees before the king and said to him, "Forgive
me!" Then the king had pity on him, and just as the militiamen wanted to
seize him and put him in prison, he [the king] said, "No! Leave him!" He
said to his servant. "You are free! Go and find out what you are able to pay
me!" Then the man left.

When he was on the path to go to his village, he met a poor man. He
looked at him and suddenly said, "It's you! I remember that a few years ago
I lent you a dollar and you have not returned it. You scoundrel! Now I recognize you. Now you are going to give it back to me at once." Then the
other man said, "Oh, I don't have the dollar that I earned. Tomorrow I am
going to bring it to you, you can be sure, but now forgive me!" Then the
other said, "No, no, no! I will not forgive you. Come to the chief. I will put
you in prison until you pay this dollar!"

Then the commander, who was in charge of the palaver and who was a
wicked man himself, said, "Yes, very well then. I will put you in prison until
you pay this dollar." And [the poor man] was put in prison, because he
owed a dollar to the king's servant who had not forgiven him. Then the
people who saw this went to the house of the king to tell him [how the man
whom the king had pardoned] had imprisoned a poor man who owed him
a dollar.

Then the king said, "What? He did that? [Send for the] militiamen,
and find me this man!" When the servant was brought back, he said to him,
"I have forgiven you thousands and thousands of dollars, and you put a
poor man in prison who owed you one dollar! I have forgiven you a great
deal, and you had to forgive only a very little bit. Then why do you want me
to forgive you? Therefore, I can no longer forgive you." And he said to the
militiamen, "Put him in prison where it is completely dark and dank! Put
him there!"

Here then, is the story that Jesus told Saint Peter. The story was told
not only to Saint Peter, but also to all of us. [In the story] the king is God.
The servant who owed him very much is the man who had committed
many sins. All that men can do to others is only one dollar compared with
all the wickedness that they have committed toward God. Therefore, even
if we forgive everyone the evil they have done, it is only as if we had the
benefit of a dollar compared with all the millions that we owe God.

Every time you do not want to forgive someone, think of this story! It is a story that I have now put into everyone's heart, and I want you to keep it. Amen.

Let us pray! O God our Father, we are poor palaverers. Place in our hearts the saying of forgiveness to men. Grant us the power always to forgive. Give us the will always to forgive. Fill our hearts with the knowledge of how much we need to be forgiven by thee. Thou art the great King and we, thy poor servants, need thy forgiveness. Amen.

30. Sunday, 20 July 1930

"Our Father"

First sermon in a series on the Lord's Prayer

Matthew 6:9–14

Last Sunday you heard me speak about the saying of Jesus in the great speech that he gave on the mountain beside the lake. In this sermon he said that we must forgive those who have harmed us. Without this, God cannot forgive us our sins. I told you the story in which the great king spoke to his head servant, and then how the head servant threw a poor man in prison who owed him a dollar. Today I will tell you another saying from this Sermon on the Mount.

In this sermon, Jesus teaches people to pray. He saw that people did not know how to pray, and that is why he wanted to teach us to pray. He taught them a prayer that all Christians pray today. It is quite brief. The pagans did not know what it means to pray. When the first missionaries came to your country, they were thoroughly astonished that the people did not know how to pray. Those Jews, before whom Jesus spoke, already knew how to pray. They knew that to pray means to speak to God. However, many of them thought that to pray meant to tell God about everything that they wanted. One man prayed so that God would give him a lot of money in his business. Another prayed that God would give him a well-thought-out argument for the palaver that he was having. Another prayed to God that he would have a lot of bananas on his plantation. They believed that God could attend to all these things, and that God did not know about the things they needed in order to live.

Then Jesus said to the men, "God knows all about what you need. He knows what you need so that your plantation will be supplied. This is why he sends the sun and the rain, so that the plantation will bear fruit. He knows that you need clothes and blankets when it is cold, and that is why he allows the plants to grow or finds sons to do these things."[23] You need only pray about things of the heart, things that are [important] to you—to your heart. That is why Jesus spoke the prayer that we must pray. This prayer is called, "Our Father," because it begins with words, "Our Father who art in heaven."

"Our Father who art in heaven." Right away the prayer says that there are no other gods, there are no idols, and there is only God, who is above all images. When, therefore, a pagan begins to pray the prayer of Jesus, in the very first word he says, "I do not believe in idols." At the same time he says, "I no longer fear spirits." He says, "I no longer believe in idols and I no longer fear the idolaters." He says, in saying this prayer, "I believe that there is only one God." This is already quite a lot!

Prior to Jesus, there were people who came to proclaim this: that there are no idols and only one God. These men are called prophets. It was the men of the Jewish people who proclaimed the Word of God. With Jesus there is something else: he says, "Our Father," and not, "Our God." Therefore Jesus teaches people to speak to God not as a being who is all-powerful, who is severe, but as to a being who is their father. He says to every poor man, "You can pray to God as if you are speaking to your father." It was the first time that a man said this. It is not altogether easy to believe that God is a father to us.

When we see a man who is very sick, who cannot speak, who cannot walk, who suffers and cries out, we ask, "Who sent sickness to this man?" We know that neither men nor idolaters sent this, only that this man is sick because it is the will of God. Then we can ask, "But if God is the father, why does he send such sad things to men?" We must say that we do not un-

---

23. The sequence of statements in this sentence appears illogical and is confusing to the reader. The transcriber may have had a lapse of concentration here or perhaps missed some additional wording. It defies reconstruction.

derstand it. Or, if we see a man who is mistreated by another, who insults him [and] makes a poor man suffer, we ask, "How can God allow that?" So we see much sadness, much difficulty, much injustice in the world, and many people who can say, "It is clear that God is not a father to men." Jesus, who was far more intelligent than all men, knew this. Nevertheless, he said, "God our Father," because he knew as well as we poor folks that we cannot know the thoughts of God.

Look at this little sheep over there! Can this little sheep understand the thoughts in a man's head? No! Isn't this true? Well, then! The difference between a sheep and a man is not as big as the difference between a man and God. So it is clear that a poor man cannot understand God. This is why Jesus says, "Believe that God is our Father, even if you do not understand it, and that everything that God wants for men, and has done for men, is good, even if you do not understand it." So it is that we Christians believe what God has spoken by the mouth of Jesus.

There are many Christians who, when they were sick, when they were sad, and when they suffered a lot, prayed, "God who art our Father." When they said, "God our Father," they said, "We know that all that thou hath done for us is good, even if I suffer." They had tranquil hearts, because the only real good in the world is for a man to have a tranquil heart. No one can be happy or have a tranquil heart except those who believe that God is our Father. That is why Jesus taught men to pray, "Our Father, who art in heaven." Amen.

Let us pray! Our Father, who art in heaven, may we, in our hearts, have the ability always to know that thou art our Father, so that our hearts may become tranquil and happy, and that we may be thy children. Amen.

31. Sunday, 3 August 1930

"Thy Kingdom Come!"

Second sermon in a series on the Lord's Prayer

Matthew 6:10

Last time we spoke of the prayer that Jesus taught to the Twelve Apostles and to the men who were around him when he delivered the Sermon on the Mount.—*There is a man over there who wants to leave. He ought to come here. He ought to be ashamed!*[24]—This prayer is quite short; it has only a few words. It begins with "Our Father who art in heaven."

I have explained to you that this means that men believe that God is all-powerful in the world and is their father. Today I am going to tell you another phrase in this prayer: "Thy Kingdom come," which is to say, "May thy Kingdom come." This means that Jesus said to men, "Pray to God that he might begin his Kingdom on earth." What does it mean that the Kingdom of God is going to come on earth? What is happening now on the earth? What sort of kingdom is there? The kingdom of men, and men are wicked. Then the kingdom of men is wicked.

When your fathers still lived here, there was a kingdom of black chiefs without [any] white men. This kingdom was wicked. The rulers you had were unjust. They were cruel and they made the people suffer. They killed them for no reason at all. The old men who are now here and who still remember those days, they know. They know that the chiefs sold poor black people for [gun]powder, lead [shot], [ ] and salt. Isn't it true? You know all this. We whites, we know it too.

The doctor, up there,[25] has among his many books one that was written by one of the first whites [to come to Gabon. This man] wrote of what he saw on this hill where the doctor now lives and where the chief of the Galoas

24. Here, the transcriber has once again recorded Schweitzer's out-of-frame remark. Someone stood up to leave as Schweitzer was beginning his sermon. Schweitzer was not pleased with the man's behavior and tried to make him stay.

25. Schweitzer may be referring to himself in the third person, as he points to a house in the hospital village.

once lived. We know that this white man was not lying, that everything he wrote in this book is completely true. He tells shocking stories of things that the chief did when he was drunk—how he slit the throats of men, only slowly, so that they suffered greatly. All these things are written in that book.

This was the kingdom of Galoan men. When we speak of the kingdom of men, we mean the kingdom of war, since all the tribes are constantly waging war against each other. This is how it is throughout the whole world, where the kingdom of men is—men who are wicked, unjust, [and who wage] war.

You know that all these men lived like that in the kingdom of men, who were unjust, [who allowed] poverty, and [who made] war. Everyone said, "That's the way it is! It's still like that and it will always be like that." You speak like this because you do not know that God is in heaven, a God who wants goodness and love. But among the whites, among the Jewish people who were children of God, there were men who knew the Word of God. They said, "No, it does not have to stay like that—war, injustice and cruelty—it doesn't need to be like that." Someday the Kingdom of God will come.

When Jesus came into the world, there were already many people who prayed and said, "Oh, that the Kingdom of God would come into the world!" But a kingdom must have a king! So it is that God sent our Lord Jesus Christ, who is the King of hearts. Then, on the day when Jesus was raised before men, and when men saw him as the King of men whom God had sent, then the Kingdom of God began. So we know the Kingdom of God began with the Lord Jesus Christ. But it has only begun. That is why when Jesus Christ taught men to pray, he taught them to pray, "Thy Kingdom come." Since Jesus came, men have prayed this prayer for many, many years: "Thy Kingdom come!" There has only been a little beginning to the Kingdom of God, and often [ ].

Oh no! The Kingdom of God has not become great; it always remains little among men! You have seen the trees that the doctor has planted—the orange, tangerine, and lemon trees. Twice a year he clears away the brush around them, but there are trees that stay small. They do not grow. Then men could say, "This tree does not grow." Nevertheless, we who see that the Kingdom of God [is] so small and poor, we believe that the Kingdom of God will one day be great.

What is the difference between black and white? It is not that the white knows many things that the black does not know, but that the white has in his heart, since he was little, this thought that the Kingdom of God must come on earth. There has always been this idea among the whites that the Kingdom of God must come. Oh, I know that there are many whites who are wicked. You know this, too. Isn't it true? But even in wicked white hearts there is always a little bit of the Word of God. They know that it does not have to be like that—that the kingdom of men does not have to be wicked, that the Kingdom of God must come—because when once someone has the idea of the Kingdom of God inside his heart, it can never be forgotten.

When a man has seen the village where he was a small child, does he ever forget the village? Doesn't he see his father's hut, his uncle's hut, and the plantation? Why can he never forget? Because it was in his heart when he was a small child. So in our hearts—in the hearts of the whites, in most white hearts—there is always the thought of the Kingdom of God. You have seen that we have sought to have not only the kingdom of men, but also something that is the Kingdom of God. We have tried to become more just, because you see that many things can be said against the whites. However, many of them seek justice.

Yesterday you saw the governor here. Well, then! When there is a palaver and one says [ ], "Here is a gift!" Do you believe that the governor will accept the present? No! He will not accept it.

You knew Mr. Garnier?[26] If men came to his house to say to him, "Here is some money; settle the palaver for us," do you think that he would have accepted it? No! He would not have accepted it. He would have said, "No, I am here to see that justice is done." So there are many, many whites everywhere on earth who seek to be just—just to the poor man and to the one who is rich. It is as if, within this poor little tree that does not want to grow, there is a small leaf—[ ]. Because there is a little leaf of the Word of God within the hearts of men, there is also pity.

Among you blacks, a man who was sick could no longer walk, [and so] you said, "He can no longer walk, he can no longer work. What do I care?"

26. Mr. Garnier was the name of the impeccably honest governor. We do not know his first name or any other details about him. There were some in Schweitzer's audience who knew him, and they agree with his conclusion about what Mr. Garnier would have done if someone had tried to bribe him. Schweitzer acknowledges their response.

But we whites, because the Word of God is in our hearts, we have made hospitals for poor black people [ ] given them food to eat. Then we heard that among blacks there are many sicknesses and much suffering. We did not say, "Oh, this is far away from us; what can we do about this? They are not our brothers." But we have come to your country, here and elsewhere, and we have built shelters for those who are ill. Isn't this true? This, too, is a very little leaf from the poor tree that cannot grow. We have seen a few leaves from this poor little tree already. But the Kingdom of God is a poor little tree. Now it has no leaves; it has no flowers; it does not give fruit. However, we believe that a day will come when the Kingdom of God will be among men. I believe it. I have friends who believe it. I know a lot of men who believe it. That is why we pray the prayer that Jesus told us, "Thy Kingdom come."

We know that we will not see the time when the tree will be great, when there will be flowers and fruit. But we pray God that one day other men may see the Kingdom of God. That is why we plant the seeds of the Kingdom of God in all hearts, and this is why I preach the Word of God to you. Amen.

Let us pray unto God! Put [your] hands together.[27] God our Father, thou knowest how wicked the kingdom of men is. Thou knowest how there are injustices, cruelties, and wickedness on the earth. That is why we pray unto thee. Send thy Kingdom speedily, the Kingdom of goodness and justice, so that men may thank thee from the bottom of their hearts. Amen.

27. Schweitzer is instructing his congregation in the proper positioning of the hands for prayer.

32. Sunday, 10 August 1930

"Send Thy Kingdom!"

Third sermon in a series on the Lord's Prayer

Matthew 6:10

I spoke to you the last time about the prayer that Jesus prayed [on behalf of] the men who were around him. Jesus taught this prayer to men when he delivered the great speech on the little mountain. In that place, it was not as it is here. When it was announced that the Word of God was going to be preached, everyone came—all who could walk from the villages. There was no need to look for the men in their huts as it is with you, where each Sunday morning the doctor is quite sad before beginning to speak.

When Jesus taught them how to pray, he began this prayer with the words, "Our Father who art in heaven." Later, after these words, is the phrase "Thy Kingdom come." I told you the difference between whites and blacks. The whites have known for a long time that there is a Kingdom of God. Whites know that the kingdom of men is wicked, unjust, [full of] lies, cruelty, and that it will always remain so. You natives have been told, "Oh, it will always be like this! There will always be cruelty, injustice, war, and lies." So you may say, "How can this be changed? Men are always going to be like this. But we [ ]."

Jesus' prayer tells us that it is always necessary to hope and believe that one day it will be otherwise, and that is why nearly all whites have the belief in their hearts that one day the Kingdom of God will be here. We know that the Kingdom of God has already begun, because God has already sent the King and the Kingdom into the world. This King is Jesus, our Lord, the King of hearts. Ever since Jesus was on earth and spoke to men and preached [to them], the Kingdom of God has begun. And ever since then, all the men who know the Word of God pray every day, "O God, may thy Kingdom come!"

Already we see the Kingdom is like a little tree, a little orange tree, a little tree that grows. Already there is more justice in the world. I have told you that among the whites there is already more justice than among you. There is no palaver, there is no lying, there is no injustice as [there is] among you. There is more goodness and there is more love. The wretched are attended to and are fed, and huts are provided for them. But among you, if someone is unfortunate or sick, you're too busy to care. So, we all hope someday the Kingdom will come.—*Wait a moment! I'll be right back.*[28]

Therefore we all wait for the Kingdom of God to come, and nobody can tell when this will be. Perhaps only the children of our children, a hundred years from now, will see the Kingdom of God. We all believe in the Kingdom of God, and we hope that it will come. We pray to God every day, in the prayer that Jesus taught, that God might send the Kingdom. If we do not see that the Kingdom is already in the world, a thing [ ] can have if it is in our heart, because the most important thing is that the Kingdom be in our hearts. It is not necessary that there always be sun in the sky, if only the sun is in our heart. If [ ] it becomes dark again and if [there is a] tornado, if joy is in the heart of a man, he is happy even if he does not see the sun in the sky. And so we pray to God, "Send thy Kingdom!"

We pray for two things. We pray to God, "Send thy Kingdom into the world among men, and we pray again, "O God, send thy Kingdom into our heart!" The one who has the Kingdom of God in his heart is as happy as if the Kingdom of God were throughout the whole world.

What does it mean, "The Kingdom of God is in the heart of a man"? It means, first of all, that he says, "My real King and chief is the Lord Jesus." I want to obey the Word of Jesus. As if [ ] the chief that [ ] and, I do thy will [ ]." This is why we proclaim to you the Word of Jesus, so that all of you who have come from far off [may say], "Oh! I know Jesus! I know that he is the King and that he must also be the King of my heart."

Until now, your heart has been like a village where there are a lot of wicked chiefs. These wicked chiefs are the bad thoughts of your heart. There is the great chief who is called "Lying." There is another chief who says, "Become rich! Steal! Tell lies to become rich!" There is yet another chief who is "Wickedness," [the chief] of palavers, [who says], "Hit hard, be wicked ones!" And yet again another chief, "Laziness." All these chiefs are chiefs in the great village that is your heart.

Well then! Now tell me, if the chief of a village is bad, can the village be happy? Tell me, can the village be happy? Well then! If the chiefs who are

---

28. The transcriber has captured Schweitzer's verbal response to an unexpected situation needing his prompt attention. He returned and continued his sermon.

in your heart are wicked, can your heart be happy? Because the heart [that is] tranquil is like [a calm river], while the heart that is not happy is like the Ogooué when a tornado begins.

If I ask each of you now, "Is your heart happy and tranquil?"—If I ask each one of you—everyone must answer, "No!" Even those among you who do not appear to be thinking, but [ ]; if I ask that, they will answer, "No, doctor!" If I listen [to] my heart I know that I am not happy. [ ], and every heart wants to be tranquil and happy. Even the most savage [men] know this. Men's hearts are all the same; they want to be tranquil and happy—the hearts of whites as well as blacks. The heart becomes tranquil and happy only when Jesus, [with] all [his] good thoughts, is the chief of hearts.

Each man has chiefs who are men. We have chiefs—Mr. Boutin, [for one]. We have the governor of Libreville and the governor above him in Brazzaville, and we have the president of the Republic. You still have "land bosses," and you know that all these land bosses are not honest. When we pray, "Thy Kingdom come," we also pray that all these land bosses may be honest—that they may not be scoundrels. All these chiefs [ ] can make us obey. They can force us to obey. They can make us pay the tax that [ ]. We may do something else, but they cannot make our hearts obey them. There is only one chief who is able to make our hearts obey him, so that our hearts may become tranquil and happy—and that is Jesus. This is why you must always think about what you do. Does this chief allow it? Do you do something that the chief does not allow? That is why I tell each of you, "Jesus must be the chief of your heart!" Then those who want Jesus to be the chief of their heart will have a tranquil heart, and they will know that this is the Kingdom of God in their heart. That is why I say to all of you today, "Pray that the Kingdom of God may come into the world, and pray that it comes into your heart!" Amen.

Now let us pray! Hands together.[29] O God, we all pray unto thee. Send thy Kingdom into the world! Cause all wars to cease, all cruelty to cease, all injustice to cease, and all lying to cease! But, we also pray thee, send thy Kingdom into our hearts! Grant that we all recognize Jesus, our Lord, as the chief of our hearts, with all the good thoughts [he has given us]. Amen.

---

29. Schweitzer is again reminding his audience about the proper position of their hands when they pray.

33. Sunday, 17 August 1930

The Will Of God

Fourth sermon in a series on the Lord's Prayer

Matthew 6:10

For the past two Sundays I have spoken to you about the prayer that Jesus told to those who were with him [to teach them] how to pray. This prayer is rather brief, having only a few words, but there is a lot to say about each of the phrases in this prayer. I have explained this to you. There is a phrase in it that says, "Thy Kingdom come." I have spoken to you about this phrase for the past two Sundays, and I want it to remain fixed in every heart. Now, today, I am speaking once more about yet another phrase of this prayer. The phrase is quite unusual.

Listen carefully! The phrase is, "May thy will be done on earth as it is in heaven." It is a strange expression.

The will of God—what is it? Look at the sun. It rises each morning at the same minute behind there, by noon it is above here, and in the evening it is there once more. Why does the sun do that every day? Because it is the will of God. At first the moon is dark, then it gets big, and then very little. It is always the same thing. There is the rainy season and then the dry season. Every year it is the same thing. There are winds. The hot winds come from there and the cold winds come from there. Every year it is the same thing. Have you ever thought about this? The more one reflects, the stranger it seems. Haven't you ever been astonished about all that you see like this? All this astonishes everyone who thinks. Isn't this true? Is there anyone among you who has not been surprised that every day the sun rises at the same time and goes down at the same time? Isn't this so?

If the sun were a man, one day he would come at eight o'clock. On another day, because he had slept for a long time, [he would come] at nine o'clock. In the evening he would speak up at four o'clock [and say], "I am tired." He would be going to sleep when all the workers would still be in the plantation. That's how it would be. But the sun is not a man: the sun is the sun of God, and that is why it always obeys. The stars that come out in the sky at night, they also obey the will of God. Each goes along the way that the good Lord has shown it—always. So everything in the sky obeys God. God also wants those who are on earth to obey him, that the will of God may be done in the hearts of men. God could force men as he forces the sun to do his will, but he does not force them. He puts his will into the hearts of men. He wants men to obey him not as slaves but as children. When a man has a servant, he says to him, "Do this! Do that!" And the servant obeys him because he is afraid. When a man has a son, a son who is good, he does not need to say to him, "Do this! Do that!" The son likes to obey him because he is his father. Even when the father is far away and cannot speak to him, the son says, "I want to do that because my father wants it." Isn't this true?—*These women are not supposed to walk around. They must come here. You don't walk around when the Word of God is being preached!*[30]

Now, how do we know the will of God? The will of God is in the hearts of all men. It is only necessary that they want to read it and to listen to it in their hearts. That is why a man who comes from far off, from the interior, cannot say, "I have not heard the Word of God." Everyone, even the most savage [of men], even though he may have heard nothing of the words of God, already has the Word of God in his heart.

When a man wants to steal, his heart does not say, "That's just fine!" even if he is a man who has never heard the Word of God from a missionary. The heart of the man always says, "It is wicked to steal." When a man wants to lie, the will of God that is in his heart tells him, "to lie: one must not. It's wrong." When a man sees another who is hungry, while he himself has something to eat and the other has nothing, he says, "This is not my brother," although the heart tells him, "Even if this is not your brother, you should give him something to eat."

When a man has an enemy, a man who has done him evil, he wants do him some evil in return, but his heart says, so that he hears it, "No! You shouldn't!" Isn't all that I have said true? However, if a man, from his childhood on, does not listen to the voice of God, the voice of God then says, "Why should I have to speak, if this man does not listen?" This is the way people [come to behave] like savages—men who have become thoroughly wicked. They say, "I do as I please. When I want to lie, I lie. When I want to

---

30. Schweitzer interrupts his sermon when his eye catches the movement of two women wandering about the area in which the service was held. He urges them to attend.

steal, I steal. It makes no difference to me. When I want to kill, I kill. I do what I want." Are these men happy? Has anyone ever said to you, "Oh, I also want to be a man just like that?" Real happiness is to have peace in your heart, and peace in your heart can be had only when one does the will of God.

When I preach the Word of God to you, I do not preach it to you as something that you have never known. We whites have to learn a lot of things that we never knew before. It is hard to make [you] understand. Now, if I drive you out in the motorboat and I want you to understand why the machine goes when gasoline is put [in it] and it runs and [ ], because there is a lot to learn. Now, if I drive you in the launch and show you the entire machine and what there is inside it, you will never understand why it runs—from here to Port Gentil, always paddling, always the same thing—without becoming tired. Not many people who would understand—perhaps only one. If a native mechanic was here among the invalids, I would say to him, "Explain to me why it runs." He would reply, "I don't know. I know only that when it runs it runs." Isn't this so?

When I speak the Word of God to you, do I need to explain to you why—why? I know that the will of God is already in your heart. When I speak the Word of God to you, who many never have heard the Word of God, the will of God is already in your heart. It sleeps.

Wake up! Wake up! This is why today I am telling you these words of Jesus, "Thy will be done!" Listen carefully in your hearts for what is the will of God. Happiness will begin in your heart when you begin to listen to the Word of God. Amen.

Now let us pray! God, our Father who art in heaven, thou who hast placed thy will in our hearts, give us the will always to listen to the will that is in our hearts, so that thy will may be stronger than the bad wills of our hearts, and that we truly become thy children. Amen.

34. Sunday, 24 August 1930

A Happy Heart

Fifth sermon in a series on the Lord's Prayer

I spoke to you last Sunday about the prayer of Jesus in which he asks that the will of God be done on earth as [it is] in heaven. That means that the will of God should be done by men. Only then, when the will of God is done, will all men on earth be happy. Then men will be happy because, if the will of God is done, there will no longer be war, there will no longer be stealing, there will no longer be cruelty, there will no longer be lying, there will no longer be all that, but men will live in peace.

We will not [live to] see this and the children who are here likewise will not see it, but we all believe in the Kingdom of God and we want to work so that this Kingdom of God may come on earth. Perhaps then, if we all want it, and we all work so that the Kingdom of God will come, it will come for the children of the children of our children. This will happen!

Isn't it true that we all want the Kingdom of God? It's clear, isn't it? But the Kingdom of God cannot come [from] outside if it is not within the hearts of men. This is why I ask you, "Do you truly want the Kingdom of God to come into your heart?" That is the reason I say to you all, "Do you truly want the Kingdom of God to come into your heart?" Answer truthfully! Ah! They are afraid already.[31]

Look! Everyone who replies truly with his heart, "I want the Kingdom of God to come into my heart," God hears him and he is happy.

Perhaps there are some among you who have not answered with the mouth but with the heart. If they have really answered with the heart, God has also heard them. Nevertheless, I want many of you today to say with the heart, "Now we know the will of God [ ] and we want the will of God to be done in our hearts." This means that, today, the one who says that wants to begin a new life.

Have any of you ever lived in an old hut where the roof was rotted

---

31. Schweitzer asks his audience for an audible response.

[through and] where the wind and the rain came [in]? Yes?[32] You have all lived in these huts, therefore, because you are all lazy and do not repair the huts. Even the Galoas, whose women wear beautiful clothing and silk stockings, live like savages in huts that are rotted. Isn't it true? Go and look at the huts at Port Gentil and at Lambaréné!

Then, finally, when [a man] says, "I am going to construct a new hut," and when there is a new hut with a good roof, then the man is happy. This man is happy because life in a new hut with a good kitchen is something quite different from a life in a hut with a bad kitchen into which the rain falls. Well, then! If a man [is happy] when he finally has a new hut, how much happier will he be when he has a new life!

Surely you have often been told, "Oh! I want to have a new hut [ ]. Someone among you reflects, "Oh! I want to have a new life!" But he does not begin a new life because he sees that all the men around him are leading the same kind of life. Today, Jesus would come to all those who [ ].

Do not look at others, but look at yourself. [ ] a new life. Only then can you be truly happy, since no one can truly be happy—even if he is rich, even if he has all that he wants—if his heart is not happy. The heart is happy only when it does the will of God. Amen.

35. Sunday, 31 August 1930

"Our Daily Bread"

Sixth sermon in a series on the Lord's Prayer

Matthew 6:11

During these past Sundays we have been speaking about the prayer that Jesus taught to those who were with him. He spoke this prayer when he gave the sermon to the people while he was seated on the mountain near the lake. This prayer is called "Our Father" because it begins with the words, "Our Father who art in heaven."

---

32. Schweitzer has asked for another response.

We have already spoken together about the part of this prayer that says, "May the will of God be done and may the reign of God come on the earth as it is in heaven." Today we speak about the part of this same prayer that says, "Give us this day our daily bread!" Therefore, Jesus teaches us to pray to God so that he may give us food, because, in the language of the whites, *bread* does not mean only the bread that the cook has made with flour, but everything that we eat.

It is much colder where the whites live than it is here. There is no cassava, there are no bananas, there are no taro roots, and there is no maize. There is only the wheat from which flour is made. The plant that provides flour is a tall plant, just about like this.[33] Therefore, if blacks have the heart to pray to God, and if they say, "Give us our daily bread!" this means, "Give us bananas! Give us cassava! Give us what we need to eat!" "How?" you say. "Is it the good Lord who gives me cassava and bananas and all the others? Certainly not! It is I who have made a clearing. The women planted, and then this grew up. It is we who work, who make what we have to eat!" Isn't it true that men say these things? When they speak like this, they talk foolishly, because a man can make a clearing [and] a woman can plant when she is not lazy, but a man cannot make a small root, a small plant, or a tree that can bear fruit.

A great chief is able to put a lot of people in prison, but he cannot make a little tree grow. The governor-general is the chief of all the soldiers of Equatorial Africa, but he cannot make a single little tree grow. Gaston, who is the president of the republic—all the soldiers are obliged to obey him, but he cannot make a cassava plant grow.[34]

We have very learned men in Europe who know how to construct a machine to fly in the air, and other machines, but if we tell them to construct a small palm tree, they cannot. Only the good Lord can make a plant grow that gives fruit. Only the good Lord can make it grow. Only he can make all the plants, since it is the good Lord who sends the sun, it is the good Lord who sends the rain. It is the good Lord who sends the wind. Without sun, without rain, without wind, without all the forces that are in

33. Schweitzer indicates the size with a gesture.
34. Gaston Doumergue (1863–1937) was president of the French Republic (1924–31). He was a well-liked statesman of Calvinist origins who was one of the first persons to use the radio to address the nation. His radio messages were often sermons.

the earth, all the plants cannot grow. If the good Lord does not send the sun, does not send the rain, does not send the wind, there is nothing for men to eat. That is why each one who eats something—bananas or cassava—must say to himself, "It is the good Lord who gives food." That is why we Christians pray before we eat and say "Thank-you" to God, who gives food. Those who live in the land of the whites know very well that it is through kindness that God gives food. They know very well why they pray to God, "Give us food every day!"

In our country it often happens that there is not enough sun for the plants to grow very well. It often happens that in winter it is so cold that the trees die, so that it is necessary to cut them down. That is why we know, much more than you, that it is the good Lord who gives food. In our villages the people are obliged to work far harder to have food than in your land. The good Lord is far better to you—much better than to us. It is not cold in your country. Plants grow easily. When people work a bit to make a clearing, then they can plant and have food.

When I tell the whites of Europe how easy it is in your land to grow maize, bananas, and taro roots, they are surprised, and say, "How good the good Lord is to people over there!" Then they ask, "Are blacks also aware of what the good Lord has done for them?" Then I say, "No!" I say, "They take it for granted that the palm tree, bananas, [and] cassava bear fruit and that they have almost no work to do. Then they say, "But why is the good God so good to them, far better than to Europeans?" Then I reply to them, "Yes, he gives them more to eat, but he gives them more sicknesses than he does in your country." Then they say, "Yes, that's the way it is. The good Lord knows what he is doing and man cannot understand it."

I am telling you all this so that you may understand the Word of God in the prayer: that all you eat is a gift of God. Every time you eat, think of how the good Lord is so good to you that he allows all the plants around you to increase and bear fruit. The man who reflects has a heart for recognizing God for all that God gives him. Look here! If the good Lord said, "I want to let the dry season in Gabon last until Christmas," what would happen? The plants would not grow and the people would have nothing to eat. That is why you must thank God when you eat, every day. [ ] the most savage of you, only if he knows how to pray to the good Lord, "I thank you for what you give me to eat," then it is really something. You who are here at the hospital, you have yet far more reason to thank God for all that he gives you. Did you grow the fruit you have eaten here? No, you haven't planted, and yet you eat nevertheless. Isn't it true? You have only brought your plate, and it has been filled for you. How does the good Lord give you food? He has given to good Christian hearts in Europe the thought that here at the hospital there are people who want to eat, and these Christians give money to the doctor so that here he can buy bananas and cassava for you to eat. So [it is] the good Lord that feeds you as well, through the good thoughts for you that he has put into the hearts of the people of Europe.

When the boat of the S.H.O. stops at the wharf and unloads twenty rice bags, it is the good Lord who sends you these bags of rice by means of the good thoughts of the people of Europe.[35] You have little comprehension that the good Lord sends you this, since there are so many lazybones among you who hide when they see this [unloading of the bags] at the wharf. I am telling you all this so that your hearts may change, so that you may become like true Christians who, every time they begin to eat, give thanks to God for what he gives them to eat. Amen.

Let us pray unto God! O God, our Father who art in heaven, we thank thee for giving, so easily to us in this country, all that is necessary for men to eat. We thank thee for making the palm tree, the banana tree, the cassava, and the maize grow—and all the other fruit. We pray thee to continue to send the sun and the rain so that the people of this country may have food to eat. And we, in this hospital, we thank thee for having placed in the hearts of the people of Europe, [the desire] to give money so that the people of this hospital may eat. And we pray thee, preserve this country, here, from all famine, and grant, in the hearts of all the natives, the joy to make good plantations, because we know that thou, who art our Father, thou dost love people who work diligently. Amen.

35. The reference to the boat of S.H.O. suggests that it was well known to the transcriber and also to Schweitzer. The abbreviation is obscure.

36. Sunday, 7 September 1930

"Deliver Us From Evil"

Seventh sermon in a series on the Lord's Prayer

Matthew 6:13

During the past few Sundays I have been explaining to you the prayer "Our Father." It is the prayer that Jesus taught to those who are Christians, so that they may pray it every day. Today, since we have looked at all the rest [of it], we are going to speak about the end of this prayer—the last words of this prayer. These last words are, "Deliver us from evil"—that is to say, "Make us free from evil, from that which is bad."

All of us in this world are surrounded by pain. To begin with, there is the pain that is the suffering of people when they are sick or when there has been a misfortune. We see a lot of that here in the hospital. There are people here who suffer a lot, who cry all night, and to whom we give all the medicines that we have. How happy we are when, with a certain medicine, we are able let a poor unfortunate, who is in such pain, get some sleep.

No one can say to us, "I will not have pain. I am young. I am in good health." You knew Gandhi, who was here—Gandhi, who lived in that hut over there.[36] He was strong. He was young. Nevertheless, from his face one could see how much he suffered. He became weaker and weaker, and when he was dead we wanted to look at his illness. Then, when we opened [him] up here,[37] we saw that poor Ghandi had a wound in his intestine. Not all [our] medicines could have saved him. He could not have been saved even with an operation.

When we look in the hut behind [us], where there are those who are disturbed in spirit, we are sad, too. We have Madoungo there who is no longer sane, who [will never be completely] cured. So it is that we pray, "O God, deliver us from evil!" He has already heard us a little bit because he

36. Since the service was always held outdoors, it was easy for Schweitzer to point to this man's hut. This is not the famous Gandhi of India.

37. Schweitzer indicates the place on his own body.

has permitted whites to discover some good medicines. Every year we discover new medicines.

It has been many long years since the doctor was here.[38] At the beginning, when he was here before the war, when he saw an invalid with sleeping sickness at N'Dende, he said, "I do not know if I can heal that." Now, when someone with sleeping sickness is brought in, who is emaciated, [he] is almost always cured. Isn't it true that you have already seen a lot of sleeping sickness cured here? The woman whom I carried [around] for a few weeks in my motorboat is completely healed. She is walking.

We know that there are men who have discovered excellent medicines, but it is the good Lord who has given them the intelligence to discover them. So when we pray to God to deliver us from evil, we say, at the same time, "Thank you," because he has already allowed us to find medicines [to fight] against evil.

There is the evil of suffering and pain, but there is still another evil, and this [evil resides] in the hearts of men. This is the great evil—the thought of stealing, of lying, of wickedness, and all the other thoughts in the hearts of men. No one can say, "I have no wickedness," because we all—whites as well as blacks—we all have wicked thoughts in our hearts.

When we pray, "Deliver us from evil," this means, "Deliver us from the wicked thoughts that lie in our hearts!" Yet can God cast out the bad thoughts from a man's heart the way a woman removes the potatoes from the pot in which she has cooked them? No! God can cast them out only if the man himself wants to help.

Every day it is necessary that the good thoughts in our hearts hold a palaver with the bad ones and drive them out from the hut of our hearts. Then, if we truly have the will to conduct a palaver with the bad thoughts, this means that God wants to help us. If we pray, "Deliver us from evil!" this means, "Give us the power to struggle in our hearts against bad thoughts!" Thus, everyone must pray to God, "Deliver us from evil! Give us the power to struggle against bad thoughts!"

All men must pray to God, the white as well as the black. Therefore, I want to inscribe in your heart this prayer— "Deliver us from evil!"—that you may carry it in your heart always. If someone really knows how to pray this prayer from the heart, he knows a great deal. And to all those who pray

38. This was Schweitzer's third sojourn in Lambaréné. He arrived in December 1929.

in their hearts, "Deliver us from pain!" God gives the power to struggle against bad thoughts. Amen.

Let us pray: O God, our Father! Thou knowest all the bad thoughts that are in our hearts, and thou knowest how weak we are to hold a palaver for the good thoughts with the bad thoughts. We all know that we are miserable as long as we have these bad thoughts in our hearts—that our hearts do not have peace or tranquility; that is why we pray, "Give us the will and the power to struggle every day against these bad thoughts so that the night may no longer be in our hearts, but instead a clear day with sunshine! Amen.

37. Sunday, 14 September 1930

The Parable of the Prodigal Son

Luke 15:11–32

Jesus often told stories to those who listened to him. Today I want to tell you one of these stories.

There was a man who had two sons. One of the sons was a good son and a worker, and the other son was an idler and thought only of how to amuse himself and spend money. One day [the idler] told his father: "I want to leave. I am very bored at home. I want to see the world. My father, you are a rich man and when you die I will inherit a lot of money. Give me now the money that I would have after your death."

The father was very sad, so he could have said, "No, go away, you will not have the money." But the father was a good man. He went to the safe and gave him the money.

The son left. He went into another country, into a great city, and spent all his money. He spent everything, all that he had, and he became totally poor. Then there was a great famine in this country and people no longer had anything to eat. Only those who were very rich could still buy rice and cassava. And this man, who no longer had anything to eat, went into a village very far off in the bush.

There he found a man who had a herd of pigs. He said to him: "Do you have any work for me?" The man said: "Yes, I have work; keep my pigs!" [This is] because where the whites live there are herds of pigs, just as here there are herds of sheep and goats. The man said: "In the morning the hut for the pigs is opened and they are left to run. In the evening they are locked up again."

And so this man did the work without receiving any pay. The only pay he had was that this man gave him a little bit to eat. When he was very hungry, he went and ate some of the corn that was given to pigs.

So he lived poorly, almost dying of hunger. This was the man who had been so rich. Then he remembered and said: "At my father's house there are many servants, and each one has a lot to eat. Here I eat with pigs. I want to return. I want to throw myself on my knees before my father. Perhaps he will forgive me."

So he traveled home through many lands where there was a famine. And he finally arrived at his father's village in the country where there was no famine. He remained standing outside a long time, looking at his father's big cabin. He did not have the courage to go in.

The father, seeing a man standing outside, recognized from afar that it was his son. When the son saw his father coming, he ran toward him, threw himself to his knees, and said: "My father, I do not deserve to be your son. Let me be the least of your servants."

He was very much afraid that his father would say: "No, go away. I no longer want to see you. You are no longer my son." But the father took him by the arm, raised him up, and said to him: "You are my son." He led him to the cabin and called all his servants and told them: "Here is my son who was lost! His loincloth is completely torn. Find a beautiful loincloth for him. Go and kill a big goat. We are going to celebrate the return of my son."

So a feast was made—a great festival. Afterward the drums were played and all the servants danced.

The other son, who had always stayed at his father's house, then returned from the plantation where he had worked all day for his father. Near the house he heard the drumming and singing. "What is this feast?" he said. And he was told: "This is your brother, the idler, who has returned, and your father is giving him a feast." Then the brother became very unhappy: "What? My father gives a feast for the one who left, and he does not give a feast for me, who have always worked. He never said to me: "Here is a goat; have a good meal with your friends."

When the father heard him speak this way, he told him: "You must understand. Don't you see? You have had the good fortune to be always with me. But he, your brother, was miserable. He was hungry. His master beat him. Don't you want me to be good to him?" So the father spoke to him. He took him by the hand, drew him into the room, and made him sit with those who were joyful.

Why did Jesus tell this story to the people? To tell them that God loves all men, even those who have gone away and sinned against him, so that every man who has sinned, and who is utterly miserable, will have enough courage to return to God. Jesus had met men who said, "Oh, no! God cannot forgive us, who have caused so much evil." Perhaps there are some among you who are looking at their hearts and saying: "No, God will never want to forgive me. I have been too wicked. I have committed too many sins. God cannot forgive me." In order to give courage to all these to return to God, Jesus told this story. Because Jesus has told this story, those who preach the Word of God can say: "God forgives everyone who has sinned." For this reason we can say to all those who live in the sad country of sin: " Walk! Go to God! In God's house you will find forgiveness. In God's house you will find happiness and peace for your heart." Amen.

Let us pray to God: "Our Father, we are all thy sons who have left thee and not served thee. We live in a world of sin. We all need thee to forgive us. Grant that in our hearts we may come unto thee and ask thy forgiveness. May we, who have sought thy nearness, have joy and peace in our hearts and acknowledge all that thou hast forgiven us. Amen.

38. Sunday, 21 September 1930

The Parable of the Sower

Luke 8:4–15

The last time, I told you a story that Jesus told to people—the story about the son who went away and came back, and his father forgave him. Today I am going to tell you another story.

Jesus said to the people, "One day a man went to put seeds in the ground." You know that when you want to plant a tomato, you take the small seeds that are in the tomatoes and you put them in the ground. When you want to plant the papayas, you take the small seeds that are in the papaya and you put them in the ground. When you want to plant an orange tree, you take the small seeds that are in the orange and you put them in the ground.

Now in the land where Jesus lived, wheat was planted more than anything else. Wheat flour is made from the seeds of large plants, and these seeds are planted in the ground. So this man was going to plant the wheat. He had a small plantation in which he had thoroughly cleared the land, since, in the land where Jesus lived, people were not as lazy as they are here. Before planting the wheat, they cleared the ground thoroughly, and then they planted the wheat. When [the man] planted the wheat, he planted a section right next to the path where the ground was hard, and this wheat had practically no roots. When the sun came, it was dry. He sowed another part of the seed where there were pebbles on the ground. Then the seed could not go into the ground, and birds came and ate it. He planted another part in ground where there were roots of especially harmful plants. Then, when the rain came, those plants grew very rapidly and suffocated the wheat so that it could not grow. Part of the seed, which he had planted where the ground was good, grew up and had a lot of wheat, which was eaten all year long by his family.

What did Jesus mean by telling this simple story? The seed is the Word of God, and the ground in which it is planted is the hearts of men. When this ground is good, the Word of God can bear fruit in the hearts of men; but when the ground is bad, the Word of God cannot bear fruit. That is why men must pay attention to be sure that their hearts are good ground for the Word of God, in much the same way as I am now preaching to you the Word of God and asking you all: Are you doing all that you can so that your hearts may become good ground for the Word of God? Pay attention to your heart, because in your heart there are thoughts that are like birds that come and eat the good seeds of the Word of God.

In your heart there are thoughts that are like pebbles, which do not allow the Word of God to take root. In your heart there are harmful plants—thoughts that are very powerful and prevent the Word of God from having roots and growing up.

You yourselves, by listening to me now, you know that there are thoughts of this kind in your hearts. So, if you listen to the Word of God, you must say, "We do not want to be like the ground where there are pebbles, where birds come to eat the seeds. In our hearts, we want to be good ground for the Word of God."

When you have made a plantation, you know that after doing so it is necessary to make a clearing once again because otherwise the maize and the potatoes and the bananas cannot grow. So it is necessary to make a clearing in the heart, to clear out the bad thoughts. I want many of you to think about that—to make a clearing so that the Word of God can bear fruit within you. Amen.

Let us pray unto God! O God our Father, we thank thee for speaking thy Word and truth in the midst of men. May our hearts be good earth for thy Word. Grant us the power, always, to clear out the bad thoughts of our hearts, which are there, so that thy Word may be able to bear fruit in our hearts and we may be happy; because we all know that we are able to be truly happy if only thy Word is in our hearts. Amen.

39. Sunday, 28 September 1930

The Love of God

Matthew 22:34–40

The last time, we spoke about a story that Jesus told, about the story of a man who went to work on a plantation. Today I will speak to you about a saying of Jesus.

Once there was a man whom everyone knew [ ], and who came to the place where Jesus was and said to him, "What is the greatest law?" [This was] because the Jewish people had written all the laws in a great book, and all the children learned all the laws by heart. Then this man wanted to know what the greatest law was. Jesus replied, "This is the greatest law: You must love other men as you love yourself, and you must love God your Father."

You must love God, and you must love other men. You must love God! This seems completely natural, because God has been good to us. He sends the sun every morning. What would become of men if there were no sunshine? He sends the rain. What would become of men if there were only the dry season? They would all die. Isn't this so? They would have nothing that could bear fruit. That's why a man who reflects [thoughtfully] loves God; and a thoughtful man, who heard the first rain fall yesterday, thanked God that the rain fell so that the bananas could grow. So we love God because he has been good to us.

But when Jesus says, "You must love other men," this seems curious, because there are men who say, "I love my parents, I love my wife, I love my children, I love my aunt, I love my mother-in-law, I love my friends, I love these people because they are good to me." There are already a lot of people like these, who love those who have been good to them.

How many times here have we seen that the patients to whom we have done much good, whose lives we have saved, leave during the night with the mosquito netting and the blanket, without saying thank you to us? It is for this reason, first of all, that each man must [ ] love in his heart those who have been good to him. But Jesus does not only say, "Love God, and affirm, with love, those who have been good to you!" Jesus says, "Love all the men that you meet and who need you!" And you natives, you still do not understand that.

It often happens that we have a patient who cannot get up, so that it is necessary to help him. Then the physician says to another patient, "You can lift well, you can already walk, and you can go as far as Lambaréné without permission. This man is sick. He needs an attendant. He cannot get up. Be his attendant!" Then you know what happens? Is this other man good? No! He [doesn't] help him. "He is not a brother to me!" This is what happens, isn't it? Yes! And if tomorrow I asked for an attendant, he would not be the only one to reply, "No, he is not a brother to me!"

Look here! If I have some sick whites in there and I ask one white to be an attendant for another during the night, the white never says, "No, this one is no brother to me!"[39] This even happens when a sick man is brought in and there is another white person present. Without my saying something to him, he says, "Doctor, I am going to be an attendant for that one." Perhaps he is not a very good white; perhaps he is a man who shouts at natives, who is not very good, but he remembers that Jesus said, "One must love everyone." [This is] because all the whites have [this saying] in their hearts, because they have heard it since childhood: "One must love all men."

I will tell you something else. You sometimes see a soldier come with prisoners. Who sent them? Did you ever see a native chief who has a prisoner who is sick, and he sends him to the doctor's? Have you ever seen this? No! Because the native, who is not Christian, says, "He is a prisoner. If he dies, fine! It wasn't me who killed him." He dies—all alone. Isn't this true? And each of you, if you became chief now, would do the same thing. But from now on you can no longer do such a thing as this, because you have learned the saying of Jesus, "You must love all men"—prisoners as well.

Someday, when all rulers learn the saying of Jesus, they will do as Mr.

39. The situation is not one of racial prejudice, but of tribalism. Schweitzer's meaning here is that a person from one tribe does not consider someone from another tribe to be a human being of equal stature. In Gabon, a member of one tribe often would refuse to assist someone from another tribe. A member of another tribe was not considered a brother or a sister. This was upsetting Schweitzer, because he believed that all human beings were brothers and sisters in the eyes of God. According to Schweitzer, whites in his hospital would help blacks and whites equally, because all whites had been taught the words of Jesus, who said, "One must love everyone."

Pégnier.[40] When he learns that a prisoner is sick, he says, "I am going to send him to the doctor's." When a prisoner returns, you see that the doctor writes [ ] a large paper. And do you know what is written on the paper? He has written there, "Dear Mr. Pégnier, I thank you because you sent the prisoner who was so sick, because if you had not sent him, perhaps he would be dead, or his hand or foot would have rotted. I thank you, since perhaps the native did not thank you." And if a prisoner returns to Mr. Pégnier's after he has been nursed or operated on, he must go to Mr. Pégnier's and say, "I thank you for sending me to the doctor's."

I [want] to tell you something else. In the place where the whites live, when there is a woman who has a small baby [who is sickly], another woman is asked, "Take the small baby and feed it." And she gives [her own milk] to this poor little child, because she loves this poor little child. And very often she doesn't even ask, "Can I have a gift?" Why does the white woman do this? Because she knows the words of Jesus: "The greatest law is that you love another human being." But how is it in your country? When a native woman is asked to take the baby of another [woman] who has died, she says, "Oh no! This is not my baby." Isn't this true? Well then! I tell you that when this woman dies, Jesus will summon her to a great palaver. You know that [up there] we have two babies whom we nourish with milk the doctor has provided, because no woman wants to give her milk. And then we have tried to find a woman just so the little baby could be with her at night. Do you want me to have the baby lie down with a native boy, or have me put it with the goats and sheep? No! A baby is placed with a woman. Isn't this true? Well then! I looked for a woman but did not find her. I promised to give her splendid gifts [ ] in addition to many fine words from me. Do you know what she said? Galoan women and Pahouin women [are] like all the rest. "Unh! Unh! Unh!" [No! No! No!] Well then! Jesus will have a palaver with them all.

At last, I was overjoyed when the wife of Dominique, who is an old servant, said, "I [will] take the baby!" And the woman did not even ask, "Can I have a gift?" I am sure that not only the doctor and the nurses rejoiced but even the Lord Jesus himself, who said, "Here, finally, is a native woman who understands that one must love others as oneself." So that you understand this—that one must love others—I have told you all this.

---

40. It appears that Mr. Pégnier was an official at a nearby prison.

When someone preaches this saying of Jesus, "The greatest law is to love others as oneself," it is like a fisherman who is seated on a raft holding a fishhook. This saying of Jesus is like a fishhook that enters into the hearts of men. Then the man can no longer do what he wants, because he has a fishhook in his heart. And Jesus says, "You must not pull this hook out." Nobody who has once heard this saying, "The greatest law is to love other men," can ever forget it. And this Sunday morning God wants all of you who have heard this saying not to forget it. Amen.

Let us pray unto God! Everyone must place his or her hands together. O God our Father, who sendeth the sun and rain, may we love [one another] with all our hearts, as thou hast been good to us. And place in our hearts the great law that Jesus has given to the world, so that we love other men—not only those whom we know, but all men who need to be loved by us—because to have the love of Jesus Christ in our hearts is the sole happiness in all the world. Amen.

40. Sunday, 5 October 1930

The Great Pearl

Matthew 13:45–46

Jesus once told a very brief parable to those who listened to him. He said, "The Kingdom of God is like a merchant who buys pearls." Do you know what a pearl is? A pearl is a small white stone that is completely round. You have seen black women and white women who wear a ring that has a small stone that shines like a light. Nurses have no pearls and the doctor has no pearls, because they are not rich people, but perhaps you have already seen people with pearls. Pearls are very expensive. Now I am going to continue the story that Jesus told.

Jesus said that a merchant had found a far prettier pearl than all others, and so he decided to buy it. He asked, "What does it cost?" He was told a price that was very, very expensive; a price that he could not pay because he did not have the money. But to have this pearl he sold his house, his beautiful clothing; he sold everything—his plantation, all that he had—just to have this pearl. The other merchant was a rich man who had all that he wanted and many servants as well, but who did not have the pearl. The first merchant was a poor man who himself had to go to work on the plantations, but now he was happier because he had the pearl.

What curious story! A pearl cannot be eaten, and one cannot dress with a pearl. Nevertheless, this man was happy, far happier than before, when he was rich and could dress as he wished. What does Jesus mean by this story? He means this: "To be happy is not to be rich, or to have a house or a plantation and everything that you want. To be happy is something completely different. To be happy means to have joy in your heart." The man in this story had joy, the joy of the pearl in his heart. But there is a still greater joy in the heart, and that is the Kingdom of God. All men must know that the greatest joy is to have the Kingdom of God in your heart. Just as it was necessary to buy the pearl at such a great price, it is also necessary to buy the Kingdom of God.

A man, who wants to have the Kingdom of God cannot have peace in his heart by having everything that another man has. Another man can become rich by injustice, but the man who wants to have the Kingdom of God in his heart cannot act unjustly. Another can have those joys that the man who wants to have the Kingdom of God in his heart cannot have; he always asks, "Is this joy just? Is this right before God?" Another man, when someone has done something to him, can say, "Ah, I want to take vengeance!" He can say, "I want to do something bad to my enemy." And when he has done something bad to him, he is happy; he has joy. But the man who wants to have the Kingdom of God in his heart cannot have this joy.

An ordinary man, when he has earned a lot of money, when he has made a lot from his plantation, can say, "I want to eat all that. With my money I can buy everything I want." But when he has the Kingdom of God in his heart, he hears the voice of God, which tells him, "You see this man who is poor?" You see this man who has not nothing to eat? It is necessary to help him with your money, with fruit from the plantation." Now someone is proclaiming to you the Word of God. I tell you that here is the pearl that you must buy.

You cannot just say, "Yes, the Word of God is lovely; it gives me joy." No, you must have it in order to have joy in your heart. And in order to have the Kingdom of God in your heart, you cannot keep all the bad thoughts that you have in your heart. It is necessary to throw them out. So the great question is this: "Do you want to buy the Kingdom of God into your heart? Do you want to throw everything else outside?" During this week you have already chosen to have those thoughts that I want you to have, such thoughts as these in your hearts. And those who choose the Kingdom of God, they will be happy. And I would like many of you to be happy in your hearts. Amen.

Let us pray to God: O God, we all know that happiness in things that are not according to thy will is not happiness; that the man who has eaten all that he desires, who has all the money he wants, and who other men call happy, is not happy in his heart. The only happiness is to have thy Word in our hearts. Let us hunger and thirst for thy true happiness, and let thy Word dwell in our hearts. Amen.

41. Sunday, 9 November 1930

The Good Samaritan

Luke 10:29–37

I want to tell you a story today that Jesus told to the people who were around him, and I want all of you here—those who have already heard the Word of God as well as those who still have not heard it—to keep this story in your hearts so that you will never forget it.

A man had been to Jerusalem and had left the city to return to his village. His way led him through a region where the thieves were very wicked. He knew quite well that there were thieves in this region, but he hoped to be able pass through it without being robbed. He was not rich enough to pay for militiamen, as others did, to accompany and protect him. The thieves saw him, and they beat him and took all his money and all his belongings—everything that he had in his trunk—leaving him for dead, lying beside the road. Then, on this same day, another man from Jerusalem passed by this place, a man who was well acquainted with the Word of God.

Everyone in his village knew that he was a man who knew the Word of God very well. But when he saw this poor unfortunate man who was lying there beside the road, he said, "Oh, thieves have gone past here. I am going to run away so that I will be safe." And he passed by the side of the poor unfortunate man without even touching or looking at him. Well, was that a good thing to do? (*General murmur.*)[41]

A little while later, another man from Jerusalem passed by on the same path. He was a man equally well known and a very good man. He also passed by very quickly, without even looking at the injured man.

Later, yet again, another man came, who was from a different tribe than the man who had been injured by thieves. He was from the tribe of the Samaritans, as they were called, and his tribe was the enemy of the tribe of the injured man. This man, then, having come and seen that the man lying there was from the other tribe, should have passed him by and left him there. But no, it was he who stopped and looked at this man. He took him up, washed his wounds, and placed bandages on him made from his own undergarments. He had come by riding on his donkey. Do you know what a donkey or a jackass is, as they are called? This is a big animal on which whites sit so they won't get too tired when they go a long distance. But instead of remaining seated on the donkey, he placed the poor unfortunate man upon it, and he himself walked beside it so that [the injured man] would not fall off the donkey. So he walked with him in the blazing sun until the next village, which was very far away. And there he laid him down in a man's hut and said to the man, "Here is all the money I have." And there he left all the money that he had in his loincloth, and said, "This is for you." And he said to him once again, "Take this! Make a good bed for him, make good bandages for him, and give him something to eat until he is healed! And if this man remains sick for a long time in your house, and if there is not enough money, I will give you more when I return from my country."

Now I ask you all, did the men from the same tribe do good to the poor unfortunate fellow, or was it the man from the other tribe? (*Murmurs, various movements.*)[42] You see, those who are "savages" answer best.

41. The transcriber of this sermon has taken the liberty of entering into the text the spontaneous responses of Schweitzer's Sunday morning congregation.

42. Another response from the congregation, followed by Schweitzer's reply to it.

Now I put another question to you. Who among you has done the same thing? I could ask a Galoan: if he ever met a Pahouin just as unfortunate [as the man in the story], would he say to him, "Here is my brother. I want to save him"? No! I know that many of you, if you found someone else from another tribe and if you had to help him with something—if you had to lend him some money or something else—I know that there would be many who would say, "No, that fellow is not my brother. I'm not going to help him."

Now I want to tell you a story that happened when the doctor first came to the country of Gabon, in 1913, before the war. There was a white man who went up from Lambaréné to N'Djolé. He spent a very dark night in a village near Samkita. During the night, there was a tornado. After the tornado, they heard someone shouting, far off on the river—someone who did not stop shouting. The white lit his lantern and ran into the village, shouting, "Come quickly! You hear this man? His canoe has overturned! He is shouting for help. Come quickly to help him!" But the people of the village said, "Yes, we have heard him; he has been shouting for a long time. But he is not a Pahouin, he is a savage." Then the white took his cook, his servant boy, and three more paddlers whom he had found and to whom he had given gifts. He himself was going to find this poor man, who was clinging to his small canoe and who was already thoroughly exhausted, by dint of having shouted so much. When he returned to the village, this unfortunate man was completely soaked. [The white man] gave him a loincloth and a blanket and laid him down in a hut. The following morning, when he left in his canoe to go on to N'Djolé, [the white] said to the men of the hut, "Here is some money. Give him something to eat, and when he is completely rested, put him in a canoe and lead him back to his village."

This white knew the story that Jesus had told. And do you know what the people of the village did? When the white left, they stole the poor man's blanket and chased him out of the village. (*Laughter, protests.*)[43] You don't believe that the story is true and that it could still happen today? I need not tell you the stories of Samkita or Talagouga or Franceville. I need only tell you stories from the village of the hospital. When a poor unfortunate is brought in who cannot walk, and who has no one to get his food or bring him water, and when the doctor says to the person in the bed next to

43. The congregation responds again.

him, who is able to walk quite well, "Be a good attendant to him," the other one replies, "This fellow is not even my brother."

So then, here is this story that Jesus told just for you. That is why I wanted to put this story into your heart—as if I had made a hole in your heart, put this story inside it, and sewn it all up again. I want it to stay in your heart so that it can no longer ever leave it. I want the time to come that whenever you have the desire to say or to think these words, "This one is not my brother," this story will gnaw into your heart like a worm, so that you may know and never forget what the Lord Jesus has said to all the peoples of the earth, whether they be white or black: that they are all brothers. Amen.

Let us pray unto God: God our Father, who art in heaven, thou knowest how wicked our hearts are. Let the Lord Jesus Christ put love into our hearts; and may this fire of love burn always in our hearts, so that we may be thy children and want to be good. Grant us the power to love all men. Grant us the strength, this week, to love all the people who are in the hospital. And this week, may we neither say nor think, "That one there is not my brother." Amen.

42. Sunday, 23 November 1930

To Love God

Matthew 22:35–40

There are many laws in the Word of God. It is forbidden to lie. It is forbidden to kill. Many things are forbidden.[44]

One day a man who read a great deal in the Word of God said to Jesus, "Dear master, what is the greatest law?" And Jesus said to him, "The greatest law is that you must love God with all your heart." And it is this law that all those who proclaim the Word of God should announce over all the

---

44. This is an abrupt beginning to the sermon summarizing two of the Ten Commandments.

earth. And when I proclaim it to you, I think that there are men among you who do not know that there is a God.

Before white missionaries came to your place, you believed that there were many spirits and fetishes. There were witch doctors and old people who taught you this, and all of you were afraid of the witch doctors and spirits. Now we tell you there is only one God. Until now, you were men who had chains on both hands and feet—not chains of iron but chains of fear that are as terrible as those [of iron].

We come to tell you not only that there is one God, but also that we must love God; and this point needs to be considered—why love God? The great news that we proclaim to you is this: to love God. We love the sun when it rises, when we see the rain, when we see bananas mature, when we see other fruit come. We believe it is there in simple fact; we do not reflect. But the man who reflects knows that God gives all this. And so you see that today the sun has risen just like that. We have to thank God for sending the sun. We can give a man something to show him that we love him, but we can give nothing to God. I wish that you all loved God and that you understood what it is to love God. I wish that the woman who put bananas in the pot would reflect and say to herself, "It is a good God that has let the bananas grow so that I can have something to eat."

There are some men—and there are already even some blacks—who believe themselves wise because they know how to read and write a bit and who say, "There is no God." They say, "I have never seen God, I have never heard God, nobody has ever revealed God. Therefore I do not believe that there is a God." These men are blind in their hearts, because those who have good hearts see by the heart and know that there is a God. So it is that we all want to understand the Word of Jesus, "The first law is that you shall love God, your Father, with your whole heart. And those who love God in their hearts are happy. And I wish that many of you might become happy by loving God in your hearts. Amen.

Let us pray to God: Oh God, we pray unto thee. Grant that we may love thee in our hearts, as we ought to love thee. We all know that a heart that does not love thee is sad and miserable. We all want to become happy. Grant us, therefore, the love of thee in our hearts so that we may be happy. Amen.

43. Sunday, 7 December 1930

The Second Sunday of Advent

You all know that in three weeks Christians will celebrate a great holiday. This holiday is called Christmas and means that Jesus, the King of hearts, is born. And these Sundays that come before this feast of Christmas—these four Sundays—are called the Sundays of Advent. During these Sundays, Christians prepare their hearts to celebrate Christmas well. And they reflect: In what sense did Jesus, the King of hearts, come into the world? And you also, who are here now with Christians, we want you to think about these Sundays that are about the coming of Jesus into the world.

We all know that the King of hearts has come to create the Kingdom of love. Kings, emperors, the president of the republic, ministers, rulers—all the great men—order other men about. They command and say, "If you do not obey, I will punish you." They protect people who kill, they protect people who steal, they command that people pay taxes, and they order many other things as well. But have you ever seen an order, or a ruler, which commanded men to love other men, to forgive them, or to be good to them? Nevertheless, are people happy in a country, or in a village, or in a family, if they are not good to each other, and if they do not love one another? This is why Jesus has come, the King of hearts who governs the hearts of men and who has said: "I want you to love one another." This is why he is the greatest of kings.

Rulers and administrators each have a small country where they are in control. When they go far away and are no longer in their country, there is no longer anyone who obeys them. But what Jesus has said, all men—the whole world, as far as there are men—have to obey. Rulers, commanders, and kings are obeyed only because they have militiamen and soldiers. If the commander did not have soldiers to catch those who do not pay their taxes, would you pay the tax? Not even Miss Mathilde, not even Miss Emma, not even the doctor would pay the tax, because no one would catch them. And in each village, it would be announced, "The commander no longer has militiamen, so it is no longer necessary to obey him; you can do what you like." Well then, the Lord Jesus himself does not have a single militiaman, but nevertheless there are thousands of men and whole peoples who obey him. When a chief or a commander or a king is dead, one no longer obeys him. You have never found someone who said, "I obey a ruler who died a long time ago." But Jesus died a long, long time ago. A hundred years have passed and yet another hundred years, and still many more years, but nevertheless people obey him even more than when he was alive. You can see that there is in my heart a voice that obeys Jesus—you see it here, before your eyes, entirely before your eyes. Who was it that built this hospital? It was not the doctor by himself. The doctor has only built [it] because the Lord Jesus told him, "You must love all the people here in Gabon and you must take care of them." This hospital is therefore a village of the Kingdom of Jesus. Therefore all of you who come to this hospital need not ask, "But is it true that there is a Kingdom of Jesus?" You see it before you, the Kingdom of Jesus.

And these Sundays before Christmas, we all thank God to have finally sent the King of hearts into the world. We wonder if Jesus is already truly the King of hearts in our hearts—if we obey him enough. All of you who are here, and also these who still have heard almost nothing of Jesus, ask yourselves, "Do we believe that there is a King of hearts and are we beginning to obey him?" I want each of you to ask, "Is Jesus the King of my heart and is it through him that I become a good man?" Because when a man gives his heart to Jesus, he is happy. He has peace in his heart. And when he does not give it, he is miserable, for he does not have peace. And I want all of you to be happy and for you to have peace in your hearts. Amen.

44. Christmas, 25 December 1930

The King of Hearts

While we are here together, all Christians throughout the world are also celebrating Christmas. I want everyone in the entire world to celebrate this holiday with a good heart. Today there are Christians among us who already know the Word of God. You see there are those who already have the book [the Bible]. There are some others among you who have never celebrated a Christmas holiday. There are some among you who know practically nothing about Jesus Christ. Nevertheless, they are able to celebrate Christmas well, since it is enough that they know the most important thing: that Jesus Christ, the King of hearts, has come into their land. What we all have to know— those who know a great deal about the Word of God and those who know practically nothing—is that there is a King who wants to reign in our hearts. What is necessary today is that you might know, and that you might sense, that your heart is poor when Jesus Christ is not the King of your heart. There is no need to explain what this means, even to those who do not know the Word very well: Jesus must be the King of your hearts. The voice of the King of hearts is heard in our hearts—in the heart of one who is far away in his village where there is no missionary and in the heart of one who is far away in his lumber camp where there is no missionary. He cannot say, "I do not know who the King of hearts is," because he hears the voice in his heart.

This is what Christmas means to all of us: believe that Jesus is the King of hearts! Listen to the voice in your heart that tells you, "This you must do; this you must not do." Those who understand the voice of the King of hearts will be happy.

We all want to be happy. When people want to become rich, why do they want this? Because, they say, "When we are rich, we will be happy." When a man has an enemy who wants revenge, he believes that when he has done a lot of bad things to his enemy, when that enemy has become very unhappy, then he will be happy. However, we know that there is a King of hearts, and that we will be happy when it is he who reigns in our hearts. This is why we want to find real happiness, so that we can celebrate Christmas with great joy—we who are old, you who are young—because we know that we are able to become happy. Amen.

Let us pray unto God: God our Father, we thank thee that thou hast sent Jesus Christ, the King of our hearts; and we pray thee, grant that he may truly be the King of our hearts. Grant that our hearts may obey him so that that we may be happy, and that we may have peace and tranquility in our hearts. Amen.

PART FOUR

The 1931 Sermons

45. n.d.[1]

The Garden of Eden (A Fragment)[2]

Genesis 1–2

You see the sun? Who made the sun? You see the plantation with the bananas, the taro, the cassava? Who made all that grow? Who sends the rain
and the sun? You see the river Ogooué? Who made it? Who made the N'-
Gounié? Who made the forest and the earth on which we walk? Everyone
knows this, so say it. Well! It is God. God has created everything. The
Word of God tells us all this.

Formerly there was neither day nor sun. It was always night and cold
like the rain in the night. There was neither the forest nor the plantation,
neither the river, nor the earth, neither goats nor chickens, neither men
nor women. There was only the night and God. But God worked without
rest and he made the sun and he ruled the day and the night. Then God
made the sky, with clouds to cover it and give rain; God worked two days to
do this. We do not know how he did this, we know only that God made the
day and the night and the sky. But the water flowed everywhere and God

1. The typewriter used in this fragment is the same as the one used to transcribe the sermons dated between 14 September 1930 and 1 February 1931. Before and thereafter, different typewriters were used. Thus this fragment probably dates between 14 September 1930
and 1 February 1931.

2. The sermon has two sections. The transcriber apparently has made an error by re-
versing the sections. We know this because the sermon follows the story of Adam and Eve in
Genesis. Therefore I have rearranged the sermon to reflect Schweitzer's intended sequence.

began to give order to it. He made such rivers as the Ogooué and the N'-Gounié, and sandbanks, and the earth to walk upon, and all the lakes, and the sea. And soon God made the grass to grow, and the trees of the forest, and trees with fruit. He made the bananas to grow, and the taro—and God was pleased because the earth was beautiful and all the work was good. But still God did not rest, because the work was not finished. God made the fish in the sea and great and small and other animals. Then in the bush he placed the antelopes and the boar and the monkeys and the birds. The leopard lay down next to the goats and neither hurt them nor ate them. The birds had no fear of snakes or tiger cats.[3]

So God worked five days to arrange all that, but still he was not satisfied. The grass sprouted where it wished. There was no one to eat the bananas and the oranges and the potatoes and all such things. Then, on the sixth day, God took some earth and formed a man, and he breathed into his nose, and there was the first man who walked. God gave him the name of Adam.

And God appointed him the chief of the earth, the master of all animals. Adam gave a name to each animal and a name to each tree. Adam arranged the plantation, and all the earth seemed to him like a pretty garden. But Adam was sad to be the only man. Then God made him fall fast asleep, and during this time he made a woman for him and called her Eve. The two of them walked without loincloths, entirely naked, and they were totally happy. Adam knew that God had given him the woman. Eve knew that God had given her Adam, and then they loved each other.

46. 1 February 1931

A Heart Prepared

It has not been too long since we celebrated the New Year. Perhaps, when we celebrated this New Year, you did not think, "Will I still be able to celebrate another New Year?" Nevertheless, it is true that there are those who

---

3. This is not from Genesis but an interpolation of Isaiah 65:25.

have celebrated the New Year with us who may not celebrate another New Year with us. I think that there are many among you who have not considered this. They have not thought that this New Year, which has come, may be the last new year of their lives. They have said to themselves, "I am young. It is only the old who are going to die." They have said to themselves, "I am not sick. It is only the sick who may die." Possibly in this way they have not thought of anything that they should be thinking about. They think only, "Am I ready to live?" They think only about earning money. They think only of living for pleasure. They think of the wicked things that they have in their hearts. They think only of the hatred they have for their enemies. But their hearts do not think, "Am I ready to die?"

All of us are servants of God—servants whom God has sent to walk far. One day he calls them to his home. He calls them to his home from this path that is life. And he will ask them, "What have you done there, in the place where I sent you into life?" And there are many there who will not know how to answer because they walked though life completely forgetting that it was God who sent them into life, and that one day he will call them back. And then God says to them, "Show your heart!" Then he looks at the horrible heart. And then God says, "You have come back to my house with a heart full of all these things!" Then the man becomes full of fear, and he trembles and says, "God, forgive me!"

When God says "Show your heart!" to a man who has considered death—a man who has cast out all his bad thoughts along the way, just as we would throw away something along a path—then God sees that he has thought of him. And he finds in this heart thoughts of God. And he sees that this man has not forgotten to think of him along the path of life, and that he has thought to return to God through death. Then God tells him, "You are a child who has returned to his father." "Be happy in your father's house!" he tells him. And so our Lord Jesus Christ, when he preached to men, always said to them, "Ponder the fact that you must die!" And so Jesus wants to say to everyone, "Bear in mind that this New Year may be the year when you're going to die!" Amen.

Place your hands together and pray unto God: O God our Father, thou who hast sent us into life and who callest us from life, let us never forget that thou wilt call us from life through death. May we always think of death, so that our hearts will be ready to return to thy house. Thou art our Father, and thou wilt receive us as a father receiveth his child. Amen.

47. 15 February 1931

Doing Good

Matthew 25:14–30

Last time, I spoke about death, and I told you that every man, when he returns to God [ ].

Today I want to tell you a story that Jesus told to men. There was a man who had a large plantation, and he went into another city. He had four chiefs among his servants. To these four chiefs he gave some money. He gave each one some money. "Here is the money that I am giving you to work with, to oversee the plantations and to conduct trade, and when I return [ ]." He did not give all of them the same amount of money. To the first he gave a lot, to the second a bit less, to the third a bit less still, and to the fourth very little. And then he went away.

He stayed away for a long time. When he returned, he called the four men. He said to them, "Show me what you have earned with my money." And the first, who had received a lot of money, told him, "Here is the money that you have given me, and here is the money that I have earned." And the master said to him, "Here is a good servant. You will have a good reward." And the second was called: "Come and account for what you have earned." "Here is the money that I have received, and here is the money that I have earned." "This is good. You will have a good reward."

The fourth came and said, "I know that you are a hard master. If I did some business and lost the money, my master would put me in prison. This is why I put the money in an iron box and hid it in my garden, and now I am bringing it back to you. You cannot say that I have stolen it from you. I am bringing you the money." And the master said, "Put him in prison, because I gave him money to earn more money for me, not to put in the ground. He has not been faithful. He is lazy. That is why he will be punished."

What does this story mean? It means that God has given life to each of us, so that we may make [ ], and when life is over and we return to God, he will ask us, "What have you done with your life? Show me the good you have done." And he will ask, "What have you done with your intelligence?"

If the man cannot reply, God will say to him, "Go away!" [The people reply] "We have obeyed people." [God responds] "This is not enough.

What good have you done? What good have you done for them?" [The people answer] "I have done good service." [God rejoins] "This is not enough. What good did you do for them? Didn't you hit them?"

And so he will ask administrators, doctors, and commanders, "What good have you done?" [But some of you may be thinking,] "However, we are poor hardworking black people living in our village. He cannot ask a lot from us. I am a pauper [ ]."

Another story. When Jesus preached for the last time, he told them that when the Last Judgment comes upon men they will be divided—these to the left, these to the right. Those on the right will be told, "You are the children of God." The others will be told, "God does not want to see you." Then they will all be surprised, and among those to the right there will be some who will say, "How frightened I was, and here I am among the good ones." And then Jesus will say, "I was a prisoner and you came to me. I was sick. I had no clothes. And you said, 'Here is a loincloth.' I was hungry and I had nothing to eat, I was thirsty and I had nothing to drink. [And you said, 'Here is something to eat. Here is something to drink.']"

Then all these people will say, "But we never saw you. When did we give you something to drink, to eat, and so on?" And Jesus will smile, and he will say, "You did not do it for me, but you did it for the poor, and what you did for a pauper is the same as if you did it for me. And all that a man does for a pauper, I know without someone telling me." And to the others he will say, "You also have met poor people. You have never been good to them, and I do not want to see you." And so God will ask us one day—everyone from the hospital of Lambaréné will be asked—"Have you helped the poor? The sick needed to drink, but you said, 'No! You are not my brother.'" And God knows all those who have cooked for others. He knows those who have fetched water for others and those who have said, "This one is not my brother." He will know these: the one who has said, "I want to cast him into the river," and those who have said, "No! He is not my brother." He will judge them according to these things. Amen.

Let us pray. God our Father, you have given a heart to each of us so that we may do good, and none of us is so small or so poor that there is no goodness in our hearts. And you will judge whether we have been good in our hearts. May we be faithful servants according to the heart, so that that one day, when we have sfinished our life, you will be able to say, "Oh come, children of God."

48. 1 March 1931

The Salt of the Earth

Matthew 5:13–16

Among the sayings that our Lord Jesus Christ said, there is one that is very curious. This saying is, "You, you are the light of the world." It says also, "You are the salt of the world." What does that mean? How can a man be the light of the world and also the salt of the world?[4]

The man who has the Spirit of God is the light of the world and the salt of the world because he brings this Spirit of God to others. A light, when it is lit, gives light to everything. When one puts salt on what he wants to eat, all the food is made good by the salt. This means that the Word of God that you hear now has to be known by others. You are here in this hospital, and on Sunday mornings you hear the Word of God. Then, when you return to your home in your village, where others do not yet know the Word of God, then the Word of God must come through you. Each of you must be like a torch that one lights in a village. Each likewise should be like the salt that is brought into the village, of which everybody says, "We are happy to have this salt."

Because, truly, if someone has understood the Word of God, he has to speak about it to others. When you return to your village, you have to speak of what you have seen. They will ask you, "What has happened to you since you left?" Then one says a lot of things. But if you return, you first have to say, "I have heard the Word of God." And when you are with someone, you have to tell him, "Now, I want to explain to you what the Word of God is." You must say that the Word of God is this: that all men must be good and not lie like some others.

We know that some men and women have already returned to their village and said, "At the hospital we have heard the Word of God." And then the people have said, "Tell us all that you know about this Word of God." You must do the same when you return to your village.

But you must announce the Word not only by what you say, but espe-

---

4. Please note that Schweitzer uses the French word *monde*, for "world," rather than the word *terre*, for "earth," throughout his preaching.

cially by your manner of life. The light does not say, "I am there," but each one sees that it is there. The salt does not speak, nor does it say, "I am there," but everyone who eats this dish feels that the salt is there, inside, and that it is good. So people have to see and feel that the Word of God is in you. They must say, "We have known this woman and this man before. He lied, he stole, he was wicked, and he showed no kindness to animals and men. This same one does not lie anymore, does not steal, and is good. It is the Word of God that has done that in him." If you return in this way, as another man because you know the Word of God, then you are like the light and like the salt for your village. And when Miss Emma and I preach the Word of God every Sunday,[5] it is with the hope that this Word will go with you to your village. And we ask that God bless our word that we address to you. Amen.

Let us pray together: God our Father, grant us strength to have thy Word in us; grant that men may see that by thy Word, we have become different men; grant that they may say that we have the Word of God in our hearts, and, thus, that all villages may know thy Word and become thy children. Amen.

49. 22 March 1931

Listen to God

You know that soon there will be a great holiday called Easter, and before the feast of Easter there is the feast of Good Friday. Good Friday is the feast of the death of Jesus, and fifteen days from today there will be the feast of Easter.

You know that Jesus died. He did not die because of a sickness; he died because men killed him. The chiefs of the people made a large cross from wood, and with nails they nailed Jesus on the cross until he was dead. Jesus knew he had to die, because Jesus had read the hearts of men. If Jesus were

---

5. Emma Haussknecht was one of Schweitzer's secretaries and nurses in Lambaréné. She also preached from time to time, but we do not have her sermons.

among us, he would know how to read the heart of each of us. So it is that he read the hearts of the men who said, "We want to kill this man." Why did the people want to kill Jesus? Because Jesus told them how wicked they were and because he told the truth to the chiefs. He told them that it was not right that they made war in order to kill men. He told them that it was not right that they cheated when they collected the taxes. He told them that it was not right how they governed the palavers—how they judged, not according to justice but according to the gifts given them. Then the chiefs said, "If we said all that to the people, the people would no longer obey us."

They also saw that Jesus won the hearts of all men. Then they said, "It is necessary to kill this man so that he does not win the hearts of men." It was the great chiefs of the city of Jerusalem who thought so, but they could do nothing because Jesus was not in Jerusalem. He was far away in the country villages, and there, where Jesus was, all the people of the villages supported him, and they surrounded Jesus so nobody could come to kill him. If Jesus had never gone to Jerusalem, the chiefs would not have been able to kill him, because he would not have been there. Therefore Jesus could not have been killed if he had not gone to Jerusalem. You understand that. It is like someone far away in the bush who cannot be made captive: only when he is here in Lambaréné can he be captured.

Jesus knew all that, but he did not say anything. He continued to preach the Word of God. He did not say, "Oh, I know that you chiefs of the people want to kill me." Because Jesus knew that he heard the voice of God in his heart, he thought only one thing: "Is it the will of God that I have to die or is it not the will of God?" Every man can hear a little bit of the voice of God in his heart. But men usually do not listen to the voice of God in their hearts. The noise of the bad thoughts in their hearts prevents them from hearing the voice of God. But when Jesus listened to the voice of God in his heart, he understood that he had to die. And he told his disciples, the apostles, "Come, we are going to go up to Jerusalem." The city was on a mountain. And when the apostles heard, "Come, we are going up to Jerusalem," they said, "No, you must not go up to Jerusalem; they are going to kill you." But Jesus did not listen to them. And he left with them to go die in Jerusalem. Amen.

Let us pray unto God. God our Father, Jesus listened to thy voice in his heart. But we poor men, we often do not listen to the voice in our hearts, and we are not obedient to thy voice. May we listen better to thy voice in our hearts, and may we become obedient as well. Amen. May the peace of Jesus be with you all. Amen.

50. 29 March 1931

Palm Sunday

Today is the beginning of the great Christian holidays. This Sunday is called Palm Sunday. You will understand why this Sunday is the beginning when you have heard the story that I am going to tell.

At the feast of Easter, all the Jewish people went to Jerusalem to celebrate Easter in the great church of Jerusalem. Easter was celebrated in the Jewish country in remembrance that God had saved the Jewish people from their enemies, the people of Egypt.

Then Jesus went to the feast of Easter at Jerusalem with all the people who came from his country. And with all these men he came to a small town before he came to Jerusalem, a town that was called Jericho. And there was a man who was blind and who sat on the road because he had heard that Jesus would pass by. And he was there when he heard Jesus pass by, and so he called out, "Jesus, have pity on me!" And when Jesus heard this man call him, Jesus said, "Bring this man!" When the man was in front of Jesus, Jesus said to him, "What do you want me to do?" And then the man said, "I want to see again!" Then Jesus healed him and the man could see again.

You know that physicians can also cure the blind by cutting with the knife as the woman doctor does, or with medicines.[6] But Jesus knew how to heal without medicines, solely by the Word. And when all the people saw that this man was healed, they were filled with joy.

And then, when Jesus entered Jerusalem, it was as a king coming into the city. Men sang hymns. Jesus sat on an ass. Where the whites live, kings

6. Some of the physicians at Schweitzer's hospital were women. This must have been the one who did eye surgery successfully. We have no further information about her.

do not go on foot, but sit on a horse or another animal. Then, so that the King of hearts did not have to walk on the ground, the people placed their loincloths on the ground so that he could walk on top of them. That is how it is done where the whites live. Others cut branches of palm trees and put them on the ground so that the ass walked on top of them and not on the dirty ground. They did this for Jesus, as for a king who enters a city. It began when he came into Jerusalem. And all the people of the great city of Jerusalem were surprised and said, "Who is this great king who comes?" And the people who came with Jesus said, "This one is Jesus, the King of hearts."

And then the rulers of the people and the priests were very sad and said, "Now this Jesus whom we want to kill has come with many people, like a king, and we cannot do anything to him!" During the day Jesus went into the great church of Jerusalem and spoke the Word of God to everyone. And in the evening he left the city in order lie down in the house of friends in a little village near the city. And so every morning he went into the great temple to speak the Word of God and in the evening he went to his friends' house. He did so for several days until Thursday evening. On Thursday, at night, the rulers took him prisoner, and Friday morning they killed him. This is the reason why we celebrate the death of Jesus on Friday. Amen.

Let us pray unto God: God our Father, today Jesus came as King of hearts to Jerusalem. May he come into our hearts as the King of our hearts. May he rule our hearts with good thoughts as the king who brings peace to our hearts. Amen.

51. 3 April 1931

Good Friday

Today is the day of the death of our Lord Jesus. I want to tell you how he died. That evening—yesterday evening, on Thursday—he returned from Jerusalem to a small village where he rested at the home of friends. He had been at dinner with the apostles, and when it was night he left. He was in a garden with great trees. And then, suddenly, the garden was filled with militiamen, rulers, and priests. As it was night, they would not have been able to recognize the Lord Jesus. But then there was one of the apostles who was wicked, and he had been given money so that he might betray Jesus. Those of you who are Christian know the name: he was called Judas. And those very rulers had given him money so that he might show them [the rulers] who Jesus was. So Judas went to him, and then the militiamen knew which one was Jesus, [even though] it was dark and they could not see. And they took him prisoner. And they brought him to the great ruler of the people, who was sitting there that night in order to conduct the palaver. And then Jesus was brought before the council of rulers to say what he had done wrong. And then they called witnesses, and no witness would say anything bad.

This surprised the rulers. They should have allowed Jesus to leave, because he was innocent. But they wanted to kill Jesus, because they knew that he was the King of hearts. And then finally the great ruler said, "Is it true that you are the Son of God according to the Spirit, and that you are the King of hearts?" Then Jesus said, "Yes." Then they said, "Now we are going kill you! How can it be that you, a poor man, are a king that God has sent for hearts?" But the rulers of the Jewish people could not kill anybody, because in their country the Roman people were the primary rulers. It is like here: the native chiefs don't have the right to kill a man. They must go to the administration. So in the morning they went to the great Roman ruler, who was called Pontius Pilate. And the great Roman administrator said, "What has this man done?" The Jewish rulers said this and that. At the end Pontius Pilate said, "I do not find anything wrong. I cannot condemn him."

And while he was sitting there, his wife sent a boy to him with a message that said: "Above all, do not condemn this man. He is innocent. I have dreamed a lot about him tonight." And while he was conducting the palaver, many people woke up and came to the great administrator's house. Then he told the people, "See, I have here Jesus, whom you like a lot, and here is a man who has done much evil. He is called Barabbas. Soon there will be a great feast. To make you happy, I want to free a prisoner. Do you want Jesus or Barabbas?" He thought that they would all say, "We want Jesus!"

But then the rulers went among the people and said to them, "No, don't ask for Jesus. You must ask for Barabbas." Then they all shouted, "No, we don't want Jesus, we want Barabbas." And then the great adminis- trator said, "What must I do with Jesus?" And they said, "Make him die upon the cross!" So the great administrator, Pontius Pilate, said, "Well, let him be killed!"

Then militiamen took Jesus and stripped him of his garments, beat him, and put a crown on him with branches of thorns that sting greatly, and they said, "So, you are a king. You will be crowned." And after that they led him to the cross on a small mountain near Jerusalem. And there, with two other men who had each been put on a cross, they nailed his hands and feet to the cross. And then one of these two who were on the cross—the one who was very wicked— said, "Well, you who are a king, now help us!" And the other said, "You who are a king, think of me when you come into your kingdom." And Jesus said to him, "Even today you will be with me in heaven." And Jesus said still a few more words, and he called God his Fa- ther, and suddenly he died.

And when he was dead, there was a man who was very pious. He was called Joseph, of the village of Arimathea. And this man went to the great administrator and said, "Give me the body of Jesus, I want to bury it." And the great administrator said, "You can take it." And then he left. He took the body from the cross. He wrapped the body and placed it in a tomb that he had carved for himself in a rock. At that time the people did not make tombs as we make them, but they carved them in a mountain so that they could go inside. And he put the body in a large white linen cloth and placed it in the tomb and put a large rock in front of the tomb to close the entry. And when he was finished, it was evening, like now, and he went back. Amen.

Let us pray unto God: O God our Father, we thank thee that thou hast sent the Lord Jesus Christ into the world. The Lord Jesus Christ has to be the King of hearts. The men who lived with him killed him because they wanted to be the King of hearts and because they did not believe him. But we know that he is the King of hearts and that he died in obedience to thee, because it was thy will that he die. And may he be King of our hearts. Amen.

52. 5 April 1931

Easter

Today is Easter. Easter means that Jesus did not stay in the tomb, that he is not dead for always, but that he lives—that he lives also in our hearts. The rulers of the people believed that Jesus was dead; the apostles were afraid and hid themselves. But this was not so, because when Jesus was dead, suddenly the apostles saw him. We cannot explain how this happened, but it was certain. The Lord Jesus was not dead forever. But they understood what Jesus had told them: "God will allow me to die and only then will I be the real King of hearts." So then, instead of hiding, they went into the streets and said, "Jesus is the real King of hearts. He is not dead. He lives as spirit near to God."

Then many others believed the same thing. And even when the rulers of the people put them in prison, even when they killed some among them, they nevertheless had no fear. And if we celebrate Easter, we should think also of all these first Christians who were thrown in prison, who were mistreated by the militiamen, because they said, "Jesus is the King of hearts as spirit." And today we say, "We believe that Jesus is the King of hearts, although he is no longer among us, except as spirit."

You also believe in spirits. In your country there are people who say that they have seen spirits in the forest. Is this not true? When we say, "Jesus is spirit," it is a completely different thing. This is not a spirit such as you believe you see in the forest. We say, "Jesus is a spirit who must live in our hearts, who must be alive in our hearts."

Today, many people celebrate Easter. And the ones who celebrate Easter most joyfully say, "Jesus, King of hearts, I open my heart to you so that you are the King in my heart." And to those among you who are celebrating Easter, I wish that he might become the King in your heart, beginning today. Amen.

Let us pray unto God: Today in all the world we celebrate that Jesus is not dead but lives as spirit in the house of God and in our hearts. This also we want to believe, and we want to open our hearts to Jesus and to all the good thoughts that come from him. Amen.

53. 19 April 1931

No False Witness

Matthew 27:3–5

When I told you last time about the death of Jesus, I also told you the name of Judas. You know that Judas was one of the Twelve Apostles. And when a Christian says the name of this man Judas, he says it with great sadness, because Judas is the apostle who betrayed the Lord Jesus, and he betrayed him in a palaver, with a lie. And each one of you says, "It was a wicked man who betrayed Jesus." But you know that Judas was not alone in betraying Jesus, who was his brother and who had done him good. Too often we see men who begin to betray others. Even in your own country you see a man give a false testimony about someone else. Then that one is punished, perhaps killed, and the other one thinks, "Oh well!"

And among those who are prisoners there are surely some who are innocent but have been condemned because men have lied. Isn't it true? And then the people who have lied, and perhaps have received a gift for lying, think, "Now I am happy, I have money." They do not think about the other one, who is miserable. But you know that they are not happy because they lied. Their hearts are not happy. Likewise, Judas said, "When I have the money (for betraying Jesus), I will be able to live happily ever after. I will be able to buy all that I want in the stores." And this is the way it was with Judas. But listen, what happened to him? When he betrayed Jesus, his heart began to speak. He went to the place where the rulers of the people were and said, "What I have said against Jesus is not true. Take your money, but do not kill Jesus!" But the rulers of the people laughed, "The palaver is over. We are going to kill him. You do not have to do anything more." And then Judas went to throw the money into the great church at Jerusalem, and he said, "I do not want it any longer!" And then he went to kill himself. He no longer wanted to live. And all this is written in the Word of God for all those who want to betray others for money and to be unjust, so that they might consider this and realize that they will not be happy, but only miserable. Amen.

Let us pray unto God: O God, thou art our Father. Thou knowest also that we can be tempted to betray men and to bear false witness. Thou knowest how much lying there is in our hearts and how much we are tempted to lie for gifts. Then help our hearts, that they may be strong, so that they may not prove false, and not be miserable like Judas. Let us always reflect that it is not money that gladdens, but the peace that lieth in our hearts. Amen.

54. 3 May 1931

St. Stephen

Acts 7

You know some natives who are called Stephen? Is there someone here called Stephen? He must get up! (Stephen, the uncle of Aloÿse, got up).[7] Today I am going to tell you the story of the first Christian who was called Stephen.

When Jesus was dead, the apostles hid themselves with the other Christians. They feared that the rulers of the people would also put them in prison. And they prayed in the cellars of some people. And everyone said, "It is not possible that God has sent such a poor man like Jesus, who was crucified, to be the King of hearts." There were some people who said, "Here are our kings. We don't need a King of hearts. This would be stupid." And so the people were frightened. But there were also some people who were not afraid, and one of those was named Stephen. And this Stephen called the people and the priests and said, "Come, we are going to talk." He said to them, "Take the book of the Word of God and read what is written." He showed them all the sayings of God where there was a mention of whom God was going to send into the world. They were obliged to recognize that, yes, this is what is written, and if it is written, it is true that Jesus is the King of hearts that God has sent into the world. Then some

7. The transcriber is identifying the person. Aloÿse is also mentioned in sermon 15.

men got angry and said, "This man must be killed." They did not want to listen to him.

Then they called all the people and said, "Look at this! He speaks against the priests; he speaks against the rulers. He is a wicked man—he must be killed." And they did not ask who he was. That one shouted this; this one shouted that. They saw only that he was a man they wanted to kill. They dragged him out of the city. They gathered stones and threw them at this poor Stephen until he was dead. And when Stephen was almost dead, he prayed again. He prayed, "O God, do not punish them, they do not know!"

And one of those men, who was the first to look for stones, was called Saul. And this Saul was the one who was later to become the Apostle Paul; a few weeks later he became a Christian.

Stephen is the first Christian who died for Jesus. That is why each one of you must know who Stephen is and what his name means. And if you meet a man who is called Stephen, you must remind yourself of what I have told you, that the one who is called Stephen should know what a beautiful name this is, and that he must be a good man. Amen.

Let us pray unto God: O God our Father, we thank thee today that those who want to become Christians are no longer persecuted. May we recognize that those times are gone, and that we are able to love Jesus without suffering. And may we, through this knowledge, seek to become true Christians. Amen.

55. 17 May 1931

The Conversion of Paul

Acts 9:1–31

Last time, I told you about the death of the first Christian who was called Stephen. Jewish men killed him with the stones that they threw at his head. There was a man present who said that it was necessary to kill Stephen. This man was Saul. After that, this man called Saul said, "I want to kill all the Christians." And he went to the rulers of the people to take the paper on which it was written that he could kill all Christians. And he was given militiamen and sent into all the countries to seek out Christians. And he arrived near a city that was called Damascus.

When he was on the road, this Saul suddenly fell to the ground. And he heard a voice from heaven that said to him, "Saul, Saul, why are you persecuting me?" And he said, "Who are you who speaks to me?" And the voice replied, "I am Jesus, the King of hearts. You want to disobey me, but you must obey me." And then Saul said, "Lord, what must I do?" "Go to Damascus. Then you will be told what you have to do." And then Saul got up and he was blind. And the militiamen who had accompanied him were obliged to take him by the hand and lead him. And he sat there in the house of a friend who knew him, and he waited. And then, after some days, there came a Christian who was called Ananias. (The translators repeated, "Who was called Ananias!")[8] This Ananias had heard the voice of God, who had told him to go the place where Saul was. And Ananias said to Saul, "God has sent me, and I must make you see again." And suddenly Saul could see again. And he believed in Jesus Christ and was baptized. And immediately he began to preach among the Jews and among others that Jesus is the King of hearts.

Then the Jews said, "How can this be the one who wanted to kill Christians? Now, wherever he goes, he says that Jesus is the King of hearts. We are going to kill him, too." Since they wanted to kill him, Saul was obliged to hide. And because the others thought that he wanted to leave the city, they guarded all the city gates.

The cities of the Jews were almost like the villages of the Pahouins. One could exit only here and here, and all around there was a wall. But then the friends of Saul made a basket large enough to put a man inside. And during the night they put Saul inside and lowered him over the wall. And then, when it was quiet, he began to leave the city. All night long he walked toward where the apostles were at Jerusalem. And all the Christians of Jerusalem were afraid because they said, "Formerly this man killed Christians and now he is a Christian himself. We cannot believe him." But soon they came to know that this man Saul, who had killed Christians, now

---

8. The transcriber for the sermon adds that at this point the translators repeated the words: "Who was called Ananias!"

really was a Christian. And since this man Saul had become a Christian, he was no longer called "Saul" but "Paul." And this Christian called Paul became the Apostle Paul. Amen.

Let us pray unto God: Oh God, who hath shown thy Spirit in the heart of Saul to reveal that Jesus is the King of hearts, show this Spirit also in our hearts. There are many here who know that Jesus is the King of hearts, and many who still do not know. Therefore, open our hearts, we pray thee, God our Father. Amen.

56. 14 June 1931

"You Shall Not Steal"

Exodus 20:15

Two Sundays ago we celebrated Pentecost. The feast of Pentecost is the feast of the Holy Spirit, because on the day of Pentecost the apostles of Jesus Christ received the Holy Spirit in their hearts. You know that God gave the Ten Commandments to the prophet Moses, written on stone. Christians who are here know the Ten Commandments. Today I want to speak about one of these commandments, a commandment that is always necessary to speak about in your country. It is the commandment "You must not steal!"

You know why one must always speak about this commandment in your country. Many people among you still do not know how terrible it is to steal. If I asked now for those who as yet haven't stolen to stand up where they are, how many women and men would get up? I believe that almost all would remain seated. For this reason, I want everyone to reflect on what they have stolen.

Why is stealing such a wicked thing? Those who steal think two things. The first thing they think is, "The one I steal from still has other things." And the other thought is: "I hope nobody knows what I did." Their hearts say it is bad; even savages know that stealing is bad. And then they try to think, "Oh, I haven't stolen a lot." But each theft is something terrible, because after each theft there is a palaver. The Lord Jesus said, "You must not have a palaver." You must not accuse another man in front of the chief or before the administrator. When someone steals, there comes a palaver. People are accused, and then often a man who has not committed a theft is accused and condemned.

How many innocent men do you think have already been imprisoned, beaten by militiamen posted in Lambaréné, because others have stolen? Perhaps there are people here who have stolen and know that others have been punished in their place. This is why a man who is Christian in his heart and who has stolen does not want a complaint to be filed, and perhaps another punished who is innocent.

There was someone, hired by the doctor, who saved everything he earned, including all his loincloths, in a trunk in his hut. And during the night someone stole the trunk, and this person was not a foreigner; he was someone who lived here. And you, as natives, would then have accused those who were in the hut, and then the commander would have been cross with them and made them work a long time while waiting for his judgment. And then he would have said to them, "Perhaps it is [that one] who has stolen, and he will have to stay in prison for a long time." And you know that you natives have far crueler ways to find out someone who must have stolen, and yet you always accuse the one who has not. You make a witch doctor come who claims to know everything, does all kinds of wicked things, and finally says, "It is this one who has stolen." But the witch doctor is lying, and the good Lord God will punish him one day and also the others who listen to him.

And then this hired man, who had heard the Word of God, did not file a complaint because he did not want someone to be punished who was innocent. And the doctor says that this man has done well, and the doctor loves this man as a brother. But there is someone who knows the thief for sure, and this is the good Lord. So the thief must not say, "Oh, there will no longer be a palaver. This is good!" God will pursue him and will punish him, if not today, then tomorrow; if not this week, then another; if not this month, then another; if not this year, then another—but he will be punished. And the good Lord punishes with a terrible sickness.

There are a lot of women and men who have come to the hospital. They were not sick in body, but they suffered greatly. It is the good God who has punished them. And it for this reason that all of you who have heard this commandment must say, "I want to return what I have stolen, so that the good Lord does not punish me." Obey God, so that he will not be obliged to punish you. Amen.

Let us pray unto God: God our Father, who hast filled all our hearts with sadness because of stealing, make our hearts strong so that they will no longer think of stealing. And those who have stolen, fill their hearts with sadness and fill their hearts with thy Word so that they may return what they have stolen, and so that you will not be forced to punish them. Amen.

PART FIVE

The 1933 Sermons

57. Sunday, 30 April 1933

Give Thanks to God

Albert Schweitzer's first sermon after his return to the hospital.

1 Thessalonians 5:18

Today, for the preaching of the Word of God, I have chosen a verse from the apostle Paul. It is a verse from the first letter that he wrote. The people of the village where he wrote this letter are called Thessalonians, and those of you that have a New Testament can look for this verse at the end of the first letter of the apostle Paul. This verse is as follows: "Be thankful in all things, because this is the will of God." And I am telling you about this verse today because my heart is full of gratitude toward God, and I want you also to be full of thankfulness toward God, because all of us here at the hospital have reason to be grateful to God.

When I left the hospital more than a year ago, I asked myself how it would be when I returned. I wondered, would we still have enough money to buy medicines, bandages and rations? Would we still have enough money to buy thread to sew up stomachs in operations—this thread that is so expensive? You know there is a crisis. Look at the warehouses that are closed. They no longer have goods. And then I wondered whether our friends in Europe would also tell me, "There is a crisis. We no longer have money." Then we would have been obliged to tell the people, "Do not come here anymore for operations." We would have had to send the sick people away, and finally we would have had to close the hospital and return in Europe. This was the great concern that the doctor had in his heart.

Now he has returned and the hospital can continue, because friends in Europe have said, "Yes, it is a crisis, but we know that there are a lot of sick people among the natives, and we are giving you a gift to help them."

This is why I am able to buy these things that you have seen in these boxes—the medicines, and the thread to sew up stomachs. So when the doctor saw all these things arrive in these cases on the barge from Foing, his heart was filled with thankfulness toward God. And you yourselves, you shouldn't take these things for granted; you should be grateful to God, who has sent you these things.

The doctor's heart is also filled with thankfulness toward God for something else. Each time the mail arrived in Europe, the doctor's hands trembled before opening the letters because he wondered whether the letters would say that one of the doctors or nurses was sick, or perhaps dead. And, you see, everyone has remained in good health. If someone was sick, it was not very much, and soon he resumed his work. And when the doctor heard in Europe that Doctor Bonnéma was all alone with all the work, I thought, "Perhaps he is going to get sick." See, it is the good Lord who has given him strength, so that Doctor Bonnéma was able to do the work all alone for several weeks. That is why the doctor is filled with gratitude to God.

And now that we have arrived safely, I want you to know that we are not doing this work just to please ourselves. You know that in times past there were a lot of mishaps on boats. Boats have sunk with everyone on board. Large boats have burned, with many people burned too. Then, when we went aboard the boat from Bordeaux to Port Gentile, we wondered, "Are we going to arrive safely?" One is always in danger. And you know that we arrived fifteen days late because the engine of the boat broke and there was bad weather. If the engine had broken during the bad weather, the boat would have had a mishap, but as it broke during the good weather, there was no misfortune. Now we are here, and all of us want to give thanks to God for being able to be here.

When I tell you to thank God, I tell you to also thank the men who have worked here. I tell you to thank the physicians who have done the work and who have nursed you so well.

I tell you to especially thank Doctor Bonnéma, who was all alone for such a long time, doing all the work.[1] I also want you to thank the nurses. I want you to thank Miss Emma, who preached the Word of God to you instead of the doctor on Sundays. Often on Sunday mornings, the doctor thought, "Now Miss Emma is speaking the Word of God at the hospital."

And this is also what we want to write in our hearts: the verse to be thankful to God, to be thankful to men who do the will of God. And at this time you and I should think of those men in Europe who have given a gift to buy the medicines and the thread, who do not say, "There is a crisis and I can no longer give anything," but who listen to the Word of God in their hearts and give the gift to help those who suffer. It is God who put these things in their hearts, and I want you likewise to listen to these thoughts that God has put into your hearts. Amen.

Let us pray unto God: God our Father, we thank thee for all the good that thou doest. We thank thee that thou hast permitted the hospital to be here. We thank thee that thou hast brought back the doctor and the nurses, and we thank thee for the gift that the people in Europe have given to buy medicines and thread. We pray thee, let our hearts be filled with thanksgiving so that that we may listen to thy Word, and thank thee properly for all the good thou hast done for us. Amen.

58. Sunday, 20 August 1933

Live in Peace Together

1 Thessalonians 5:13

These last Sundays I told you the story of Saint Paul: that he had been put in prison, that he traveled on the sea, and that he died in Rome. And I think that those who have heard the story of Saint Paul not only with their ears but also with their hearts say, "Here is the kind of man that God wants."

Now when Paul traveled, he wrote letters to missionary outposts. He

---

1. Doctor Bonnéma was from the Netherlands. He served as physician in Lambaréné from 19 December 1931 to July 1934.

wrote these letters to them to give his news and to remind them about the Word of God that he had preached to them. And when the people of a city had a letter, they did not simply read it and forget it; they kept it. And on Sunday, when they were united for prayer, they said, "We want to read the letter of Paul again." And so it is that the letters of Paul were kept and are written in the great book of the Words of God. In the great book of the Words of God, they have been put side by side with the words of our Lord Jesus Christ. And in the book of the Words of God there are also letters by Saint Peter the Apostle and Saint John. But the other apostles did not write as many letters as Paul. In his letters there are many beautiful words. And in the coming Sundays I am going to read to you these words and speak to you about them.

Today I read to you a passage found in a little letter that Paul wrote [1 Thessalonians 5:13]: "Live in peace with one another." This means that peace must always be with you. Here Saint Paul pronounces the word *peace* that the Lord Jesus Christ so often spoke to men. There is no need to explain to men what peace is. Everyone understands this word with his heart. This means that all people in the village and all men everywhere must be good toward one another, and that there are no palavers. And all men know that where there is peace there is happiness in the heart. And all men must seek to have peace in the villages and in the countries. And you know that there is no peace in the world.

You know that there was the Great War, in which many people were killed, and you know that there are still many wars in the world. And during these weeks the great rulers of the peoples were assembled in a great city, London, and they said, "We want peace now!" We read about it in the newspapers that have just arrived. And they said, "We want to talk about all the palavers that are between us. We no longer want people to manufacture guns and cannons, to be used by one against the other." And they said, "We know that because there is no peace there is a crisis." And this is why the people are unhappy: because there is no peace. And so it is that they were seated together in a large cabin—it is written in the newspapers. And each one began to speak. And each one said, "Our people want peace, but the others do not want it." And so they are divided again, and there is no more peace in the world than there was before. And all the men are afraid again that war may come.

And now, if we went into your villages, would there be peace? Oh, you know that there wouldn't be any. You know that your villages are full of palavers, full of the most villainous palavers. Villages that could be happy because there are good plantations and fish are miserable because there are palavers. Isn't what I say true? Can anyone contradict what I say? And now I put another question to you. We are no longer speaking about people or villages; I am speaking about you, and I ask each of you, "Do you have peace?" And if everyone had to reply to me I believe that everyone would say, "No!" Everyone would have to say, "I have a palaver with this one; I do not like that one; I say bad words about another one." And everyone would say, "I am not the cause of it; it is the other one who is wicked." And everyone would tell me these stupidities. And that is why I do not ask you, but only tell you the words of Saint Paul: "All of you, be at peace!"

The apostle Saint Paul is not asking you, "Are you right and the other wrong?" He simply asks all, "Do you have good thoughts so that you might have peace?" Because if there is no peace there will always be wicked thoughts in men's hearts. And that is why, when the apostle Paul said, "Have peace," he said to you, "Always have good thoughts!"

And so I ask you, "What are you doing to have peace? Do you know how to forgive?" You know that in all your palavers it is necessary to know how to forgive. A man must know how to get rid of the thoughts that he has against another in his heart, as if he were removing weeds, so that these palavers do not continue to be like a fire that has taken hold in the brush and that nobody can extinguish. And for there to be peace there must be men who know how to forget. Oh, our heart forgets so quickly—it forgets good things, but it does not forget bad things! They always stay written in the heart of a man: "This one said that, that one did this to me." All this is written in the heart, and that is why men do not have peace. To have peace it is necessary to know how to erase, just as a child erases what he has written on a slate.

So I speak the words of Saint Paul to you. The apostle Paul says, "Have peace!" And I say to you, this means, "Force your heart to forget; force your heart to forgive!" This is what I want. May each of you think today about all of your palavers. May each of you of you think, "I want to begin to forget." And God hears you and gives you the power in your heart to do it. Amen.

Let us pray unto God: God, our Father, thou who readest the heart, have pity on the world. Thou knowest how many wars and misfortunes there are in the world because people do not know how to make peace. Thou knowest how much we are troubled because we do not have peace with those who live with us. Grant us the power to want the peace that Jesus Christ brought into the world. Amen.

59. Sunday, 10 September 1933

Why Jesus Christ Died

Last time, I spoke about the letters of Saint Paul that are found in the great book of the Word of God. In many of his letters he speaks about the death of the Lord Jesus Christ, and he seeks to explain its meaning. You know that the Lord Jesus Christ told his disciples, "I die for men." He did not explain that to them. He only told them, "If I die, it is the will of God. The rulers of the Jewish people could not kill me if God did not want me to die." And that is why the Lord Jesus Christ, when he knew that they wanted to kill him, did not flee into the bush, but went right there, where the rulers were, because he knew that the will of God had to be done. And then he told them, "I die for the sins of men. I die in order that the Lord God may send the Kingdom of God on earth." The Lord had not sent the Kingdom, because men were too full of sins. And that is why, when the Lord Jesus died for men, they said, "Now God forgives us our sins." Then Saint Paul the Apostle explained with many words what this means. Was it necessary for God that the Lord Jesus be killed so that God could pardon the sins of men? No, because the Lord God can do everything that he wants to. This is why what the Lord Jesus Christ said—"When I am dead God will forgive you your sins"—remains a secret, a secret no one can explain. Then Saint Paul the Apostle said, "It is very important to try to understand the death of the Lord Jesus." And he said, "No one can understand the mystery of why God wanted the Lord Jesus Christ to die." We will understand this secret once we are in heaven with the Lord Jesus Christ. But one thing we can already thoroughly understand today, and that is that the Lord Jesus wanted to die for us. And by this he wanted to give us an example. All men say, "I want to live for myself." But the will of God is not that men live for themselves.

We see men who do not live for themselves. A canoe capsizes in the wind. Someone falls into the water who does not know how to swim. Then someone jumps into the water to save him. This man or this woman is perhaps someone who is not good. Perhaps it is a man or a woman who has previously lied or stolen. But at the very moment when he jumped into the water to save the other person, he understood the Word of God. At this moment, when he jumps into the water, he doesn't say, "No, I don't want to drown." He knows only, "Here I have to save someone, and I alone can save him." Then this man or this woman has followed words of the Lord Jesus, who died for others.

When the mail arrives and we open the papers, we read, "A large cabin has burned, because in Europe there are a lot of cabins that are tall and hold many men—one cabin on top of another, and another one under it, and still one more underneath, as high as a mountain.[2] When the cabin burns down, there are children and old men who cannot get down quickly and who can be burned. Then we read that some old people jumped into the fire and climbed up the stairs to look for others. And often we also read that they did not leave with children in their arms, but that they were burned in the cabins.[3] These also have followed the Lord Jesus. That is why Saint Paul the Apostle said, "Jesus died for us all, so that we may live not for ourselves but for others": so that we may not live only for ourselves in both great and small things. The Kingdom of God is present already when people do not live only for themselves in both great and small things.

Oh, when you have a palaver you say, "I have just cause; it is my right." Perhaps it is your right; perhaps your cause is just. And then you say, "I want to win my palaver," and so that is why there is a palaver in your village. But the Lord Jesus who died tells you, "It is not for you to seek to win a palaver. Instead, leave the palaver. It is like a piece of yourself—this law. Remove this piece of yourself as if it were dead and then you will be happy."

2. The "tall cabins" are apartment buildings.
3. The idea is that "some old people" went into a burning apartment building to rescue some children trapped there but died in the attempt.

In this way, be gentle throughout your life. Walk away from men who say that you are wrong when you know that you are right. This is how you do the will of Jesus Christ, who died for us.

Men believe very wisely when they say, "I want justice." But the real wisdom is that which comes from the Lord Jesus Christ—the wisdom of goodness, the wisdom not even to think of oneself. This is the real wisdom that puts peace into the hearts of men. Christ died for us all so that we might not live for ourselves but for others.

Let us pray to God. Lord God, may we consider in our hearts that the Lord Jesus Christ died for us. We do not understand why thou didst wish him to die, but we know that it was according to thy will that this was done. And that is why we ask thee to give us the power to follow his example, so that we may live not only for ourselves, but also for others and fulfill thy will, and also that of the Lord Jesus Christ, who died for us. Amen.

60. Sunday, 24 September 1933

The Spirit of God Is Love

I told you that we are speaking about the words of Saint Paul the Apostle. Many of St. Paul's words speak of the Spirit of God that is in men, because he found that when he came to the missionary stations, some men said, "We have the Spirit of God more than others." There were people who were proud and who said, "We are greater than the others." And there were people who said, "We have more of the Spirit of God because we know the Word of God better than what is written in the great book of the Word of God." And there were some others who said, "No, it is we who have the most Spirit of God, because we understand the words of God the best." Then, when the people discussed it, St. Paul wrote to them, "I am going to explain to you how one sees if someone has the Spirit of God."

The greatest amount of the Spirit of God appears when a man has goodness. The Spirit of God appears in a lot of things. The Spirit of God appears in all that we have in the head and in the heart. If men are very learned, far more learned than other men, that is good. It is the Spirit of God that has given them this.

There are people in Europe who know the name of all the stars and who know how stars travel in the sky. You have seen something before that is very rare: that the moon becomes completely black in a full moon. You may remember that some years ago the moon became completely black. And you also know that it is possible for the sun to become black too. This is even more rare than the moon becoming black. There are men in Europe who can calculate this and who can say, some years in advance, "On such a day, at such an hour, the sun will become black." And how learned were those men who invented the machines that are on boats! And how learned are those who have invented machines to fly in the air, so that men have become like birds! And how learned are those who have invented all the medicines that are in the pharmacy! It has taken years to invent the medicine for sleeping sickness. Well then, in all these learned men there is the Spirit of God, because only the Spirit of God has taught them what they know. But if these men were proud and said, "It is I who have the greatest amount of the Spirit of God," St. Paul would tell them, "No!"

There are many sorts of light: there is the light of the torch, there is the light of the lamp, there is the electric light that you see at the hotel, there is the light of the stars, there is the light of the moon, there is the light of the sun. Likewise, there are many sorts of light of the Spirit of God. Perhaps there are scientists who have the electric light or the light of the moon from the Spirit of God. But the greatest light of the Spirit of God is love, and this is the only real light. Because if you light a torch during the day, the torch cannot be seen, and if you light an electrical light during the day you can hardly see it. That is why the clearest light of the Spirit of God is love. This light of the sun of love is in the hearts of us all, but clouds of wicked thoughts hide this light of the sun of the love of God, and that is why we do not see the light of the love of God in our hearts. We pray God that the light of his love may become strong in our hearts.

Let us pray to God: God our Father, we thank thee that thy Spirit may be in our heart, and we are sad that our wicked thoughts do not let our Spirit become clear. May we truly have the Spirit of thy love, because the Spirit of thy love is the greatest wealth of our life. Amen.

61. Tuesday, 10 October 1933

"Let Your Gentleness Be Known"

Philippians 4:5a

I will read you a passage today from a letter of Saint Paul the Apostle. It is very short. It has only a few words: "Let your gentleness be known to all men." *Gentleness* means "goodness," and Saint Paul the Apostle, by saying these words, which mean, "May everyone know goodness," only repeats what the Lord Jesus said himself. And this phrase has special meaning for our time.

When the mail arrives and we open the newspapers, we are always very sad, because we read the news of all the wickedness and cruelties that have happened in the world. When I was young, newspapers were also read. There was also a lot of news in the newspapers. But in those days one did not read so much news about the wicked things that happened in the world. One said, "Yes, the Spirit of Jesus Christ is slowly penetrating into the world, and goodness is beginning to happen. We have hope." But then the Great War came, and then the wicked spirit came once again into the hearts of men. What we are reading in the newspapers every month is terribly sad. We now read that a country in Asia has killed all the Christians. And the people of this country did not say, "It is wicked to kill all these Christians." They said, "That's fine." And these are not savages. These are people who have cities and schools. They said, "If we want to kill Christians, that's all right."

In another nation, all the people who are Jewish have been persecuted. When they had a place to work, they were sought out and told, "We do not want Jews." And yet they had not done anything bad. When we open a newspaper, we always see news of cruelties that one people have done to another. Sometimes we say that the natives are happy because they don't read the newspapers and learn about all the cruelties of the world. We wonder what the world is coming to. You see in the cabin of the insane those who have lost the use of their reason.[4] Today there are likewise many people who are losing the use of their hearts.

---

4. Schweitzer built a place for the mentally ill at his hospital in Lambaréné.

We hear a lot of people say or write, "It is no longer necessary to listen to the heart; it is only necessary to do what you want." We wonder how God, who is good, can allow men to lose the use of their hearts. We don't understand it. It is as if God meant to say, "I have shown you my light and you haven't listened. Well then, now stay in darkness. You will stay in darkness until I hear, once again, the prayer 'God send us thy light and thy Word.' " We wonder what we can do in this terribly sad time. We can't turn the hearts of men around. We don't have the force to make them listen to the Word of God if they do not want to hear it. Yes, but we have the force to make ourselves do what the Word of God tells us to do.

What can we do—we, the people who are seated here in prayer at the hospital of Lambaréné? In what way can we show goodness? If each of you had to say now how he had done good to others during this past week, through words or by helping, what could he say? I fear that for many of you there would be very few things to say. I fear that many of you would be obliged to say, "The wicked things I have done to men are more than the good things I have done." That is why Saint Paul the Apostle wrote in this letter, "God wants us to turn our hearts to everyone, because God wants us to have goodness in our hearts."

God has made some very intelligent men. He has made some men rich, others poor. He has made some masters, others servants, but he has given to them all the same means to become good.

God is goodness. When he wants to do something good for a man or a woman—for a sick person, for someone who is sad—he looks for a man to do it, because God cannot come here himself. The Spirit of God is going to knock at the heart of this man and say, "Don't you want to do this for the sake of goodness?" But it is like a town where all the men have gone fishing. All the cabins are closed. Then the Spirit of God returns sadly to heaven and says, "I have not found anybody who wants to do what you ask." So it is that the Spirit of God has already knocked at your heart and said: "Go help. Go say a good word, go console the one who is sad!" and you have not listened. That is the reason why your heart has remained poor and sad and cold. Our hearts become truly happy only when they listen to the spirit of God. The spirit of God says to our hearts: "Be good, show kindness to men!" Now when he speaks to you, listen to him and become servants of the goodness of God.

Prayer: God our Father, thou hast made our hearts to hear thy Word.

Thou hast made our hearts to put goodness inside. Thou dost desire that we be servants of goodness and that we do goodness toward men. Open our hearts that they may understand what thou desirest. Make our hearts become a source that always has clear water for those who need water. Amen.

62. Sunday, 22 October 1933

Real Happiness Is Peace in Your Heart

Philippians 4:7 "The peace of God, which passeth all understanding, shall keep your hearts and minds through Christ Jesus."

Last time I read you a verse from a letter of St. Paul that he wrote when he was in prison. Today I am going to tell you about another verse that is written next to the one that I have already explained to you. And that verse is this one: "And the peace of God, which passeth all understanding, shall keep peace in your hearts."

In this verse, first of all, there is the word *peace*. Our heart is like a man who left his village—who left to go to other villages—but who thinks all the time about his village and says, "My village was the prettiest." So peace is something that all men wish to have. Peace is the most precious thing in the world. But there is no peace in the world. Now, in the time we live in, there is war everywhere in the world. Someone who reads the newspapers thoroughly can tell you, "This one is at war with that one, that one with this one." At this very moment—as we are seated here under the palm trees, where we hear birds singing—men are being killed with guns and cannons, prisoners are being taken, and many people have nothing to eat today, because all the plantations have been burned. It is war. And you—if there were not administrators here, you would make war. So peace is the most precious thing for men, because only a perfectly tranquil heart has good fortune.

A man who is rich is still not happy. A man who is a chief and issues orders, to whom all men say "yes," is a powerful man, but he is not a happy man. A man who is clever and intelligent, who knows how to do everything he wants, is not a happy man. But the poorest man is happy if he has peace in his heart; that is why the apostle Paul wrote to his friends in a letter, which we keep, that peace, which is the most important thing, you must also keep.

Peace is when the thoughts of a man are tranquil: not thoughts of wickedness, thoughts of lying, thoughts of revenge and hostility against the other men. But thoughts in our hearts are like lake waves when there is a tornado. Why don't you say, "Oh, you thoughts in my heart, become tranquil!" Only men who think about God can tell their thoughts to become tranquil. We must consider how short our life is. We have only a few years of life. God has called us for a few years of life, after which he will call us back to himself and he will ask us, "What did you do in life?" Then, when a man knows how short life is, he thinks, "No, real happiness is peace."

Peace comes from God. Only people who think of God have peace in their hearts. Well then, you who have heard St. Paul's words about peace, reflect today if there truly is peace in your heart. There are many people who are sick and don't know it. That is the reason why they do not come to seek medicine, and so they die. Likewise, there are many people who don't have peace in their hearts, but don't know it because they have never felt what peace is. That is why I want you to thirst after peace: so that God may give you peace in your soul. Amen.

63. Sunday, 5 November 1933

The Soul Must Return to God

Sermon on the Sunday after the Feasts of All Saints and All Souls

There was a feast this week—really two feasts. The first of November is called All Saints. The second of November is the Feast of the Dead. In Europe now all the trees have lost their leaves. All trees seem to be dead, and it is cold and dark. And when in nature everything is dead, men think of those men who are dead. And then at the beginning of the season of winter—at the beginning of the great cold and dry season that lasts until May—on the first and second of November, the Christians in Europe think of the dead. On the first of November they think of the great Christians who died, who are called saints. They think of Christians who are dead, who were killed because they were Christian. And they think also of their own deaths. And on the second of November they think of all the dead Christians. And then everyone goes to the tombs of their relatives and places flowers and lights there.

And this is the difference between whites and blacks, because you blacks, when you have buried a dead person, you no longer go to see him, you no longer go to the place because you are afraid of the spirits of the dead. And this is wrong because the spirits of the dead are no longer on earth, and spirits of the dead are not wicked because the spirits of the dead are with God.

And now, today, we are going to speak about death, and you all are going to think about your death. The Lord Jesus Christ wants Christians to think about death and doesn't want someone to say, "Oh, I am young; it is still a long time before I die," because you know that even youths, and the littlest children can die. Jesus wants us to think about our death and to ask ourselves, "Are we ready to die?"

What happens when a man is dead? One buries him, and then he rots. When one reopens a grave, one finds bones thoroughly decayed, like those of a beast. But does that mean that all of the man has decayed? Oh, there are people who say, "Then it is finished." But it is not finished, because there is something in the man that cannot rot. It is the soul—that which is in the man and cannot be seen. Each of you has a soul, even the most savage of you, even the one who does not know that it is from the good Lord. Even the one who says, "I want to do evil," even he has a soul. God has given this soul to men, and this soul must return to God. But we do not know how, because there is still no man who has seen how our soul returns to God, who is far away in heaven.

How does God speak to the soul, and how does he ask it, "What did you do in life?" How will the soul be near God? All this we do not know. We will know it when we are dead, because then we will see God, and then we will hear him speak, and then we will know all the things that we still do not know, and then we will be happy. And this is why we are thinking about death, so that our soul may rejoice to return to the house of God, as a child who has been gone for a long time rejoices to come back to his mother's village.

There is still a question: What will happen to those souls who were wicked in the world? Will God judge these souls and say, "I do not want to see you" and put them in hell? Oh, we know that if God wanted to judge souls and to put them into hell, our souls would go to hell. But we know that God is love and that God forgives, and this is why we believe that God will ultimately forgive all those souls, and that if he punishes those who did not obey him in life, this will be only for a time, and in eternity all souls will come back to him. But we who know God, we know his Word and we want to keep our soul pure, so that we may bring a soul to him that has obeyed him in life, so that when we die our soul may return joyfully to God's house. Amen.

Let us pray to God: O God, who hast given us a soul in our life, let us consider that this soul must return to thy house; and may we keep this soul pure for thee, that this soul may obey thee here in this life when it is far away from thee. So may it be. Amen.

64. Sunday, 3 December 1933

The Message of the Prophets

Sermon on the first Sunday in Advent

Today is a great Sunday. Today there are still three Sundays until the feast of Christmas. Christmas is the feast in which Jesus, the King of Hearts, came into the world—Jesus, who came to announce that the Kingdom of God has come into the world. And during these four Sundays before Christmas we think of the prophets—the prophets of the Jewish people— because these are the men who announced the Word of God for the first time; the first who announced that the King of hearts, sent by God, would come; the first who said that the Kingdom of God would come.

I will tell you the names of these prophets who came a long time before

Jesus Christ. Their words are still written in the Book of the Words of God. They are Elijah and Elisha, Amos, Hosea, Isaiah. Then there is also the prophet Jeremiah and the prophet Ezekiel. There are still the lesser prophets, whose words are also written in the book of the Words of God. You won't retain all these names, but I'm mentioning them to you because you ought to hear the names of these men at least once, these men in whom God placed his words, for the first time,—these men, into whose spirits God sent his Spirit, to speak his words through their mouths. And therefore these prophets, who lived a long time before Jesus Christ, were the first to announce that there would be the Kingdom of God.

At that time there was, like today, war throughout the world. Encircling the Jewish people, who were a small nation and who lived in the mountains, there were many great nations, and all these peoples made war. They came to burn the villages from one year to the next. So instead of being happy, they were very unhappy. Often they heard the news, "There is another nation that is going to come and make war on us." Often they were seated together and said, "We are stronger than the other people. We are going to make war on them. We are going to burn villages, take goods, steal women, kill children and men." And everyone thought that it had to be this way. As animals tear each other apart, so also the people tore each other apart.

Nevertheless, they knew God. They built temples to him. They killed beasts and offered them to him. They sent prayers to God, and when they went to war they prayed, "Let us be stronger than our enemy." They never thought, "Does the good Lord want war?" They didn't wonder if the good Lord wants war. They didn't wonder what the good Lord wants. They only asked to be stronger than their enemy. And they were among people who lied. There were some who put poor people in prison, and nobody asked, "Is this good?" They thought that it was supposed to be like this—that rich men and strong men had to be wicked toward others. And the poor people thought that it had to be this way—that we are not to seek soldiers to protect us from others who are wicked toward us, who put us in prison and who beat us.

Then, suddenly, the voices of the prophets were heard, and others began to say to those where were acting wickedly, "Have you considered what you are doing? Do you truly believe that God has a spirit as wicked as yours, that God wants men to kill and to do evil, that God wants war, that God wants the weak to be mistreated by those who are strong and rich?"

"Certainly you don't believe such things!" said the prophets "Ponder that fact that God can only be good and that those who believe in God must become good, just as the Spirit of God is good."

God does not want war. God does not want a man to be wicked toward another. God does not want lying. God wants goodness; he wants each man to be good toward all men. God wants the chiefs to be just and to judge the palavers with justice. God does not want war; he wants all peoples to be at peace with each other. God does not want a man to say, "This man is not from the same people as I am, and he doesn't resemble me; I can do with him whatever I want." No, God wants a man to say, "All men are my brothers." That is how the prophets spoke the Word of God. They spoke it in the mountains of the Jewish people.

These prophets were poor men. Then the people said, "What do these poor men want who open their mouths and say such new things, things that no one has ever heard before—that strong men must not do as they please with the weak, that they must no longer be permitted to kill men when they want to, to take their goods to become rich?" And truly, it was said, they believed that there would come a day when there would no longer be any war. And the chiefs laughed and mocked and said, "We want to make war." And they said, "Be quiet, we no longer want to listen to these words!" And they believed that these poor men were going to be quiet and return to their villages. They were surprised that these men did not remain quiet. So the prophets said, "It is God who commands, not these men." Then the soldiers were sent to seek them out and put them in prison, and they were obliged to hide in the bush. Others took them and killed them. But there was something new that had opened their mouths.

And so it was that long before Jesus Christ came into the world there were prophets who announced that God is good, and that a day will come when all men will live in peace. In all the churches of the world, when people today unite for prayer, the prophets are spoken of. And we too think of them, and we thank God that he sent them into the world. Amen.

Let us pray unto God: Oh God, who hath spoken by the mouth of the prophets, thou hast spoken the truth for the first time through their mouths. And the people did not want to hear the truth. Put the truth in our hearts so that we may understand it and do what is good in thy sight, each one in his house and in his village, so that we may be thy children, so that the Kingdom of God may come into the world. Amen.

65. Monday, 25 December 1933

Christmas

Today is the great feast of Christmas. Throughout the whole world, wherever there are Christians, no one does any work, even when it is Monday, because it is the great feast of Christmas. And everywhere people rejoice that God has sent the Lord Jesus Christ, the King of Hearts, into the world.

It has been a long time since then. One can hardly count the years. Jesus was born of very poor parents. But because in the Word of God the prophets wrote that Jesus would be a great king, the whole world thought that Jesus would be born in the great cabin of a chief. His parents were from the family of the greatest king of the Jewish people—King David. But even though Jesus was the son of a family of kings, he was still poor. The people of that time did not understand that, but we understand it. We know why the Lord God sent the Lord Jesus as a poor man into the world—because God wanted him to be the sole King of Hearts.

Other great kings, chiefs of great peoples, lived at the same time as Jesus. They are dead. On the day that they died no one obeyed them any more, but instead obeyed other kings. We still know the names of some kings who lived during this time, but there are many that we no longer know. But the name of Jesus is still known throughout the whole world. And Jesus continues to reign, to be King. He reigns through the words that we know from him. He is a Spirit who speaks to the hearts of men by his words. And he said to all men, "I want to reign in your heart." He said to each man: "Remove the bad words from your heart, sweep out your heart for me, because I want to enter your heart." And he said, "I want to reign in your heart." He said it to all men, even to those who have never heard his Word, who are hearing it today at the hospital for the first time. And he tells the same thing to those who have been Christians for a long time.

And perhaps a Christian says, "But it was a long time ago, when I was very small, that I first took the Lord Jesus into my heart." Then the Lord Jesus smiles when a Christian tells him this, and he says, "I am only the smallest of kings in your heart. I want to fill it completely." And so Jesus speaks all around him to all men, and he asks them: "Do you truly want me to become King of your heart?" And those men who reflect upon this today and who say, "Is Jesus truly the King of my heart? He must fill it completely!"—these are the ones who have truly celebrated this great feast of Christmas. Amen.

Let us pray unto God: Oh God, thou hast sent the Lord Jesus Christ that he may be the King of hearts for all men. Send him to be the King of our hearts as well. For this reason let us consider that he truly is the King of our hearts. May we be sad when we see that he is so insufficiently the King of our hearts, and may we open the door of our hearts to him so that he may enter into our hearts. Then it will be the most beautiful festival of Christmas in our hearts. Amen.

66. Sunday, 31 December 1933

The Last Sunday of the Year

Today, on the last Sunday of the year, we should consider the fact that we are all going to die. God has given to each man only so many years to live. God knows how many years—he knows how many years each of us who is here still has to live. He knows which Sunday will be the last one of the year for each of us. We will no longer be here because he will call us to his home. And it will be not only the old and the sick who will die, but also the youths who are as yet completely well and who say, "I still have many years left to live." And that is the reason why today, in all Christian churches, one thinks, "How many years does the good Lord still give me to live?" That is why we too are gathered together on this last Sunday of the year. We think, "How many years does the good Lord still give us to live?" And first of all we thank God for having given us these years to live. And we thank God for all that he has done for us this year.

Now let each of you think about what he has to thank God for. And I am sure there are some among you who are saying, "I don't have a lot to thank God for. I am a poor man. I am a poor woman. I am not rich." Nevertheless each of you has to thank God. God has given you health. And these that are sick here—they thank God today that he has given them this hospital. And when you see men who are very unhappy, who suffer much in the body, who have lost children, tell yourself that you are happy because God has not sent you these sad things.

Every banana you eat is a gift from the good Lord, for who sends the sun and the rain that make the banana grow? It is God. All the good things in your life are gifts that God gives you. That is why this day, the last Sunday of the year, you all have to say, "O God, we thank thee for all the goodness that thou hast done for us."

And still another question, "What did you do this year?" Perhaps there are some here who say, "Oh, I've done nothing in particular. I haven't been more wicked than anyone else." You can say this to other men; you cannot say this to the good Lord. The good Lord knows all the evil that you have done. Today God wants you to think about this: "What did I do during this year?" If each of you wants to remember, you know that you have lied a lot, that you have been wicked toward men, that you have stolen, that you have cheated, and all that is a burden that you carry into the New Year. And that is why I say, "Think of all the evil that you have done this year and be sad and ashamed." And think about what you need—that all we need is for God to forgive us for all we have done this year.

Ask God to forgive you. I am telling you this once more. On this last Sunday of the year, you should say—"I must thank God for the good he has done for me. I must ask God to forgive me for all the evil that I have done." And so this is the way you will be able to live well on this last Sunday of the year. Amen.

Let us pray to God: God, it is the last Sunday of the year, and we thank thee for having kept us alive during this year. We thank thee for all the good thou hast done for us. God, give us a grateful heart, because only a grateful heart knowest thee. And forgive us all the evil that we have done this year, because this is the greatest kindness thou hast done—to forgive us. Amen.

PART SIX

The 1935 Sermons

67. Sunday, 24 March 1935

The Will of God

You know that there are some great holidays in Christianity. One great holiday is Christmas. It is the day when the Lord Jesus Christ was born as a baby. This holiday is behind us. And now a new holiday is before us. You all know what this holiday is called. It is Easter, when the Lord Jesus Christ became alive again after he had died. And before Easter there is yet another holiday that is called Good Friday, and this special day is the holy day of the death of our Lord Jesus Christ. You know how our Lord Jesus died. He did not die from an illness. The chiefs of the Jewish people killed him, and he was killed in a terrible manner. They made a large cross of wood, and they nailed the hands and feet of the Lord Jesus to the cross while he was still living, and they left him to die of pain, hunger, and thirst. And for hours he was suffering on the cross. In a few weeks it will be Good Friday. And today, in all churches of the world, all those who preach the gospel speak of the death of our Lord Jesus Christ. We too are going to think of the death of our Lord Jesus Christ.

Why did the Lord Jesus die? God promised a messiah to the Jewish people, that is to say, the King of hearts. And prophets had for many years told the people, "One day there will be a King of hearts, and he will command the hearts of men." The people waited for a very rich man, a son of a chief of the country, who would be the King of hearts. When Jesus came into the world he was the child of very poor people. And when he grew up he was a poor man. Then people said, "This cannot be the King of hearts.

This man lies." But there were a lot of people who understood. They understood that the words that Jesus Christ said were the Words of God. And when some went away after hearing him, they told others: "The Lord Jesus is there—you should go to hear him speak." And they came from all the villages. They came to listen to the Word of God that came from his mouth.

Then some people said to the chiefs, "There is a man who speaks and all the world listens to him and says, 'He is the King of hearts.' " The chiefs were angry. They said, "We are the chiefs." And others said, "We are the priests. What does this poor man want?" And then they were afraid. They said, "He is going to gather a lot of men. They are going to come to Jerusalem and have palavers and say, "Jesus is now our King." They did not say, "We want to hear him, to hear if the words that come from his mouth are the Words of God." Instead they said, "We want to be the chiefs." They said, "The people must not listen to any word other than ours." And then they said, "When he comes to Jerusalem, we will kill him." So it was that Jesus, the King of hearts, had to be killed by the chiefs of the Jewish people. But this is only a piece of the truth, for Jesus died not only because the chiefs wanted him to die, but because it was the will of God.

Everything that happens is the will of God. Nothing can happen in the world that is not the will of God. Everything that happens to each of you is the will of God. He is a true child of God who says about everything that happens, "It is the will of God." Jesus was the Son of God. He was the true child of God. And when he heard that the chiefs had said, "We want to kill him," he did not say to his followers, "Take axes and lances. We should defend ourselves." He did not say, "We are strong. We are going to Jerusalem and there you will say, 'Jesus is King!' " Jesus would have been able to speak this way, because there were a lot of people around him, but he said nothing. He reflected and said, "It is the will of God. I want to understand it. I want to die, if it is the will of God." Then he took the book of the prophets, in which were all the Words of God up until that time. He read all the words that God had said about the King of hearts who was going to come. Then he read all the words that the great prophet Isaiah had said, including the words where the prophet said that the King of hearts had to die. Then he understood. "It is not I, a man who walks and speaks, who must be the King of hearts, but my spirit when I am dead." He understood that he had to become the King of hearts, and then the people would understood that by dying he was doing the will of God. This is the way he became completely serene, and peace was in his heart. He said, "I want to bear the will of God." He did not utter words against the chiefs and the people, but he was utterly serene. He had peace in his heart because he wanted to do the will of God.

This is the way I wanted to tell you about the death of our Lord Jesus Christ and to teach you one thing. You likewise, in all that may happen to you through the wickedness of men, must not defend yourself, but say, "It is the will of God." If people say bad things, lies, and nonsense, do not say, "I want to defend myself," but say, "It is the will of God that I suffer this, as it was the will of God that Jesus died." As he obeyed it, we also have to obey. And as he found peace in his heart, despite all the stupidity and the wickedness of men, we must find peace in our hearts by doing the will of God.

To recognize the will of God in the wickedness that men do to you: this is the secret. To have peace in the heart by obeying God: this is the great truth. It is necessary that we learn this truth, because only when we know this truth are we children of God. This is the truth that we are thinking about with all Christians when we reflect on the death of the Lord Jesus Christ. Amen.

Let us pray to God: Oh God, thou art the Father of all men, and men are thy children. May we be thy children as Jesus was thy child. Let us know thy will. Let us know thy will in the wickedness and the lying of men against us. Let us be obedient and become serene, and have peace in the heart. Let us learn that our Lord Jesus went to his death because he did thy will. Amen.

68. 7 April 1935

We Must Give Our Life

I told you that these Sundays are Sundays when we are thinking about the death of our Lord Jesus Christ. And I explained to you when we had prayer together the last time that the Lord died because it was the will of God. He knew that the chiefs of his people wanted to kill him. They wanted to kill him because Jesus was the King of hearts. They were afraid that the people would say, "Now we are obeying the King of hearts; the chiefs are no longer anything." But Jesus knew that if the chiefs wanted to kill him, it was the will of God. And then he said, "I obey God." This I told you last time. And I told you that when there is sadness and misery in our lives, we have to say, like Jesus, "It is the will of God," and that when people are wicked to us, we must not say, "I want to defend myself," but we must say, "It is the will of God." And this is the great thing that each of us has to learn in life—to recognize the will of God in misfortune. Those who learn this are happy, because they have peace in their hearts, while others are miserable. That is the reason why, during these Sundays when we think about the death of Jesus, we must learn this. And now, once again, we want to reflect on the death of Jesus, because Jesus, when he died, knew that it was the will of God and that he would die for others.

When the missionaries came for the first time into this land, they proclaimed, "You have God in heaven," and also, "You have the Lord Jesus Christ who died for men." But what does that mean: "The Lord Jesus died for men"? The Lord Jesus died for men so that God could forgive their sins. But then we ask, "Is God not able to forgive sins without someone being killed?"

When a child is wicked, the father forgives him. He forgives him by goodness. And so we believe that God is our Father and that he forgives us by goodness. This is true. But when the Lord Jesus knew that it was the will of God that he die, then he knew that he was bearing the punishment of men. You have already seen in some palavers that when a man is punished he has to go to prison. And then his brother comes and says, "Let me carry the punishment. I am stronger than my brother. I can handle prison better." And so through love he wants to go to prison. Well then, it is the same thing with the Lord Jesus. When he knew that it was the will of God that he die, he also knew that God allowed him to bear the punishment for others. And when he died, he died through love for others. So it is that we know that Jesus died through love for us. He died so that God would not punish men. This we know. But the Lord Jesus never explained to the apostles why he died. It was something that only he and God knew. And we do not know the justice of it. St. Paul the Apostle tried to understand it, and the great missionaries tried to understand it, but we do not understand it completely. We understand only that it was the will of God that Jesus died for us, through love for men.

The Lord Jesus left an example. St. Paul the Apostle, who knew the thought of Jesus best, once said, "Jesus came and died so that we do not live for ourselves, but so that we know that our life does not belong to us. It belongs to God, and we have to give part of this life to others and we have to help them." That is why, during these Sundays, the missionaries preach so that we might know that we must not live for ourselves. Jesus is our master. He has not kept his life for himself. He has given it through love for others. And if we are brothers of Jesus, we too must give our lives.

Consider this. When God asks you to give a part of your life to others—to give the money that you have, to give supplies—obey, and be glad that God does not ask you to die for others; that he only asks you for part of your life. And give this part of your life, because this what the Lord Jesus wanted when he died. He wanted to give us all an example and, to all those who have truly understood the life of Jesus, he gives us a part of his life. Amen.

Let us pray to God: Jesus our Lord died for us and wanted to give an example. He did not keep his life for himself; he gave it to men because it was the will of God. Oh God, put in our hearts the thought of giving a part of our lives to others. Oh God, teach us thy will. Teach us to obey thy will. Amen.

69. Sunday, 21 April 1935

Palm Sunday

Next Friday is the great holiday of the death of the Lord Jesus Christ. And today is the Sunday that we call Palm Sunday, because this Sunday the Lord Jesus entered the great city of Jerusalem and the people cut branches of palm trees to put on the road, just as one puts down mats. So we call this Sunday Palm Sunday. I want to tell you all about this.

Every year all the people of the country came to celebrate the festival of Easter, because Easter was a festival of the Jewish people. The people had been captive in the kingdom of Egypt, and through Moses, God had liberated them and led them to the country of Canaan. And this people celebrated the day of Easter. And every year on the festival of Easter, which was in the spring, the people went up to Jerusalem. Jesus had been far away from Jerusalem in the villages, but as Easter approached, he said, "Let us go to Jerusalem." I told you how an apostle once said, "Oh Lord Jesus, do not go up to Jerusalem. They are going to kill you." But the Lord Jesus said, "It is the will of God." And so he went up to Jerusalem. While he walked, more and more men came and walked with him. And in the evening when he rested in the villages, he spoke the Word of God. Then the hearts of many people were touched, and they said, "This man speaks the Word of God." And then he came to Jericho. There, there was a blind man who said, "If only the Lord Jesus would heal me!" He was seated among the people who were waiting for the Lord Jesus to pass by. The people were crowded in. He could not walk. He was seated there, that poor blind man, and he spoke as loudly as he could, "Lord Jesus, heal me! Have pity on me!" And Jesus passed by. There were many people there, and from the other side of the road the blind man thought that the Lord Jesus would never see him. But suddenly the Lord Jesus stopped. He had heard the poor blind man who called out, and then he said, "The man must come." The people said, "He is calling you." And there were good people who took him by the hand, parted the others, and led him there, to where the Lord Jesus was. When the blind man was before the Lord Jesus, he asked him, "What do you want me to do for you?" "Lord Jesus," the blind man replied, "let me see the light again." Then the Lord Jesus healed him.

We can also heal the blind by cutting into the eye and using medicines. And you know that already there have been blind men among you who have gone away healed. But Jesus Christ healed by the Word. This we do not understand. God gave him the power. Everyone saw that he healed this blind man.

When Jesus approached Jerusalem there were still more people on the road. In a village the Lord Jesus found an ass to ride. (You know that the whites have animals upon which they can sit. The large animals are horses. The small animals are asses. Where the whites live there are no porters. Only the horses or the asses carry things.) Now, it was written in the Word of God that the King of hearts would enter Jerusalem on an ass. Important kings are seated on large horses; only poor people are seated on asses. It was written in the Word of God that Jesus would be seated on an ass, in order to show that Jesus was not like any other king, but that he had a heart for all the people.

And so Jesus entered into Jerusalem according to the Word that God had spoken concerning the King of hearts. The people sang when Jesus entered Jerusalem. By humbling himself, Jesus showed us that he truly was the King of hearts. That is why we celebrate Palm Sunday; on this Sunday we think about how Jesus wants to be the King of our hearts also. He asks us if the path to enter our hearts is well prepared. Is there enough goodness and gentleness in our hearts that the King of Hearts can enter? And so today, throughout the world, at this very hour, many Christians are thinking about this very thing. We too want to think about this and to celebrate this Palm Sunday with good thoughts in our hearts. Amen.

Let us pray to God: Jesus, today thou hast entered into Jerusalem as the King of hearts. Thou art also the King of our hearts. Enter into our hearts. Fill our hearts with thy goodness. Be our King so that we may listen to thee, for that is our joy, our sole joy. Amen.

70.　Sunday, 5 May 1935

The Apostle Peter

When the Lord Jesus left this earth, the apostles preached the Word of God. Before the Lord Jesus there had been prophets of the Jewish people who spoke the Word of God. Today I want to speak to you about the apostles. Those of you who are Christian know that there were twelve apostles. One apostle died—Judas, who died after he betrayed the Lord. After his death the apostles gathered together and said, "We want to be twelve apostles again." They chose a man who had known the Lord Jesus and who loved the words of Jesus. So it is told in the Bible. So there were twelve apostles again, and later yet another great apostle, Saint Paul. But the apostle Paul did not become Christian until a long time after the death of

Jesus. He was baptized later, and it was only much later that he became an apostle.

Now I am going to name the names of the best-known apostles. Those who are Christians, whether Protestants or Catholics, know them. There are three: St. Peter, St. John, and St. Paul. I want to tell you about Saint Peter the Apostle.

Saint Peter the Apostle was a fisherman. In the region of the Jewish people there was a lake almost as big as Lake Azingo. There the men went fishing, and they sold the fish in the villages. But they were not lazy fishermen like you—fishermen who come to ask for line, fishermen who come to ask for hooks, fishermen who come to ask for advances and afterward do not bring any fish, fishermen who sleep the whole night long in their huts instead of going fishing. No, not fishermen like that, but good fishermen—those who stayed outside all night long to catch fish and to bring them to those who had given them advances. That is why the Lord Jesus liked them and was often with them and went with them in the canoe and spoke with them.

One time they fished all night long and caught nothing. Then the Lord Jesus said to them, "Throw the net once more!" and they pulled up the net full of good fish. Then they realized that Jesus was not an ordinary man. One day Jesus said to Peter and his brother, "Stop fishing! Until now you have been fishers of fish; now you will be fishers of men for the good Lord. Until now you have cast the net; now you will cast the Word of God among men." And then he said, "Come with me." And they did not ask what the monthly wage would be. They did not ask what the pay at the end of the month would be. They did not say, "Perhaps we will come later." When Jesus said, "Come," they left their net and canoe and walked with him. They went all around the villages. They heard the Word of God spoken. The apostles understood the Lord Jesus better. When he walked on the path, Peter next to him, the Lord Jesus told Peter, "One day you will be chief."

Saint Peter was a weak man. The night when the Lord was arrested, Saint Peter walked behind the soldiers who led Jesus, and they came to where some people had made a fire near the house of the chief. There he sat and listened to those who came with Jesus. Suddenly a woman said, "I know you. You were also with this Jesus whom they have brought before the court." Then Saint Peter should have said, "Yes, I know him. He is the

King of hearts." But Saint Peter was afraid and said, "I do not know him." It was night, and they heard the cock crow. Another said, "But you were also with Jesus." And Peter said again, "I do not know him." And the cock crowed again. Once again someone said, "You were with Jesus." And once more Peter said, "I do not know him," and the cock crowed yet again. Then Peter remembered that Jesus had said, "You will renounce me [three times before the cock crows]." Then Saint Peter cried and left. This is the apostle Peter when he was weak.

But after the Lord Jesus died, he was no longer weak. He was no longer afraid of the soldiers. He was no longer afraid of the chiefs, but he spoke in the Temple to the people of Jerusalem, telling them: "Jesus, whom the chiefs have killed, is the King of hearts." The soldiers said, "Silence, or you will go to prison!" But he was no longer afraid.

One time he was going up to the temple and he saw a man who could not walk, who could not even move his hands and feet, and Peter said, "If the Lord Jesus were here, he could have healed this man." Then he heard the voice of God: "You, too, can heal." So he took the man's hand and said, "Get up and walk!" And the man walked. Then everyone realized that Peter was an apostle. The chiefs put him in prison, had a palaver, and said, "We do not want the Word of Jesus to be spoken." But Saint Peter said, "I'am going to do it anyway." And the chiefs beat him and mistreated him, but they did not dare kill him.

Saint Peter was always among the people, speaking the Word of God. He was often in prison, often beaten by the soldiers, but he was always courageous. Saint Peter did not want only the Jewish people to hear the Word of God; he also wanted to bring it to pagans. He left Jerusalem and went on some big trips, farther than M'Bigou, and he announced the Word of God. And this is the way it was for several years. He was the chief of the Christians. And at the end of his life he went to the great city of Rome. There, in Rome, lived the emperor of all the great kingdoms, an empire larger than France and Gabon and the whole of Equatorial Africa: the emperor Nero.

Nero did not like Christians. When servants came to tell him, "Your majesty, there are Christians in your city," he said, "I do not want them." Then there was a great fire in the city and half the city was burned and the misfortune was great. Then people said, "The Christians started the fire." This was not true, but you know how much people like to tell lies. So Nero had all the Christians killed. He had them eaten by leopards. He put resin on them and torched their bodies. It was in Rome, during the persecution of Christians, that the apostle Peter died. The Lord Jesus had told Peter that he would die for him. We all love the apostle Peter—the weak man who became the courageous man. Amen.

Let us pray to God: Oh God, thou hast spoken through the voice of the apostles. It is through the apostles that we know the Word of the Lord Jesus. May we keep this Word in our hearts. May we be courageous Christians who tell everyone that they love Jesus. Amen.

WORKS CITED

INDEX

Works Cited

Archival Material

Designations for Depositories

Günsbach   Archives centrales A. Schweitzer, Maison Albert Schweitzer, Günsbach, France
RSM   Personal Collection of Rhena Schweitzer Miller
Syracuse   E. S. Bird Library, Syracuse University, Syracuse, New York [manuscripts originally RSM]

Schweitzer, Albert. The 1913 African Sermons. Nos. 1–6. RSM. Manuscripts in Schweitzer's hand. [The author worked from transcribed typed copies made by Rhena Schweitzer Miller.]

———. The 1914 African Sermons. Nos. 7–12. RSM. Manuscripts in Schweitzer's hand. [The author worked from transcribed typed copies: nos. 7–9 by Sonja Poteau-Müller; nos. 10–12 by Rhena Schweitzer Miller.]

———. The 1930 African Sermons. Nos. 13–25. RSM. Typescripts made by various transcribers from their notes taken during the delivery of the sermons.

———. The 1930 African Sermons. Nos. 26–36. Syracuse. Typescripts made by various transcribers from their notes taken during the delivery of the sermons.

———. The 1930 African Sermons. Nos. 37–39. Syracuse and Günsbach. Typescripts made by various transcribers from their notes taken during the delivery of the sermons. Each of these three sermons was apparently transcribed twice; the two versions are similar but not identical. The Günsbach set of sermons was typed on one typewriter, the Syracuse set on another. [No. 37 has been previously edited and published by Jean-Paul Sorg: *Études Schweitzeriennes* 4 (1993): 133–35; and Sorg 1955: 352–55.]

———. The 1930 African Sermons. Nos. 40–44. Günsbach. Typescripts made by various transcribers from their notes taken during the delivery of the sermons. [Three 1930 sermons have been previously published by Jean-Paul Sorg in

Études Schweitzeriennes 1 (1990): no. 41 appears on pp. 35–36; no. 43 on pp. 37–38; and no. 44 on p. 38.]

———. The 1931 African Sermons. Nos. 45–56. Günsbach. Typescripts made by various transcribers from their notes taken during the delivery of the sermons. [No. 48 has been previously edited and published by Jean-Paul Sorg: *Études Schweitzeriennes* 1 (1990): 39.]

———. The 1933 African Sermons. Nos. 57–66. Günsbach. Typescripts made by various transcribers from their notes taken during the delivery of the sermons. [No. 64 has been previously edited and published by Jean-Paul Sorg: *Études Schweitzeriennes* 4 (1993): 135–37.]

———. The 1935 African Sermons. Nos. 67–70. Günsbach. Typescripts made by various transcribers from their notes taken during the delivery of the sermons.

Books and Articles

Brabazon, James. 2000. *Albert Schweitzer: A Biography.* 2d ed. Syracuse, N.Y.: Syracuse Univ. Press.

Byers, Jeannette Q., trans. 1996. *Brothers in Spirit: The Correspondence of Albert Schweitzer and William Larimer Mellon, Jr.* Syracuse, N.Y.: Syracuse Univ. Press.

Gollomb, Joseph. 1949. *Albert Schweitzer: Genius in the Jungle.* New York: Vanguard.

Ice, Jackson Lee. 1994. *Albert Schweitzer: Sketches for a Portrait.* Latham, Md.: University Press of America.

Jack, Homer. 1984. *The Words of Albert Schweitzer.* New York: Newmarket.

Marshall, George, and David Poling. 1989. *Schweitzer: A Biography.* New York: Doubleday.

Mattison, Joel. 1992. "Lessons from Lambaréné." *Bulletin of the American College of Surgeons* 77 (Sept.-Oct.) 1992. Reprinted by Joel Mattison, n.p., n.d.

Schweitzer, Albert. 1931. "Un culte du dimanche en forêt vierge." *Cahiers Protestants* 2 (Mar. 1931): 3–7. [An English translation by the editor appears on pp. xxxi–xxxiv of the introduction to this book.]

———. [1923] 1939. *Christianity and the Religions of the World.* Translated by Johanna Powers. New York: Holt.

———. [1931] 1955. *The Mysticism of Paul the Apostle.* Translated by William Montgomery. New York: Macmillan.

———. [1924] 1963. *Memoirs of Childhood and Youth.* Translated by C. T. Campion. New York: Macmillan.

———. [1906] 1968. *The Quest for the Historical Jesus.* Translated by W. Montgomery. New York: Macmillan.

————. 1969. *Reverence for Life*. Translated by Reginald H. Fuller. New York: Harper and Row. Originally published in German as *Strassburger Predigten*, ed. Ulrich Neuenschwander (Munich: C. H. Beck Verlag, 1966).

————. [1922, 1931] 1976. "On the Edge of the Primeval Forest" and "More from the Primeval Forest." Translated by C. T. Campion. 1948; reprint, New York: Macmillan.

————. [1933] 1990. *Out of My Life and Thought*. Translated by Antje Bultmann Lemke. New York: Henry Holt.

————. 1992. *Albert Schweitzer: Letters, 1905–1965*. Edited by Hans Walter Bähr. Translated by Joachim Neugroschel. New York: Macmillan.

Sorg, Jean-Paul. 1995. *Albert Schweitzer, Humanisme et Mystique*. Paris: Albin Michel.

Index

Acts: 2, xlix, 75; 7, 147–48; 9:1–31, 148–50; 9:23, 17:17, xlix–1; 18:33, 1; 23, lii

Adam, 134

adultery: as mocking love of the gospel, 8; Schweitzer preaching against, xli, xliv; sickness caused by, 10; "You Shall Not Commit Adultery," 52–54

Advent: first Sunday of, 1913, 14–15; first Sunday of, 1933, 169–72; second Sunday of, 1930, 128–29

agape, xxxviii

alcohol, xliv, 10, 12–13, 15

All Saints, Feast of, 167–68

All Souls, Feast of, 167–68

Amos, 170

Ananias, 149

animals: God creating, 134; killing of, xx, xlii, 40; showing kindness to, 139

animism, xliii

Apostles, the: after death of Jesus, 7, 64–67, 75, 145, 147, 183–84; James, 65; Jesus appearing to on Easter morning, 64, 145; John, 65, 68, 83, 158, 184; Judas, 62, 65, 143, 146, 183; Philip, 65; receiving the Holy Spirit, xlix, 32, 65, 75, 150–52. *See also* Paul the Apostle; Peter the Apostle

Assembly of the Synod (1914), 21–26

Association des Amis de l'Hôpital Schweitzer, L', xlv

Bach, J. S., xxii

baptism, 69–70, 76, 83, 85

Barabbas, 143–44

Bibellese (Schweitzer), xxxvi

Bible, the: Pauline letters, 67, 155, 157–59, 160, 166; in Schweitzer's sermons to Africans, xxxii, xlii, xlvi, xlviii–lvi; at worship with hospital staff, xxxv, xxxvi. *See also* New Testament; Old Testament

blindness, healing of, 141, 182

Boegner, Alfred, xxiii

Bonnéma, Doctor, 156–57

Boulinghi, 59, 88

Canada, Mrs. (Lillian Russell), xxxi, xxxin, xxxii, 39, 44, 47, 66, 77

Christmas: Advent preceding, 128, 169; 1933, 172–73

Christol, Mrs., 20

cleanliness, lii, 51, 61

clothing, 46, 58, 107

colonialism, xxv, xxvi

compassion, liii

conversion, 14

1 Corinthians 6:19, 32